Teaching Mathematics to Middle School Students with Learning Difficulties

WHAT WORKS FOR SPECIAL-NEEDS LEARNERS
Karen R. Harris and Steve Graham
Editors

Strategy Instruction for Students with Learning Disabilities
Robert Reid and Torri Ortiz Lienemann

Teaching Mathematics to Middle School Students
with Learning Difficulties
Marjorie Montague and Asha K. Jitendra, Editors

Teaching Mathematics to Middle School Students with Learning Difficulties

edited by

Marjorie Montague
Asha K. Jitendra

Series Editors' Note by Karen R. Harris and Steve Graham

THE GUILFORD PRESS
New York   London

Library of Congress Cataloging-in-Publication Data
    Teaching mathematics to middle school students with learning difficulties / edited by
Marjorie Montague, Asha K. Jitendra.
       p. cm.—(What works for special-needs learners)
    Includes bibliographical references and index.
    ISBN 978-1-59385-306-8 (pbk.)
    ISBN 978-1-59385-307-5 (cloth)
    1. Mathematics—Study and teaching (Middle school) 2. Learning disabled children—
Education. I. Montague, Marjorie II. Jitendra, Asha K. III. Series.
    QA135.6.T428 2006
    371.9′0447—dc22
                                                                    2006007899

About the Editors

Marjorie Montague, PhD, is a Professor of Special Education at the University of Miami, where she directs the graduate programs in learning, attention, and behavior disorders. She received her doctorate from the University of Arizona in 1984. Dr. Montague conducts research on cognitive strategy instruction for improving mathematical problem solving and composition for students with learning disabilities. She also studies academic, personal–social, and behavioral outcomes for children and adolescents at risk for learning and emotional–behavioral disorders. Dr. Montague has published more than 60 articles, chapters, curricular materials, and books. She serves on the editorial boards of several journals, including *Learning Disability Quarterly* and *Learning Disabilities Research and Practice* and served on the executive board of the Council for Exceptional Children—Division for Research and the International Academy for Research in Learning Disabilities. Dr. Montague regularly presents at national and international conferences on topics related to understanding and remedying learning, attention, and behavior disorders.

Asha K. Jitendra, PhD, received her degree in curriculum and instruction (special education) from the University of Oregon in 1991. She is a Professor and Coordinator of Special Education and on the faculty of the Center for Promoting Research to Practice—School, Families, and Communities in the College of Education at Lehigh University. Dr. Jitendra's research focuses on designing effective instruction and assessment in mathematics and reading for students with learning disabilities as well as on the analysis of school-based materials and tasks (e.g., mathematics, reading). She has published more than 50 articles in peer-reviewed journals, and she and her colleagues were recognized by the American Psychological Association with an award for an outstanding article in the *Journal of School Psychology*. She serves on seven editorial boards and served as the associate editor of the *Journal of Learning Disabilities*. Dr. Jitendra has presented nationally and internationally on effective instructional strategies for enhancing the academic performance of children with learning disabilities.

Contributors

Brian R. Bryant, PhD, Department of Special Education, University of Texas, Austin, Texas

Diane Pedrotty Bryant, PhD, Department of Special Education, University of Texas, Austin, Texas

Janet R. DeSimone, EdD, Division of Education, Lehman College, City University of New York, New York, New York

Anne Foegen, PhD, Department of Curriculum and Instruction, Iowa State University, Ames, Iowa

Paula Hartman, MA, Department of Special Education, University of Texas, Austin, Texas

Asha K. Jitendra, PhD, Department of Education and Human Services, Lehigh University, Bethlehem, Pennsylvania

Sun A. Kim, MA, Department of Special Education, University of Texas, Austin, Texas

Diane Kinder, PhD, Education Program, University of Washington, Tacoma, Washington

Marjorie Montague, PhD, Department of Teaching and Learning, University of Miami, Coral Gables, Florida

Rene S. Parmar, PhD, Department of Administrative and Instructional Leadership, St. John's University, New York, New York

Marcy Stein, PhD, Education Program, University of Washington, Tacoma, Washington

Delinda van Garderen, PhD, Department of Educational Studies, State University of New York at New Paltz, New Paltz, New York

John Woodward, PhD, School of Education, University of Puget Sound, Tacoma, Washington

Yan Ping Xin, PhD, Department of Educational Studies, Purdue University, West Lafayette, Indiana

Series Editors' Note

Students in today's middle schools are expected to master an increasingly sophisticated array of mathematical skills, concepts, and strategies. *Teaching Mathematics to Middle School Students with Learning Difficulties* provides teachers and other practitioners with an effective set of tools for meeting this challenge with those youngsters who find mathematics most difficult.

This volume is the second in the series "What Works for Special-Needs Learners." This series addresses a significant need in the education of learners with special needs—students who are at risk, those with disabilities, and all children and adolescents who struggle with learning or behavior. Researchers in special education, educational psychology, curriculum and instruction, and other fields have made great progress in understanding what works for struggling learners, yet the practical application of this research base remains quite limited. This is due in part to the lack of appropriate materials for teachers, teacher educators, and inservice teacher development programs. Books in this series present assessment, instructional, and classroom management methods with a strong research base and provide specific "how-to" instructions in the use of proven procedures in schools.

Teaching Mathematics to Middle School Students with Learning Difficulties features extensive use of practical examples drawn from classroom teachers and their students. Readers are also provided with a framework for evaluating and improving their current approach to teaching mathematics. The instructional and assessment procedures, adaptations and modifications, and guidelines for evaluating instruction presented in this book are designed to ensure that youngsters with learning difficulties can access and master the intricacies of middle school mathematics. An invaluable resource for practitioners, this book is also suitable for use in a methods course.

Future books in the series will cover such issues as word learning, reading comprehension, social skills instruction, writing, and working with families. All volumes will be as thorough and detailed as the present one and will facilitate implementation of evidence-based practices in classrooms and schools.

KAREN R. HARRIS
STEVE GRAHAM

Contents

Introduction

MARJORIE MONTAGUE and ASHA K. JITENDRA

Are any of these middle school students in your mathematics classes?

- Juan reverses numbers when copying from the book or the chalkboard.
- Suzie gets the assignment "wrong" because sloppy writing led to misreading and misalignment of numbers.
- Jeff has not yet memorized the multiplication tables.
- Gerard cannot remember the procedural sequence for division computation.
- Amy cannot "decide what to do" when solving math word problems.
- Alfredo cannot "remember" algebraic formulas.

The reality is that approximately 5–8% of school-age students have memory or other cognitive deficits that interfere with their ability to acquire, master, and apply mathematical concepts and skills (Geary, 2004). These students with mathematical learning disabilities (MLD) are at risk for failure in middle school mathematics because they generally are unprepared for the rigor of the middle school mathematics curriculum. Middle school mathematics teachers are considerably different from elementary school teachers. They usually have a higher level of content knowledge and have different expectations for their students. They expect their students to have mastered the basic math skills required for higher-level learning in mathematics. That is, students are expected to enter their mathematics class with basic conceptual knowledge of numbers and to have the declarative and procedural knowledge required for higher-level learning. They are also expected to be self-directed, independent learners who are able to comprehend what they are

1

learning and connect that learning to what they have previously learned. Middle school teachers expect their students to attend in class, ask questions when they do not understand the assignment, complete and turn in accurate homework, understand how to take tests, and to work compatibly with other students.

Why do so many children have difficulty in mathematics? Children with MLD vary considerably in the cognitive functions that support development of mathematical ability. Geary (2004) identified three subtypes of MLD that may help to explain these difficulties. His MLD subtypes include children with predominate procedural deficits, semantic memory deficits, or visuospatial deficits, all of which interfere with their ability to learn mathematics. Procedural deficits interfere with the development of number sense and math concepts, counting strategies, and the necessary shift from procedural-based problem solving to memory-based problem solving. These children frequently display working memory, memory storage, and monitoring problems. Semantic memory deficits interfere with retrieval and recall of math facts and with solving simple arithmetic and word problems. These deficits seem to be due to the inability to represent and manipulate information associated with the language system. Visuospatial deficits are most notably associated with difficulties in geometry, estimation, and complex word problems. These difficulties also seem to be due to an inability to represent and manipulate information but are related more to the visuospatial system and executive functioning than the language system.

Compounding the challenge of teaching mathematics to children with MLD are the expectations for teachers and students as a result of changing curricula. Most states and, as a result, school districts, have adopted curricula that follow the National Council of Teachers of Mathematics (NCTM) *Principles and Standards for School Mathematics* (NCTM, 2000). NCTM's six basic principles are (1) equal opportunity for all students, (2) a comprehensive and coordinated curriculum across grades, (3) excellent teachers who have the content and pedagogical knowledge for assessing and instructing students, (4) active construction of knowledge by students who are empowered mathematically, (5), appropriate assessment that provides direction for instruction and supports learning, and (6) technology as an essential component of mathematics teaching and learning. Mathematics teachers have had to adjust to these new curricula, which represent a dramatic departure from traditional, more didactic models of instruction. These new curricula emphasize problem solving, conceptual understanding, and communication about mathematics.

Students with MLD generally fare poorly in this teaching and learning environment because they characteristically are poor problem solvers, have deficient conceptual knowledge, and have difficulty formulating and verbalizing concepts. They frequently lack necessary strategies that good problem solvers use. If they have acquired important problem-solving strategies, they often are unable to access and use them appropriately. Given the teacher, classroom, and curricular expectations in middle school mathematics, students with MLD are clearly at a disadvantage in a general mathematics class because they often do not have the necessary background knowledge or student behavior required for success. These students need adaptations and accommodations in mathematics classes if they are going to succeed in the typical mathematics classroom.

Students' poor performance in mathematics is of paramount concern at the national, state, and local levels. Middle school mathematics represents a special challenge for educators because teachers assume that students will have acquired the foundation for higher-level mathematics. This foundation includes understanding of mathematical concepts, mastery of basic skills, and problem-solving strategies. Unfortunately, many students enter middle school without this foundation. This book addresses the problems in providing an effective mathematics program in middle school and the critical issues and concerns surrounding mathematics education for students with MLD. The focus is on improving instruction for middle school students with MLD.

The first chapter, by Bryant, Kim, Hartman, and Bryant, describes the *adaptations framework*, a model for implementing the NCTM *Principles and Standards* in middle school mathematics classrooms. The mathematics curriculum for sixth through eighth grades includes number, operation, and quantitative reasoning; patterns, relationships, and algebraic thinking; geometry and spatial reasoning; measurement; probability and statistics; and underlying processes and mathematical tools. This curriculum is reflected in states' accountability measures that are increasing the stakes for student performance and subsequent high school graduation. Additionally, reform efforts aimed at improving mathematics instruction for all students have stressed the need for a focus in mathematics instruction on inquiry-based learning with an emphasis on problem solving. The authors describe how the *adapations framework* can facilitate the implementation of curriculum reform for students with mathematics difficulties.

Building upon Chapter 1, in Chapter 2, Woodward describes how to make reform-based mathematics work for academically low-achieving middle school students. Results of the Third International Mathematics and Science Study confirm the importance of conceptually guided instruction in mathematics. Unfortunately, remedial and special education is particularly weak in mathematics instruction, and, as a result, there has been a primary emphasis on the acquisition of basic skills and traditional arithmetic. This focus is increasingly untenable given the profound role of technology in reshaping the world of mathematics and work. The chapter first describes the impediments to successful, standards-based instruction and then presents a more extended discussion of promising practices. At the heart of these practices is a careful evaluation of the mathematical topics that must be made meaningful to students in school if they are going to succeed in the world of work. Put simply, remedial and special education professionals must do more than simply modify traditional mathematics textbooks. Instead, they must examine school mathematics topics in terms of "valued knowledge." As a consequence, some skills, such as multidigit multiplication, long division, and operations on large decimal numbers, are best handled through calculators and strategies for approximating answers to problems. This kind of analysis also reveals critical topics that are either neglected or undertaught in remedial and special education (e.g., data analysis, geometry). The chapter provides multiple examples of how important topics can be modified for middle school students with mathematics difficulties.

Schema-based strategy instruction for improving mathematical problem solving for students is the focus of Chapter 3, by Xin and Jitendra. Key variables involved in problem solving and a research-based instructional program are described. The essential features of schema-based strategy instruction and how to solve multiplication and division problems using this instructional approach are detailed. The chapter includes examples of scripted lessons, story situations, word problems, schema diagrams, and problem-solving checklists.

Embedded in schema-based problem solving instruction is the use of diagrammatic representations. In Chapter 4, van Garderen describes how to improve mathematical problem solving for middle school students using visual representations. A commonly endorsed strategy for solving mathematical word problems is to "make a drawing." Yet, for many students, in particular students with learning disabilities, drawing a diagram is not as straightforward or easy as it seems. This chapter provides teachers with research-based practices to help students with mathematics difficulties improve their ability to generate and use diagrams to understand and solve mathematical word problems. The chapter describes what a diagram in mathematics is and the benefits associated with using diagrams as a representational strategy for solving problems. Suggestions on how to develop "diagram literacy" and how to use diagrams appropriately for these students are given. Van Garderen details how to generate a diagram and use that diagram to reason through the problem. She concludes with a discussion of other instructional considerations (e.g., using a cognitive strategy that incorporates diagramming to solve word problems). Potential problems that students with mathematical learning difficulties have in generating and using their diagrams to solve problems (e.g., conceptual knowledge difficulties may hinder diagramming a problem) are also discussed.

In Chapter 5, Montague discusses the importance of teaching self-regulation strategies to middle school students with mathematics difficulties. Middle school students with learning difficulties characteristically have deficits in self-regulation strategies that interfere with academic success. The chapter focuses on self-regulation as it pertains to effective and efficient performance in mathematics. Research on self-regulation is reviewed, and an instructional program that incorporates self-regulation to improve performance in mathematics is described. Proven instructional techniques that classroom teachers can use to promote self-regulation and academic competence in students are presented along with practical guidelines for implementation.

Foegen, in Chapter 6, describes various tools and strategies for monitoring student progress in middle school mathematics. Even the best-researched interventions are not guaranteed to be successful with all learners. As a result, it is imperative that teachers have tools they can apply to evaluate the effectiveness of their instruction for individual students. Foegen provides teachers with the skills and knowledge they need to implement curriculum-based measurement as a means of monitoring middle school students' progress in mathematics. The content includes an overview of basic concepts underlying curriculum-based measurement and its use in monitoring progress, as well as specific applications in middle school mathematics. Sample measures and graphs that teachers will find helpful are included, as are techniques for monitoring student progress (using curriculum-based measurement).

In Chapter 7, Kinder and Stein present a set of guidelines for evaluating instruction for middle school students with mathematics difficulties. The quality of commercially developed mathematics programs must be closely scrutinized because these programs are largely the foundation of mathematics programs in middle school. It is important that teachers are able to evaluate the curriculum and the instructional program. They provide a curriculum evaluation framework derived from the available evidence on effective instructional practices in mathematics and on sound principles of instructional design. Teachers can use this framework to evaluate the quality of commercially developed mathematics programs. With the framework, teachers can develop research-based criteria to assist curriculum adoption committees in selecting curricula and instructional programs. Additionally, teachers can use the framework to help them identify weak areas in the programs they currently use. Specific recommendations for designing curriculum modifications for students with special learning needs in mathematics are given.

Teacher collaboration in inclusive middle school mathematics classrooms is the topic of the final chapter, by Parmar and DeSimone. They believe that professional collaboration is the basis for effective mathematics instruction for middle school students with mathematics difficulties. The importance of collaboration as a key ingredient to program success is supported by data from a national survey of middle school mathematics teachers. The discussion focuses on collaboration among middle school mathematics teachers, special education teachers, paraprofessionals, and school administrators. Various forms of collaboration that support successful programs are described and strategies to promote a team approach to instruction presented. The importance of educators holding a shared understanding of the educational goals for included students is stressed. Positive outcomes from collaboration such as modified instructional techniques that can benefit all students in the class are presented. Included are vignettes of effective collaboration for middle school topics (e.g., polynomials), which are taken from actual classroom observations and teacher interviews.

REFERENCES

Geary, D. C. (2004). Mathematics and learning disabilities. *Journal of Learning Disabilities, 37,* 4–15.

National Council of Teachers of Mathematics. (2000). *Principles and standards for school mathematics.* Reston, VA: Author.

CHAPTER 1

Standards-Based Mathematics Instruction and Teaching Middle School Students with Mathematical Disabilities

DIANE PEDROTTY BRYANT, SUN A. KIM,
PAULA HARTMAN, and BRIAN R. BRYANT

Mrs. Martinez is teaching her sixth-grade students ways to represent fractions. Following a review of fractions and examples of comparing and ordering fractions, she has students work in small, mixed-ability groups to compare and order fractions as a first step before they apply this knowledge to solve problems. Mrs. Martinez provides students with number lines to help them visualize the relationships to make comparisons. As she circulates among the small groups, she listens to group discussions as they work with the fractions and number lines. She notices that one of her students who struggles with mathematics seems confused by the number line. She listens as he talks about the comparative size of the fractions. She decides that this student might better conceptualize fractional portions with different material. She gives this group fraction strips as another type of material to help them visually depict the fractional parts to make comparisons about and order fractions. She notes in her assessment notebook the change in instructional material for one group and for one student member of the group in particular. As she circulates among the groups, she notices another student with mathematical disabilities who seems to be struggling; she makes the material adjustment for him as well. Mrs. Martinez calls the small groups back together for a whole-class discussion. Using the number line and fraction strips designed to be displayed on the overhead projector, she calls on several students to demonstrate to the class the strategies they used to compare and order the fractions. She also solicits from other students ways that they figured out size and ordering of the fractions. She follows up the lesson with a short, progress-monitoring quiz that students complete independently. Mrs. Martinez checks all papers with particular attention to those students who need extra help with the skill and may continue to need adaptations during the week's lessons.

This scenario depicts standards-based mathematics instruction, including adaptations for students who are exhibiting problems learning the curriculum. In this scenario, Mrs. Martinez is providing instruction that reflects the intent of the *Principles and Standards for School Mathematics* (referred to as the *Standards*), which were developed by the National Council of Teachers of Mathematics (NCTM, 2000). She begins the lesson by reviewing the concept and giving students examples prior to small-group practice. Through small, interactive student groups and the use of manipulatives to visualize fractions, Mrs. Martinez has her students work on a skill that, for many sixth-grade students, requires considerable instruction and practice. During observation, she realizes that some of her students require further assistance, and through monitoring student work, she decides how to adapt instruction to benefit *all* of her students. Finally, she uses individual assessment to monitor student performance. She recognizes that in her classroom there is a range of abilities, including students with mathematical disabilities who may have challenges with grasping, discussing, and applying concepts for contextualized problem-solving situations. For many of these students, adaptations are necessary ingredients of instruction to help them learn the skills and concepts embodied in the *Standards*.

In today's middle school classrooms, mathematics instruction focuses on having students investigate and develop multiple problem-solving solution strategies for "authentic" problems (NCTM, 2000). In these environments, students are also expected to interact with their teachers and peers to develop an understanding of mathematics concepts or skills. Students are expected to explain their mathematical reasoning to others and follow the explanations of their peers (Baxter, Woodward, & Olson, 2001). Even though students continue to learn basic computational skills in these environments, more of their time and effort is devoted to solving open-ended, challenging problems that can be solved using different strategies (Baxter et al., 2001). To engage in standards-based mathematics instruction, students need the knowledge and skills to communicate using mathematical language or representations, to invent or understand problem-solving strategies, and to build their own knowledge about mathematical concepts through classroom interactions. Yet, we know that between 5 and 8% of school-age students exhibit some form of mathematical disability (Badian, 1983; Geary, 2004; Gross-Tsur, Manor, & Shaley, 1996; Ostad, 1998) that makes it difficult for them to learn and apply the mathematical skills and concepts discussed in the *Standards*. In addition, for some of these students, their mathematics performance plateaus at the fifth- to sixth-grade levels (Cawley, Baker-Kroczynski, & Urban, 1992). It is troublesome that many students with mathematical disabilities struggle learning the mathematical skills and concepts associated with the middle-grades *Standards*. This knowledge is supposed to prepare them for advanced high school mathematics in preparation for postsecondary education, which many students with learning disabilities pursue after high school. For students with mathematical disabilities, adaptations are necessary to help them engage in classroom discourse and learn mathematical skills and concepts embodied in the *Standards*. The purpose of this chapter is to illustrate how standards-based mathematics instruction for the middle grades can be adapted to enhance the ability of students with mathematical disabilities to learn the skills and concepts in the *Standards*. Examples of instructional vignettes are provided throughout the chapter to guide teachers. We use the following questions to structure the chapter:

- What are the NCTM's *Principles and Standards for School Mathematics*?
- Why do students with mathematical disabilities have difficulty learning the *Principles and Standards for School Mathematics*?
- How can teachers adapt mathematics instruction to help students with mathematical disabilities benefit from instruction?

WHAT ARE THE NCTM'S PRINCIPLES AND STANDARDS FOR SCHOOL MATHEMATICS?

In response to national and international mathematics assessment results and the influence of developments in cognitive science on mathematics education, NCTM published the *Principles and Standards for School Mathematics* (NCTM, 1989, 2000). This publication spurred standards-based reform in mathematics education and teacher preparation programs to better prepare America's children and youth for the mathematical challenges of the 21st century (Program for International Student Assessment [PISA], Lemke et al., 2004). The standards-based reform effort was built on beliefs that *all* students can better understand mathematics concepts, skills, and procedures through student-centered, inquiry-based, and discourse-driven instruction grounded in contextualized problem solving (Woodward & Baxter, 1997).

Reform efforts aim to improve mathematics instruction for all students and are reflected in states' accountability assessments, which are increasing the stakes for student performance and subsequent high school graduation. Most states have adopted the *Standards*, thus influencing school district curricula. Further, lessons in mathematics textbooks correspond with state standards and the NCTM *Standards*; this curricular alignment provides a certain "muscle" to the *Standards*. According to NCTM, the *Principles* explain the characteristics of a "high quality mathematics education," and the *Standards* focus on the content and processes that students must learn and understand. We provide an overview first of the principles and then the standards. Further details can be found on the NCTM website at www.NCTM.org.

Principles

Six principles are included: equity, curriculum, teaching, learning, assessment, and technology, which together form the foundation for a high-quality mathematics education. Each principle is described briefly.

Equity Principle

This principle embraces the belief that high expectations and teacher support are to be provided for *all* students. The equity principle is based on the expectation "that reasonable and appropriate accommodations be made as needed to promote access and attainment for all students" (NCTM, 2000, p. 12). Following criticism for not including students with disabilities in its 1989 version of the *Standards*, NCTM's recognition of diverse learners' needs, including those of students with disabilities, is more visible in the 2000 edition of the *Standards*. The equity principle acknowledges the need for appropriate professional development and teacher preparation regarding the special learning needs of all students, including learning characteristics and appropriate adaptations. We also know that campus-based support is imperative to ensure that struggling students can indeed benefit from instruction and access the general education curriculum.

Curriculum Principle

This principle is based on the premise that a coherent curriculum is critical for a high-quality mathematics program. Coherence is described in terms of opportunities that link and build upon mathematical ideas to help students develop an increasingly deeper knowledge and understanding of mathematics. Such a curriculum should prepare students to learn challenging mathematical concepts and skills across the school years in lessons that are coherently sequenced across units and connected to the "big ideas" of mathematics. Applying this principle to students with mathematical disabilities, as an example, we see classroom teachers helping students activate their prior knowledge about the topic to be studied. Students can use a Venn diagram to compare and contrast similarities and differences between fractions and decimals. Students can bring in examples of data representations from the newspaper or a magazine in preparing to discuss the use of statistics in daily life. These examples help students with mathematical disabilities by using a graphic organizer (Venn diagram) to show their understanding of numerical relationships and by identifying concrete examples (e.g., newspaper or magazine article) of everyday uses of statistics.

Teaching Principle

According to this principle, teachers should understand what students know and the curriculum should be taught so that they can be responsive to various learning needs and challenge and support students' learning through the experiences they provide. Teachers should possess an understanding of various pedagogical strategies and recognize that not all students benefit from one way of learning. Thinking about this principle as it relates to students with mathematical disabilities translates into how instruction is presented and how teachers can support student learning. For example, students with mathematical disabilities and other struggling students may need explicit instruction to help them learn new skills. Modeling, examples, and extra practice may be necessary to help students grasp new skills. Students may need manipulatives (e.g., fraction strips) or representations (e.g., number line) to foster understanding when multiplying mixed fractions. A fact table for quick reference or a calculator may be needed for those students who continue to struggle with basic arithmetic combinations even when manipulatives and representations have been used. Instruction may need to be broken down into smaller steps so that problems are not overwhelming to students. Through various teaching techniques that are responsive to individual needs, students with mathematical disabilities can benefit from instruction.

Learning Principle

The learning principle views mathematical understanding as being acquired through active experiences that build new knowledge by incorporating prior knowledge. The "vision of school mathematics in the *Principles and Standards* is based on students' learning mathematics with understanding" (NCTM, 2000, p. 20). The understanding and application of mathematical procedures, concepts, and processes is the heart of the *Standards*. In many cases, students with mathematical disabilities can benefit from standards-based instruction with adaptations. For instance, the concrete–representational–abstract (CRA) instructional routine is a way to promote understanding (Butler, Miller, Crehan, Babbitt, & Pierce, 2003). Using the CRA process, geoboards (concrete) can be used to create two-dimensional shapes. These shapes can be transferred into drawings (representational) using coordinate grids and by using "dynamic geometry software" (NCTM, 2000). Students can be given problems (abstract) that require the application of geometric principles using lines, angles, and shapes. Active student engagement using the CRA instructional routine is just one example of how the *Learning Principle*, which emphasizes active experiences, can be implemented for students with mathematical disabilities.

Assessment Principle

This principle is based on the idea that careful assessment supports learning and provides teachers with information about student progress related to instruction. According to the *Standards*, assessment should be not only a test at the conclusion of a unit but also an ongoing process that informs instructional decision making. Assessment should become part of instructional routines and tap various sources of evidence that inform instruction. In *Adding It Up* (Kilpatrick, Swafford, & Findell, 2001), assessing students' informal knowledge is discussed as an important part of instruction for students with special needs. As an example, for students with mathematical disabilities, the assessment principle can be applied to assessing student understanding of the vocabulary related to a particular math lesson. If there is a lesson on fractions, then determining student understanding of terms such as *denominator, numerator, part-to-whole,* and *mixed fractions* might be important for advanced instruction that involves multiplying or dividing fractions. In our opening scenario, Mrs. Martinez used a short quiz at the end of her lesson to assess student learning. Assessment information can inform instructional decision making about adaptations that may be needed to help struggling students.

Technology Principle

This principle, an important component of teaching and learning, calls for tapping of technological tools that allow students to focus on "decision making, reflection, reasoning, and problem solving" (NCTM, 2000, p. 24). The use of technology can deepen students' learning by presenting visual representations and models of mathematical ideas using computers or calculators. Finally, technology can be used as an adaptation for students with disabilities who may require support with basic procedures (e.g., arithmetic combinations, whole-number computation).

Now that you have finished this section, reflect on how these principles can be implemented in a classroom. Provide your own examples of how the principles ensure that all students have opportunities to learn and master the skills and knowledge in the *Standards.*

Standards and Expectations: Understanding, Knowledge, and Skills: Grades 6–8

The standards are descriptions of the understanding, knowledge, and skills students should acquire from prekindergarten through 12th grade. The mathematical areas include the Content Standards—Number and Operations, Algebra, Geometry, Measurement, Data Analysis and Probability—and the Process Standards—Problem Solving, Reasoning and Proof, Communication, Connections, and Representation, which focus on how knowledge is acquired and used. Each of the standards for the middle grades 6–8 is summarized in Table 1.1. As you read each standard, identify skills that are needed for those lessons. For example, to work with numbers, operations, and algebra found in middle grades mathematics lessons, students must have the following requisite abilities: knowledge of counting and place value of multidigit numbers; fluency with arithmetic combinations; accuracy in computing whole number operations; understanding of the associative, commutative, and distributive properties; recognition and understanding of numerical

TABLE 1.1. NCTM Content and Process Standards for Grades 6–8

Content standards

Number and operations standards
- Understand numbers, ways of representing numbers, relationships among numbers, and number systems.
- Understand meanings of operations and how they relate to one another.
- Compute fluently and make reasonable estimates.

Algebra standards
- Understand patterns, relations, and functions.
- Represent and analyze mathematical situations and structures using algebraic symbols.
- Use mathematical models to represent and understand quantitative relationships.
- Analyze change in various contexts.

Geometry standards
- Analyze characteristics and properties of two- and three-dimensional geometric shapes and develop mathematical arguments about geometric relationships.
- Specify locations and describe spatial relationships using coordinate geometry and other representational systems.
- Apply transformations and use symmetry to analyze mathematical situations.
- Use visualization, spatial reasoning, and geometric modeling to solve problems.

Measurement standards
- Understand measurable attributes of objects and the units, systems, and processes of measurement.
- Apply appropriate techniques, tools, and formulas to determine measurements.

Data analysis and probability standards
- Formulate questions that can be addressed with data and collect, organize, and display relevant data to answer them.
- Select and use appropriate statistical methods to analyze data.
- Develop and evaluate inferences and predictions that are based on data.

Process standards

Problem-solving standards
- Build new mathematical knowledge through problem solving.
- Solve problems that arise in mathematics and in other contexts.
- Apply and adapt a variety of appropriate strategies to solve problems.
- Monitor and reflect on the process of mathematical problem solving.

Reasoning and proof standards
- Recognize reasoning and proof as fundamental aspects of mathematics.
- Make and investigate mathematical conjectures.
- Develop and evaluate mathematical arguments and proofs.
- Select and use various types of reasoning and methods of proof.

Communication standards
- Organize and consolidate mathematical thinking through communication.
- Communicate mathematical thinking coherently and clearly to peers, teachers, and others.
- Analyze and evaluate the mathematical thinking and strategies of others.
- Use the language of mathematics to express mathematical ideas precisely.

Connections standards
- Recognize and use connections among mathematical ideas.
- Understand how mathematical ideas interconnect and build on one another to produce a coherent whole.
- Recognize and apply mathematics in contexts outside of mathematics.

Representation standards
- Create and use representations to organize, record, and communicate mathematical ideas.
- Select, apply, and translate among mathematical representations to solve problems.
- Use representations to model and interpret physical, social, and mathematical phenomena.

Note. Adapted from the National Council of Teachers of Mathematics *Principles and Standards for School Mathematics* (2000).

symbols; and identification and application of numerical patterns, to name a few. These requisite abilities (or skills) are needed to do advanced, middle-grades mathematics. Review the standards in Table 1.1 and identify the requisite abilities students must have learned from elementary school mathematics to be prepared for middle-grades mathematics. Now that you have reviewed the standards, what requisite abilities did you identify? In the next section, we discuss reasons why some of the skills and concepts of the standards might be difficult for students with mathematical disabilities to master.

WHY DO STUDENTS WITH MATHEMATICAL DISABILITIES HAVE DIFFICULTY LEARNING THE PRINCIPLES AND STANDARDS FOR SCHOOL MATHEMATICS?

Mathematical disabilities stem from a variety of problems including difficulties associated with memory, language processing, and cognitive development. We describe these difficulties and provide examples of how these difficulties may influence the ability to learn mathematics successfully without the use of adaptations.

Students may be identified as having problems with working memory, long-term memory, and executive functioning (Hallahan, Lloyd, Kauffman, Weiss, & Martinez, 2005). Working memory focuses on simultaneously processing and storing information. Long-term memory is a permanent storage of information that is facilitated by how information is stored using associations and organizational formats. Executive functioning refers to one's ability to self-monitor using working memory, inner speech, attention, and rehearsal (Swanson, Cooney, & O'Shaughnessy, 1998). Students who exhibit memory problems (Garnett & Fleischner, 1983) and who are slower in processing information (Geary, 1993) lack the automatic ability to retrieve arithmetic combinations (i.e., facts) that are needed to solve numeric problems typically encountered in middle school mathematics. Memory difficulties cause problems with the ability to recall and execute the multiple steps that are needed to solve complex problems such as word problems (Bryant, Bryant, & Hammill, 1990). Hallahan et al. (2005) offer a student example of how memory problems affect mathematics: Shannon, a sixth-grade student, explains, "I know I won't make it in algebra—there's just too much to learn. Even now in math, I sometimes just give up because there is no way that I can remember all the facts *and* how to do the problem. It doesn't really matter if I study or not" (p. 226). As is evident in Shannon's words, not only is she demonstrating memory problems, but her motivation for learning advanced mathematics appears to be waning.

Language processing difficulties can be manifested both receptively and expressively (Hallahan et al., 2005). Receptive processing refers to listening and reading ability and expressive processing relates to speaking and writing skills.

Both listening and reading difficulties interfere with student ability to access information successfully. Especially, it is well documented that many students with mathematical disabilities have concurrent reading disabilities that contribute significantly to their learning problems (Jordan & Montani, 1997).

Related to mathematics instruction, receptive language processing can affect students' reading and understanding of the vocabulary contained in the middle school curriculum. For instance, students need to be able to understand the meaning of terms such as *numerator, factor, prime number,* and *equation* as they listen to instruction about these concepts and engage in discussions within peer-mediated groups to solve problems. Abstract symbols (e.g., Σ, σ, π, $\geq$) connote their own meaning about concepts and processes. Each symbol must be recognized and its meaning understood to allow students to solve problems. Years ago, Wiig and Semel (1984) noted that the vocabulary of mathematics is "conceptually dense," meaning that students must be able to identify and understand the meaning of each abstract mathematical symbol because unlike reading, contextual clues are limited or nonexistent. Moreover, language difficulties are manifested in students' inability to read and comprehend word problems, including understanding what the problem is asking, comprehending the sentence structure complexity, and discerning extraneous information; difficulties with any of these language-related skills can interfere with the identification and implementation of accurate solution strategies (Rivera, 1997).

Expressive language processing difficulties can impact student ability to engage in small and whole-group discussions. Students may have difficulty expressing their thoughts coherently as part of classroom discussion (Baxter at al., 2001; Woodward, 2004). Unfortunately, students with mathematical disabilities tend not to contribute during whole-class dialogue (Baxter et al., 2001), which for some may be attributable to difficulties with expressive language processing. For instance, returning to our opening scenario, during whole-class instruction, students with mathematical disabilities may refrain from explaining their solution strategies to the whole group. Finally, for students with written language difficulties, activities and assignments that require extensive writing may not be the best way for students to demonstrate their knowledge. For these students, oral discussions or tape-recording their responses may be alternative ways to share their understanding.

Problems with cognitive development are another source of difficulty for students with mathematical disabilities. Problems may be attributable to how students process information and to their developmental problems (Hallahan et al., 2005). Cognitive development involves understanding and using declarative knowledge (i.e., understanding of factual information), procedural knowledge (i.e., rules and procedures), and conceptual knowledge (i.e., understanding relationships). Cognitive development problems may be manifested in difficulties with understanding number systems, noting relationships among numbers (e.g., fractions, decimals), solving word problems, and using effective basic calculation strategies (e.g., counting on, doubles + 1) (Geary, 1990). For example, Montague (1997) found that middle school students differed from their typically achieving peer group both quantitatively and qualitatively in types of cognitive strategies they use to solve word problems (see Chapter 5 for information about strategy difficulties of students with mathematical disabilities). Students who demonstrate difficulty with noticing the reasonableness of answers (i.e., "Does the answer make sense?"), identifying solution strategies that go beyond one basic answer (i.e., "How many different ways can you represent ¾ using the geoboard and grid-lined paper?"), and finding ways to represent data in word problems ("Can you create a chart for the information?") may be struggling with the coordination of declarative, procedural, and conceptual knowledge. We know that these students benefit from a combined approach of explicit instruction with strategy instruction (Swanson, Hoskyn, & Lee, 1999), including questions they can use to monitor their problem solving whether engaged in algebraic word-problem solving, measurement activities, or computational procedures involving rational numbers.

To conclude, evidence-based findings have shown that students with mathematical difficulties or disabilities demonstrate developmental *delay* in procedural strategies; however, other problems such as difficulties with counting strategies and word-problem solving show developmentally *different* characteristics. This persistent pattern of mathematical difficulties can affect an individual's ability to be successful in middle school mathematics classes. For many middle school students with mathematical disabilities, accessing the general education mathematics curriculum may be problematic. These students likely will need adaptations to help them learn the middle grades standards.

HOW CAN TEACHERS ADAPT MATHEMATICS INSTRUCTION TO HELP STUDENTS WITH MATHEMATICAL DISABILITIES BENEFIT FROM INSTRUCTION?

Returning to the scenario at the beginning of the chapter, Mrs. Martinez engaged in practices that effective teachers use during instruction. She provided explicit instruction and then used student-directed mixed-ability small groups for students to solve mathematical tasks. She monitored student progress by circulating and listening in on conversations. It is important that she adapted instruction for those students she observed as struggling with the assigned task.

Adaptations are described as "appropriate adjustments, accommodations, and modifications to instruction or supports that allow students to meet academic requirements and conditions of the curriculum, most often the general education curriculum" (Vaughn Gross Center for Reading and Language Arts [VGCRLA], 2001). There is a need for differentiating or adapting mathematics instruction to respond to students' needs (Gersten, Jordan, & Flojo, 2005) so that students with mathematical disabilities can benefit from standards-based mathematics instruction.

Adaptations share three common characteristics. They are *individualized*, focusing on the strengths of an individual while allowing for or circumventing the struggles students face. They are *relevant* to the objective being taught to all students and should not be viewed as "watering down" the curriculum. Finally, adaptations must be *effective*. We make adaptations so students will learn. If the initial adaptation fails, we continue to make adaptations until the student meets the objective. Teachers can use the Adaptations Framework to help them make decisions about selecting adaptations.

What Is the Adaptations Framework?

Bryant and Bryant (1998) proposed an adaptations framework (AF) as a means for identifying appropriate adaptations for students with disabilities. The AF has four components: setting-specific demands, student-specific characteristics, proposed adaptations, and evaluation. Figure 1.1 shows the connections among the four components. Notice the arrows that show how to work within the framework. Oftentimes, we work back and forth between the components until we find the right adaptation that works well for each student. The following is a description of each component.

Setting-Specific Demands: Tasks and Requisite Abilities

This first AF component involves the tasks that students are expected to perform and the requisite abilities that are needed to perform the identified tasks. Let's look at an example. In the middle school mathematics class (setting), the task related to the standard "understands numbers, ways of representing numbers, and relationships among numbers" might be the following:

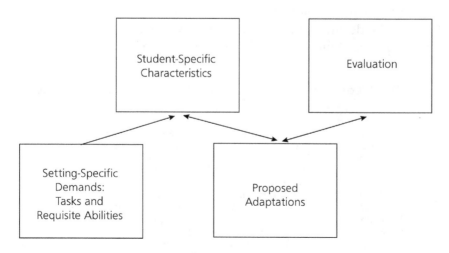

FIGURE 1.1. Components of the adaptations framework.

Representing Fractions and Decimals

Examine the box:

a. If the box represents ⅔, then draw a box that shows ½, ¾, and ⅓.
b. Create a number line to show the location of the numbers in relation to 1.
c. Write the decimal for each fraction.

The requisite abilities include understanding the comparative size of fractions and understanding the relationship between fractions and decimals. Without these requisite abilities, students will have difficulty completing this simple task. We now examine possible requisite abilities for the measurement standards. Include your ideas of requisite abilities for each standard listed in Table 1.2. Once we examine the setting-specific tasks and requisite abilities, the next step is to identify student-specific characteristics as they relate to the tasks and requisite abilities.

Student-Specific Characteristics

The second AF component includes examining the student's strengths and struggles related to the requisite abilities needed to perform the mathematics tasks. For students with mathematical disabilities, strengths and struggles can be identified using information from special education assessments and teacher knowledge of the student. Research studies have shown that teachers know their students well enough to make valid decisions about their strengths and struggles (Gresham, MacMillan, & Bocian, 1997) and can use this information to determine if students possess the requisite abilities for the instructional tasks.

Looking back at our "Representing Fractions and Decimals" example, teachers may already know whether students possess the requisite abilities. If not, they can conduct a quiz to determine if students understand fractions (e.g., identify simple fractions) and the relationship between fractions, decimals, and percents (e.g., given ¼, write the decimal [0.25] and percent [25%] equivalence). A written or oral quiz on the requisite abilities for skills and concepts to be taught will give teachers

TABLE 1.2. NCTM Measurement Standards and Possible Requisite Abilities

Standards	Possible requisite abilities
• Understand measurable attributes of objects and the units, systems, and processes of measurement. • Apply appropriate techniques, tools, and formulas to determine measurements.	• Recognize and name two- and three-dimensional geometric shapes (e.g., parallelogram, triangle, rectangle, trapezoid). • Identify the properties of geometric shapes. • Understand vocabulary such as area, perimeter, right angle, obtuse angle, area, parallel, volume, and vertex. • Know formulas for computing length, area, and volume. • Know benchmark angles (e.g., 45° angle, 90° angle). • Compare angles using appropriate tools (e.g., protractor). • Know the names of tools. • Be able to provide a reasonable estimate for a measurement based on benchmark measures.

TABLE 1.3. Possible Requisite Abilities (Skills) for the NCTM Number and Operations Standards

- Recognizing numbers.
- Remembering numbers (counting) sequentially.
- Discriminating quantities.
- Using place value to recognize numbers and to understand quantity.
- Remembering arithmetic combinations and recalling the combinations fluently (quickly).
- Applying the use of arithmetic combinations in whole-number computation.
- Using effective cognitive counting strategies to retrieve arithmetic combinations.
- Remembering the meaning of *commutative, associative, distributive* (language).
- Discriminating abstract symbols.
- Lining up numbers so that correct calculations can be completed.
- Computing whole-number operations.
- Understanding the associative, commutative, and distributive properties.

valuable information about the performance levels of students before more difficult skills and concepts are introduced.

Let's examine how some of the difficulties or struggles associated with mathematical disabilities, which were discussed earlier in this chapter, can affect students' success with the requisite abilities for the number and operations standards. Table 1.3 lists possible requisite abilities for the number and operations standards. Think of how the requisite abilities, if they are struggles for a particular student, can cause problems in successfully completing the task. Identify how the learning difficulties (i.e., memory problems, language processing [receptive and expressive] difficulties, cognitive development) discussed in an earlier section of this chapter can cause some of these requisite abilities to be struggles for students with mathematical disabilities. If teachers learn that requisite abilities for skills and concepts are lacking, then adaptations may be in order for struggling students.

Proposed Adaptations

The third component of the AF, *proposed adaptations*, can help students complete the task, thereby increasing the likelihood of learning the standards. We use the word *proposed* because we think the adaptations will work, but we are never completely certain. Adaptations can be made in the following four areas (Rivera & Smith, 1997):

1. *Instructional delivery*—how the activity is taught, including grouping practices, instructional routines, and the instructional language (discourse). Explicit or direct instruction is included in instructional delivery. Examples of explicit instruction include modeling (the teacher provides a demonstration of processes or steps to solve the problem); prompts or cues (the teacher provides assistance to increase the likelihood of correct responses); corrective feedback (the teacher provides immediate, corrective feedback for error responses); and guided practice (the teacher provides opportunities to respond and practice).

2. *Instructional materials*—aids such as textbooks, kits, hardware, software, representations, and manipulatives.
3. *Instructional content*—skills and concepts (i.e., NCTM *Standards*) that are the focus of teaching and learning.
4. *Instructional activity*—the actual lessons used to teach and reinforce skills and concepts.

Below are examples of potential adaptations. Recall that adaptations mean doing something different during instruction that helps students better understand what you are teaching.

HOW CAN WE ADAPT THE INSTRUCTIONAL DELIVERY?

Initial instructional delivery: Student-directed
• Students figure out how to solve problems using their own solution strategies.

Adapted instructional delivery: Teacher-directed
• Teachers demonstrate how to solve a problem by going through the steps of the process.
• Teachers use "thinking aloud" to demonstrate the thinking processes for problem solutions. As seen in Figure 1.2, a "thinking-aloud" character can be created and posted for the teacher to remind students that she is using the "thinking-aloud" process to demonstrate how to use a cognitive strategy to solve certain problems or how to get started with an activity. "Thinking aloud" involves the teacher saying the cognitive steps she is using to start an activity and to solve a problem.
• Teachers give specific steps for students to use coupled with questions for solving a word problem. Key questions can include the following:
   1. When reading the problem—"Are there words I don't know?" "Are there number words?"
   2. When restating the problem—"What information is important?" "What is the question asking?" "What are the facts?"

FIGURE 1.2. Thinking-aloud prompt.

3. When developing a plan—"How can I organize the facts?" "What operation will I use?"
4. When computing the answer—"What steps do I use?" "What is the answer?" "Did I get the same answer using the calculator?"
5. When determining the reasonableness of the answer—"Does this answer make sense with the information I used?"

- Teachers give "key questions" sheets to help students solve a problem. For example, in dividing whole numbers, key questions can include: What does the problem say? What are the steps? What step did you just do? What step comes next?

Initial grouping
- Students are grouped in mixed-ability small groups.

Adapted grouping
- Students are paired with higher-performing students to complete activities (see Figure 1.3).
- Student pairs then join into foursomes to share their ideas. Foursomes can turn to a foursome next to them and each group again shares their solutions.
- Teachers use flexible grouping arrangements so that some groups have students who require additional teacher assistance and other groups can function independently.

Initial discourse
- Teachers ask students to think about different ways to solve problems.
- Students discuss problems together.
- Students share solution strategies with the whole class.

Adapted discourse
- Teachers provide specific questions for students to answer: "What if . . . ?" "How do you know . . . ?" "How can you show . . . ?" "What is another way to explain . . . ?" "What steps did you use to . . . ?"

FIGURE 1.3. Student pairs.

- Teachers have students write their responses in a journal. This ensures every student has a chance to respond. The journal is a good alternative for students who prefer not to respond orally in class in front of their peers.

HOW CAN WE ADAPT THE INSTRUCTIONAL MATERIALS?

Initial materials: Representational and abstract level
- Representational: Tallies, pictures, graphs, number lines
- Abstract: Numbers, formulas

Adapted materials: Concrete level
- Calculators
- Place-value charts, base-10 blocks
- Geoboards, protractors, three-dimensional shapes
- Fraction strips, fraction/decimal/percent equivalencies charts
- Basic facts charts, cubes
- Graphic organizers

HOW CAN WE ADAPT THE INSTRUCTIONAL CONTENT?

Initial instructional content
- Teachers provide lessons to teach specific instructional objectives related to the *Standards.*

Adapted instructional content
- Teachers break tasks down into smaller steps and teach the steps.
- Teachers teach the vocabulary of upcoming lessons.

HOW CAN WE ADAPT THE INSTRUCTIONAL ACTIVITY?

Initial activity
- This is the lesson teachers provide to all students.

Adapted activity
- Teachers provide "mini-lessons" on smaller steps of the original lesson.
- Teachers provide "mini-lessons" on requisite abilities.

The following is an example of making adaptations in content, activity, and delivery. The teacher is going to teach a lesson on the process of multiplying and dividing fractions. First, she begins by giving students the following problems to solve in small, mixed-ability groups to check their ability with computational procedures involved in multiplying and dividing fractions:

$$\frac{1}{3} \times \frac{1}{3} = \qquad\qquad \frac{1}{3} \times \frac{3}{4} = \qquad\qquad 6 \times \frac{3}{4} =$$

$$\frac{\frac{2}{4}}{\frac{4}{8}} = \qquad\qquad \frac{7}{14} \times \frac{14}{7} = \qquad\qquad \frac{3}{5} \times 0 =$$

As she circulates and "listens in," she identifies several incorrect computational procedures. She also hears some students misidentifying the terms *numerator* and *denominator,* or not knowing the terms at all. Here are the incorrect answers from several groups including students with mathematical disabilities. See if you can identify the error patterns.

1. $\frac{1}{3} \times \frac{3}{4} = \frac{3}{12}$ 2. $6 \times \frac{3}{4} = \frac{18}{24}$ 3. $\frac{3}{5} \times 0 = \frac{3}{5}$

Problem 1: The answer was not reduced to lowest terms.
Problem 2: The whole number was multiplied by the numerator ($6 \times 3 = 18$) and the denominator ($6 \times 4 = 24$).
Problem 3: The any number $\times$ 0 rule was not followed.

Here is how the teacher handles the issue that some students lack the requisite abilities for multiplying fractions. First, based on error analysis assessment, she recognizes three procedures (instructional content) that are problematic and conducts "mini-lessons" (instructional activity) on those three procedures (e.g., reducing fractions, the times-zero rule). She teaches the procedure of reducing fractions and the times-zero rule explicitly (instructional delivery).
Here is how she teaches the times-zero rule:

"Today we are going to learn the times-zero rule. It is important for you to know this rule because it will help you solve problems with times-zero quickly and correctly.
"Here is the rule: Any number times zero is zero. What is the rule? [Students respond together with the teacher.]"

The teacher calls on several students to state the rule.

"Here are some problems that use the times-zero rule: $9 \times 0 = 0$, $1,000,000 \times 0 = 0$, $\frac{1}{4} \times 0 = 0$. What do you notice about these problems? [They all have $\times$ 0 and they all equal 0.] Now, you make up problems showing the times-zero rule and share with your partner."

The teacher uses the active participation cards (see below for a description) to check student understanding.
Second, she implements a warm-up activity that focuses on the vocabulary related to fractions (e.g., *numerator* and *denominator*) prior to all activities involving fractions. She uses different ways to check students' understanding (see evaluation section below) of the terms and then moves on to the lesson.
With proposed adaptations, we need to keep in mind that they should focus on the individual student's strengths and struggles as they relate to the tasks and requisite abilities. For example, to solve these problems (task)—$\frac{1}{3} \times \frac{3}{4} = ?$, $6 \times \frac{3}{4} = ?$, $\frac{3}{4} / \frac{4}{8} = ?$ and $\frac{3}{5} \times 0 = ?$—the student needs to know how to multiply, the times-

zero rule, and how to reduce fractions to the lowest term (requisite abilities). Our student had difficulties (struggles) with these abilities; thus, the teacher adapted the lesson by providing a "mini-lesson" using explicit instruction to teach procedures and a rule, she taught the vocabulary, and she reduced the instructional content demands of the lesson initially.

Evaluation

The fourth component of the AF is evaluation, which helps teachers determine if an adaptation is successful. Simply making an adaptation does not mean that it will be successful. If the adaptation is not effective, we continue to make adaptations until the student meets the objective. The following are examples of ways to evaluate student learning.

- Use active participation cards to check students' understanding. The "yes/no" or "true/false" card can be used for students to respond to questions you pose. For example, a 90° angle is a benchmark to use when figuring out degrees of other angles. "Pinch cards" can be developed and laminated to evaluate student understanding of vocabulary, formulas, and other content that lends itself to this evaluation method. Possible answers are recorded on the cards. The teacher poses a question, then asks students to "pinch" the correct response. With both types of cards, it is easy to scan the classroom to see which students need more instruction. In Figure 1.4, the first card is a "yes/no, true/false" example. The second card is a pinch card, where, for example, teachers can give the definition or attributes of shapes, and students can pinch the correct response. For the third card, teachers can provide a formula and students can pinch the correct term. Students can use the active participation cards in small groups to test each other.

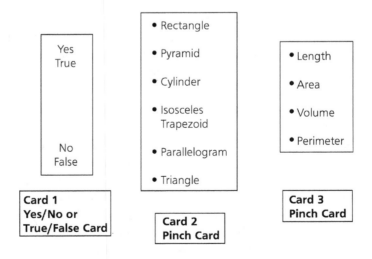

FIGURE 1.4. Active participation cards.

- Observe students engaged in activities; collect anecdotal notes on their engagement, contributions, solution strategies, and ability to engage in discussions.
- Have students use self-monitoring sheets to evaluate their own work. The sheet can contain questions to which students can check yes, no, or not certain. Questions might include: "Did I follow the procedures?" "Did I contribute one idea to the group?" "Did I circle the signs?" "Did I use my cue sheet?" "Was the calculator helpful?"

We have discussed the four components of the AF and examples of types of adaptations that teachers can make. Now, we will look at the AF in action.

ADAPTATIONS FRAMEWORK IN ACTION: INSTRUCTIONAL LESSON—BUYING SOD FOR THE BACKYARD

Objective: The student will use a strategy to solve a multistep problem.
- **Instructional materials:** measuring tape, graph paper
- **Vocabulary:** area, square, foot

Setting-Specific Demands

Task: Use mathematical concepts, skills, and procedures to solve a problem (instructional content: NCTM standards—measurement, algebra, problem solving)

Requisite abilities: Knowledge of measurement vocabulary, setting up and solving equation, representing problem, computational skills, ability to use calculator

Student-Specific Characteristics (Hypothetical Student)

Strengths: Basic computational skills
- **Struggles:** Knowledge of measurement vocabulary, setting up and solving equations, representing problems, ability to use calculator
- **Activity:** Before the lesson, the teacher provides an adaptation by reviewing the vocabulary (instructional content) because she knows that several students may require a quick review of the terms *area, square, foot*. She then provides directions to the whole class for the activity:

  "In small groups, you are going to work together to generate a solution to the following problem. You are going to lay sod in your backyard. Sod is sold in 12" × 12" squares. The backyard is 30′ × 20′. Draw a diagram of your backyard area you wish to sod on graph paper. Sod goes for $.85 a square. How much will the sod cost to complete the project? Solve the problem and record your group's answer and reasoning."

The teacher circulates among groups asking questions to facilitate discussion and problem solving. The teacher provides another adaptation by modeling (instructional delivery) one way to solve the problem for one group of students who are struggling with the problem. Two additional proposed adaptations include "key questions" and the use of a calculator. She provides the group with "key questions" (instructional delivery—discourse) to answer and demonstrates how to use the calculator (instructional material).

Evaluation

1. The teacher observes during the group activity, recording anecdotal notes about student performance.

2. Each group presents their findings orally to the class using two overhead transparencies. One lists the steps of their process. The other is a diagram illustrating their sodded area. Based on the class presentation by one group, the teacher realizes that some students require additional instruction because they demonstrated difficulty representing and solving the problem. She proposes and implements an adaptation to this group by doing a 10-minute "mini-lesson" on computational procedures (instructional activity and content) while the rest of the class continues with other exercises.

CONCLUSION

We know that many middle school students with mathematical disabilities are taught mathematics in the general education setting. In today's classrooms, instruction involves investigations of a variety of problems to teach the *Standards*. Students spend time interacting with their peers in small groups to solve problems and discuss findings. We know that students with mathematical disabilities may have difficulties accessing the general education mathematics curriculum due to problems with memory, language processing, and cognitive development. The Adaptations Framework is a useful tool to help teachers reflect on their instruction (setting-specific demands) and their students' individual needs (student-specific characteristics) as they relate to mathematics instruction. The Framework provides ideas for making adaptations in instructional delivery, instructional content, instructional activity, and instructional material. Finally, teachers evaluate the effect of these adaptations on their students' ability to master the curriculum.

REFERENCES

Badian, N. A. (1983). Dyscalculia and nonverbal disorders of learning. In H. R. Myklebust (Ed.), *Progress in learning disabilities* (Vol. 5, pp. 235–264). New York: Grune & Stratton.

Baxter, J., Woodward, J., & Olson, D. (2001). Effects of reform-based mathematics instruction in five third grade classrooms. *Elementary School Journal, 101*, 529–548.

Bryant, D. P., & Bryant, B. R. (1998). Using assistive technology adaptations to include students with learning disabilities in cooperative learning activities. *Journal of Learning Disabilities, 31*, 41–54.

Bryant, D. P., Bryant, B. R., & Hammill, D. D. (1990). Characteristic behaviors of students with LD who have teacher-identified math weaknesses. *Journal of Learning Disabilities, 33*, 168–177.

Butler, F. M., Miller, S. P., Crehan, K., Babbitt, B., & Pierce, T. (2003). Fraction instruction for students with mathematics disabilities: Comparing two teaching sequences. *Learning Disabilities Research and Practice, 18*, 99–111.

Cawley, J. F., Baker-Kroczynski, S., & Urban, A. (1992). Seeking excellence in mathematics education for students with mild disabilities. *Teaching Exceptional Children, 24*, 40–43.

Garnett, K., & Fleischner, J. E. (1983). Automatization and basic fact performance of normal and learning disabled children. *Learning Disability Quarterly, 6*, 223–231.

Geary, D. C. (1990). A componential analysis of an early learning deficit in mathematics. *Journal of Experimental Child Psychology, 49*, 363–383.

Geary, D. C. (1993). Mathematical disabilities: Cognitive, neuropsychological, and genetic components. *Psychological Bulletin, 114*, 345–362.

Geary, D. C. (2004). Mathematics and learning disabilities. *Journal of Learning Disabilities, 37*, 4–15.

Gersten, R., Jordan, N. C., & Flojo, J. R. (2005). Early identification and interventions for students with mathematics difficulties. *Journal of Learning Disabilities, 38*(4), 293–304.

Gresham, F. M., MacMillan, D. L., & Bocian, K. M. (1997). Teachers as "tests": Differential validity of teacher judgments in identifying students at-risk for learning difficulties. *School Psychology Review, 26*, 47–60.

Gross-Tsur, V., Manor, O., & Shaley, R. S. (1996). Developmental dyscalculia: Prevalence and demographic features. *Developmental Medicine and Child Neurology, 38*, 25–33.

Hallahan, D. P., Lloyd, J. W., Kauffman, J. M., Weiss, M., & Martinez, E. A. (2005). *Learning disabilities: Foundations, characteristics, and effective teaching.* Boston: Allyn & Bacon.

Jordan, N., & Montani, T. (1997). Cognitive arithmetic and problem solving: A comparison of children with specific and general mathematics difficulties. *Journal of Learning Disabilities, 30*, 624–634.

Kilpatrick, J., Swafford, J., & Findell, B. (Eds.). (2001). *Adding it up: Helping children learn mathematics.* National Research Council, Mathematics Learning Study Committee, Center for Education, Division of Behavioral and Social Sciences and Education. Washington, DC: National Academy Press.

Lemke, M., Sen, A., Pahlke, E., Partelow, L., Miller, D., Williams, T., et al. (2004). *International outcomes of learning in mathematics literacy and problem solving: PISA 2003 results from the U.S. perspective* (NCES 2005–003). Washington, DC: U.S. Department of Education, National Center for Education Statistics.

National Council of Teachers of Mathematics. (1989). *Curriculum and evaluation standards for school mathematics.* Reston, VA: Author.

National Council of Teachers of Mathematics. (2000). *Principles and standards for school mathematics.* Reston, VA: Author.

Ostad, S. A. (1998). Comorbidity between mathematics and spelling difficulties. *Logopedics, Phoniatrics, Vocology, 23*, 145–154.

Rivera, D. P. (1997). Mathematics education and students with learning disabilities: Introduction to the special series. *Journal of Learning Disabilities, 30*, 2–19, 68.

Rivera, D. P., & Smith, D. D. (1997). *Teaching students with learning and behavior problems* (3rd ed.). Boston: Allyn & Bacon.

Swanson, H., Cooney, J. B., & O'Shaughnessy, T. E. (1998). Learning disabilities and memory. In B. Wong (Ed.), *Learning about learning disabilities* (2nd ed., pp. 107–162). San Diego, CA: Academic Press.

Swanson, H. L., Hoskyn, M., & Lee, C. (1999). *Interventions for students with learning disabilities. A meta-analysis of treatment outcomes.* New York: Guilford Press.

Vaughn Gross Center for Reading and Language Arts. (2001). *Effective instruction for struggling readers: Research-based practices.* Austin, TX: Texas Education Agency.

Wiig, E. H., & Semel, E. M. (1984). *Language assessment and intervention for the learning disabled* (2nd ed.). New York: Macmillan.

Woodward, J. (2004). Mathematics education in the United States: Past to present. *Journal of Learning Disabilities, 37*(1), 16–31.

Woodward, J., & Baxter, J. (1997). The effects of an innovative approach to mathematics on academically low-achieving students in mainstreamed settings. *Exceptional Children, 63,* 373–388.

CHAPTER 2

Making Reform-Based Mathematics Work for Academically Low-Achieving Middle School Students

JOHN WOODWARD

Randy Nealman used to begin his middle school special education class by making sure that students were quiet as he passed out the day's worksheets. After showing students how to perform an operation or answer a simple, one-step word problem, he'd spend the rest of the period working with students individually and managing behavior problems.

"One of the biggest challenges that I had when I used a drill-oriented approach was student motivation. I found it hard to get students interested in math. They would groan and complain, 'When am I ever going to use this stuff?' Even worse were those students who filled out worksheets carelessly because they didn't care about math anymore."

Over the last year, Mr. Nealman has been trying a more reform-oriented approach to teaching his middle school students. Even though each day begins with brief, independent practice, it is followed by multiple opportunities for students to work on math as a group, not an isolated set of individuals. Nealman makes an effort to discuss concepts with students before they practice a small set of problems. He has also been encouraged by the effects of manipulatives and drawings on student understanding. "I never realized how important it was for students to think and show their understanding of operations and concepts. Talking with students about math helps me foster strategic thinking. I have also found that good, application-oriented activities are an effective way of answering the question, 'Why do I need to know this stuff?' It's much more work teaching math this way, but I can see big differences in motivation and understanding."

For many years, special educators have perceived competence in mathematics to be fluency in math facts and computational procedures as well as the ability to solve problems quickly and accurately. This image of basic skills mastery is alluring because these targeted outcomes are relatively straightforward. They lend themselves to hierarchical instruction, with each step in the sequence taught to mastery. This perspective, however, is a great distance from what the National Research Council's *Adding It Up* (Kilpatrick, Swafford, & Findell, 2001) recently described as mathematical proficiency: (1) conceptual understanding; (2) procedural fluency; (3) strategic competence, the ability to formulate and represent problems; (4) adaptive reasoning, the capacity for logical thought, explanation, and justification; and (5) productive disposition, the belief that mathematics makes sense and is useful. These dimensions of proficiency make for an ambitious agenda for moving American students to much higher levels of mathematics achievement.

Initially, many special educators were skeptical of the mathematics reform of the early 1990s, labeling it elitist and characterizing it as recycled efforts from the new math of the 1960s (see Woodward & Montague, 2002). However, continued efforts to reform math in the United States based on ongoing research and new curricula, as well as the impetus of new National Council of Teachers of Mathematics (NCTM, 2000) *Standards* suggest that mathematics reform is far from an educational fad or pendulum swing that will eventually return to basic skills instruction. In fact, arguments today are less about whether standards should guide math education and more about which standards should be adopted and how they should be implemented (Loucks-Horsley, Love, Stiles, Mundry, & Hewson, 2003).

The gap between typical special education practice and the current state of mathematics reform can be explained on at least four grounds. The first stems from fundamental assumptions about instructional interventions in special education. The professional literature and the way in which graduate students are prepared in special education tend to focus on broad-based instructional interventions, particularly instructional and classroom organization strategies, over in-depth knowledge of a specific discipline. Consequently, the research in the field is filled with studies on curriculum-based measurement, peer tutoring, direct instruction, strategy-based instruction, and the like. For many researchers, the specific content and structure of a discipline (e.g., math, science, social studies) is secondary to these broader interventions. The way special educators tend to think about instruction also tends to place a great emphasis on the skills in a discipline. This is one reason why math (a discipline) is easily confused with skills instruction (e.g., phonics).

A second and related reason is historical. In the late 1970s and early 1980s, prominent research in remedial, special, and general education research coincided. Effective teaching research and direct instruction shared many common principles (Becker, 1977; Brophy & Good, 1986). In an effort to help students develop mastery of basic skills, teachers were encouraged to move through a lesson at a brisk pace, model new procedures, ask low-level questions that allowed immediate feedback, and provide extended opportunities for students to complete carefully supervised seatwork or homework. Many of these practices were called into question two decades later through mathematics research in the United States (see Grouws, 1992; Putnam, Lampert, & Peterson, 1990) and international comparison studies (e.g., the Third International Mathematics and Science Study [TIMSS]).

A third major reason for the distance between the common special education vision of mathematics instruction and the wider view held in the mathematics education community is a deep distrust of constructivism, which is commonly associated with math reform. Some special educators present oversimplified accounts of constructivism, suggesting that it is nothing more than discovery learning (Carnine, 2000). Geary (2001) provides a good example of the confusion around constructivism in his recent essay on the evolutionary dimensions of learning. He seems to dismiss constructivism as opposed to the kind of skills instruction needed in math. At the same time, he acknowledges the importance of classroom discussions, particularly opportunities for children to explain their thinking to others. The latter practice is fully consistent with social constructivism. Some of this confusion undoubtedly stems from the asymmetry between constructivism as a theory of learning and what has appeared over time as a diverse set of instructional principles. There are multiple visions of constructivist practice, and thus it is a mistake to characterize its instructional methods in one way. The concept of scaffolding, which is central to constructivist practice, suggests that constructivism is much more than open-ended discovery learning. Nor is it the case that constructivism prevents teachers from focusing on skills. As the section below on number sense suggests, skills instruction needs to be thoughtfully integrated with more meaningful activities.

A final reason for the gap between current math reform and special education practice has to do with learner characteristics, particularly children who are broadly labeled as having learning disabilities. Most mathematics intervention research is conducted on this population of students. Unfortunately, this special education category is notoriously ill defined. Some would claim that the vast majority of students with learning disabilities (LD) are misclassified, and that their main difficulties are reading problems (Lyon et al., 2001). Others in the field intimate that a distinct subset of students with LD suffers from dyscalculia, and that these students have a difficult time acquiring basic skills like math facts if they can learn them at all (Geary, 1994, 2004). Still others question the construct of learning disabilities from a philosophical and sociological standpoint (Reid & Valle, 2004). Their accounts suggest that social and cultural factors significantly outweigh neurological impairments as an explanation for why students end up (or should end up) being labeled LD.

Even more problems with the LD category can be found by examining the math intervention literature. When studies are conducted in naturalistic settings, the accessible samples often possess a wide range of characteristics because cooperating districts, not researchers, qualify these students as LD. As a consequence, many students who under other conditions would be labeled as mildly developmentally delayed or behavior disordered are classified as LD. The sum effect of all of this is that it is difficult to link one best practice to such a heterogeneous population of students. Put in a mathematical context, some students classified as LD would be best served with consumer math and daily living skills rather than a continuum of instruction that leads them toward increasingly ambitious mathematics.

ALIGNING MATHEMATICS INSTRUCTION FOR STUDENTS WITH LEARNING DISABILITIES WITH MATHEMATICAL PROFICIENCY

The remainder of this chapter describes new ways of conceptualizing math instruction for many students with LD. The different sections draw on emerging directions in the field of special education where researchers are attempting to rethink or broaden the instructional experiences for these students. It is hoped that this perspective will move students toward increased mathematical proficiency as articulated in *Adding It Up* (Kilpatrick et al., 2001). Finally, as suggested above, LD as they exist in schools (vs. idealized accounts in the professional literature) are markedly heterogeneous. Thus, what is presented may not be well suited to *all* students in the category of LD.

Developing Number Sense

Special educators have recently become interested in the development of number sense as a foundation for mathematics understanding. Gersten and Chard (1999) suggest that intense remediation in number sense will better prepare primary-grade students at risk for special education to be competent in the skills needed to start learning topics like addition and subtraction. Their argument draws on 20 years of mathematics research, beginning with Gelman and Gallistel's (1986) seminal work with 3- to 5-year-olds. This work established a clear progression in the ability to make a one-to-one correspondence between counting words and objects and the principle of order irrelevance (i.e., the ability to count objects in any order). Subsequent research by Siegler (1996) and others underscores the complexity of this kind of development. In fact, Siegler documented how students can demonstrate a range of mathematical strategies in the early primary grades, and the choice of a strategy often depends on the task. This line of research has culminated in Griffin, Case, and Siegler's (1994) Right Start program, which presents counting skills in the context of number line games.

Promising as early number sense interventions might be, they can be problematic on two accounts. First, there is the danger of transforming number sense activities into direct instruction drills. Current efforts in early reading make the notion of drill on basic skills plausible. However, there is a vast difference between the kind of convergent, drill-based instruction that might lead a student to identify the letter *f* and say its sound and the kind of understanding associated with a number like 4. Figure 2.1 shows the range of concepts associated with this number, virtually all of which can be learned in the primary grades.

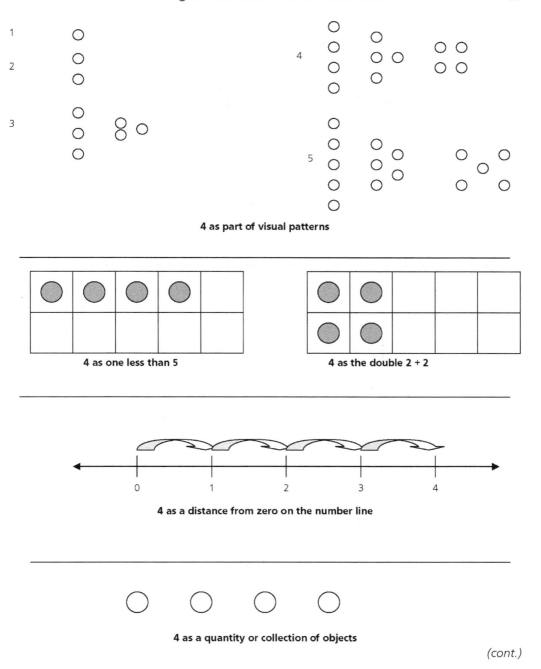

4 as part of visual patterns

4 as one less than 5   **4 as the double 2 + 2**

4 as a distance from zero on the number line

4 as a quantity or collection of objects

(cont.)

FIGURE 2.1. Understanding the number 4.

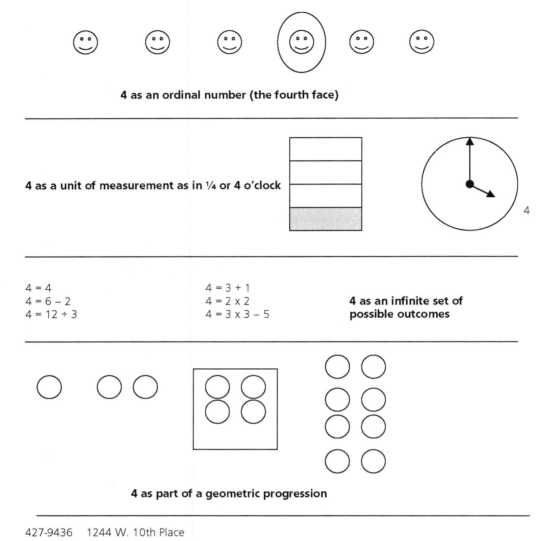

4 as an ordinal number (the fourth face)

4 as a unit of measurement as in ¼ or 4 o'clock

4 = 4	4 = 3 + 1
4 = 6 – 2	4 = 2 x 2
4 = 12 ÷ 3	4 = 3 x 3 – 5

4 as an infinite set of possible outcomes

4 as part of a geometric progression

427-9436   1244 W. 10th Place

4 as an arbitrary number

4 + 4 ≠ 8   as in 4 dollars + 4 dimes

different units of 4

FIGURE 2.1. *(cont.)*

Clearly, many of these representations are learned over time as students move through the primary grades, and as Fuson (1988) pointed out, number lines are potentially confusing for young learners because of the number of tick marks (i.e., there are five tick marks that are used to represent the distance of 4).

The second problem is the implication that number sense development is a primary grade phenomenon. Liping Ma's (1999) now classic interviews with U.S. and Chinese teachers present tacit examples of how number sense develops throughout the elementary grades. Arguably, number sense develops concurrently across the entire mathematics experience. As one example of Ma's research, teachers in the United States tend to show students only one method for solving subtraction problems like the one below.

$$
\begin{array}{r}
5 \\
\cancel{6}\ ^{1}2 \\
-3\ \ 9 \\
\hline
2\ \ 3
\end{array}
$$

In contrast, Chinese teachers show students multiple ways of solving the problem. Each method turns on the ability to decompose numbers by place value and work efficiently with facts. For example, students can learn how to work "from the top" by decomposing 62 into 50 + 12, and 39 into 30 + 9. Once this is accomplished, students can subtract 50 – 30 and 12 – 9. This yields 20 and 3 or 23. An alternative method would be to decompose 62 into 50 + 10 + 2 and 39 into 30 + 9. Once it is broken up this way, students can learn to subtract in this fashion: 50 – 30 and 10 – 9. Students then add 20 + 1 + 2 to get an answer of 23.

To be sure, it is unclear at this point how many methods are suited to academically low-achieving students in the elementary grades. There is little reason to believe that exposing all students to multiple (or invented) algorithms will ensure success for everyone. Figure 2.2 presents a more conservative array of methods for helping students think about addition.

At the top, students learn the traditional algorithm and contrast this understanding with an expanded algorithm. The advantage of the former is that it is efficient. The advantage of the latter is that students explicitly see two key concepts: place value and regrouping. This understanding is enhanced through the use of number blocks, which also help students understand the regrouping process.

The next portion of Figure 2.2 shows how the same addition problem can be presented horizontally and the numbers decomposed by place value. It should be apparent that this kind of presentation informally introduces students to the commutative property and, more generally, the horizontal structure of mathematics found from middle school onward. In all likelihood, this kind of presentation is best suited to academically low-achieving students in the intermediate or middle school grades.

Finally, Figure 2.2 shows the value of approximations as a core dimension of number sense. Students need only learn a limited number of strategies for rounding and then approximating answers to problems. The first strategy encourages students to round up or down to the nearest decade or hundred if applicable. An extension of this strategy is to compensate with problems like 44 + 24. In other words, both call for rounding down. However, the effects of rounding both numbers down can be contrasted with rounding one of the numbers down and the

Traditional and expanded algorithm and number blocks

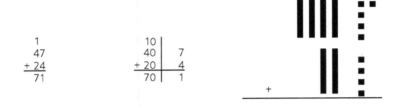

Horizontal addition by place value

$$74 + 24 =$$
$$40 + 7 + 20 + 4 =$$
$$40 + 20 + 7 + 4 =$$
$$60 + 11 =$$
$$60 + 10 + 1 =$$
$$70 + 1 = 71$$

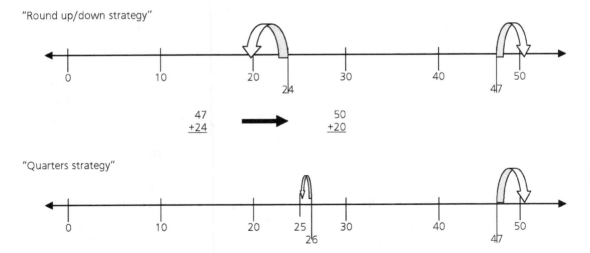

FIGURE 2.2. Developing number sense.

other one up. Consequently, the compensation approach yields a closer approxima-tion than rounding both numbers down. The quarters strategy builds off the con-cept of money and has students round to 25, 50, or 75. As students are introduced to different strategies over time, opportunities arise for discussion regarding which strategy is best suited to a particular context. Moreover, it is critical that number sense arise from informal as well as formal contexts.

Some math researchers feel that students are most likely to expand their understanding of numbers when it is part of a classroom "environment" (Greeno, 1991). It is equally important that number sense is an agenda that develops concur-rently with every mathematical topic. For example, being able to use benchmarks to talk about decimal numbers such as 0.3147 as about $\frac{1}{3}$ is important number sense as well as a way to connect two types of rational numbers. Identifying compatible numbers and commuting to simplify the following algebraic expression also involves number sense.

$$17 + 6x + 9 + x + 3 + 4x \rightarrow 17 + 3 + 9 + 6x + 4x + x \rightarrow 29 + 11x$$

These kinds of activities, which occur across the grade levels as students learn mathematics, help develop conceptual understanding. Naturally, this needs to be coupled with the development of procedural fluency, particularly in math facts and extended facts (e.g., $4 + 5 = 9$, $40 + 50 = 90$). The emphasis on strategies for learning facts as well as on the use of approximation in solving mathematical problems also fosters the kind of strategic competence described in *Adding It Up* (Kilpatrick et al., 2001).

Conceptual Understanding

A central theme in mathematics education since the mid-1980s has been the impor-tance of conceptual understanding to mathematical competence. A series of influ-ential texts on mathematical concepts written over the last 15 years emphasize the importance of conceptual understanding as a guide to procedural fluency (e.g., Carpenter, Fennema, & Romberg, 1993; Hiebert, 1986; Leinhardt, Putnam, & Hattrup, 1992; Ma, 1999). The importance of conceptual understanding was rein-forced recently in reflections on the results of the Trends in International Mathe-matics and Science Study (TIMSS). Schmidt, one of the senior authors of the TIMSS research emphasized the importance of conceptual understanding as a common thread in successful mathematics instruction around the world (Math Projects Jour-nal, 2002; Schmidt, McKnight, & Raizen, 1997).

The role of conceptual understanding is certainly not restricted to the manipu-lation of numbers. Other core topics such as measurement and geometry are excel-lent venues for exploring concepts and problem solving. Furthermore, math research indicates that elementary and secondary students are prone to significant misconceptions in topic areas such as geometry (Barrett, Clements, Klanderman, Pennisi, & Polaki, 2001; Toumasis, 1994). Regrettably, there is little research in the special education literature on topics such as geometry. Carnine (1997) offered a rare description of geometry instruction for students with learning disabilities. Using what he called an instructional design perspective, he described how an understanding of volume formulas for common three-dimensional objects can be reduced to variations on base • height. This organization enables students to see the "sameness" between the objects that is otherwise masked by a disparate set of formulas. For example, the volume formula for a cylinder is base • height. However, the formula for the volume of a sphere is typically written as $\frac{4}{3} \pi r^3$. Carnine showed an alternative formula for a sphere written as base • $\frac{2}{3}$ • height. The alternative formula uses the area of a circle as a base and a perpendicular diameter that intersects this base as the height. However, it is not clear if the students ever compare the traditional formula with its alternative to see how they are equivalent.

The potential advantage of this kind of treatment is that it does more than draw attention to the common role of base and height in volume formulas. If these concepts are presented with physical models, students can explore the relationship between two- and three-dimensional objects. Carnine does not indicate if this is a complementary activity, and one is left wondering if the ultimate purpose of this sameness analysis is to facilitate an easier method for memorizing formulas for various pyramids, prisms, and a sphere.

An alternative and much richer framework for thinking about geometry concepts comes from the work of van Hiele (Fuys, Geddes, & Tischler, 1988). Rather than focus on vocabulary and memorizing formulas, the van Hiele system places considerable emphasis on the role of observation and problem solving in the early stages of learning about geometric objects. The system then gradually builds toward the more formal geometry that is studied at the high school and college levels. Fuys et al. argue that textbooks in the United States frequently emphasize memorization of formulas in the elementary and middle grades and then move quickly to theorems and deduction in high school. Consequently, many students do not receive an adequate foundation in geometric thinking and fail to achieve complex levels of understanding. This is less of an issue for students with disabilities because of the focus on computations and one- or two-step word problems in the research literature and of the fact that most day-to-day instructional settings largely ignore geometry.

A system like van Hiele's can be a constructive way of thinking about geometry instruction for students with LD. Examining different shapes and then grouping them into different categories (e.g., objects with straight sides, objects with at least one acute angle, objects with convex surfaces) can be a problem-sovling task that promotes logical thinking. Finding lines of symmetry on cut-out objects and creating tessellations as ways to slide, flip, and turn objects are possible early, informal activities.

As students move toward higher levels of geometric understanding, they have the opportunity to explore the underpinnings of many of the formulas used for two- and three-dimension objects. This aspect of the van Hiele system is particularly crucial, because it enables students to visualize properties of objects and the rules or formulas used to describe these objects. For example, triangles can play a significant role in many two-dimensional shapes. For a higher-level activity, students can investigate different types of triangles using metric rulers and protractors to measure the sides and angles and then discuss their results. Examples of the kinds of triangles that could be used for this kind of instruction are shown in Figure 2.3.

A discussion of the properties of the six different triangles should yield the observation that triangles A and C have equal sides and equal angles (i.e., equilateral triangles), triangles B and E have two sides and two angles that have the same measurements (i.e., isosceles triangles), and triangles D and F have unequal sides and angles (i.e., scalene triangles). The potential benefit of this approach is that it turns the rote memorization task of simply identifying three different types of triangles into one where students need to create classifications based on common features.

An investigation of triangles can be extended into area formulas for many two-dimensional objects. For example, it is relatively easy to communicate the formula for the area of a square or rectangle through arrays as shown at the top of Figure 2.4. Students can readily see that the area formula for these two objects is length • width or, to use consistent language for two-dimensional objects, base • height.

Students can see how other area formulas were derived through a series of prolem-solving activities. For example, bisecting a rectangle into two congruent triangles as shown in Figure 2.4 helps students see that the area of the triangle is ½ base • height. Manipulating the triangular portion of a parallelogram (e.g., cutting and then reassembling) helps students see that the area of a parallelogram is the same as that of a rectangle.

A similar logic applies to the formula for the area of a trapezoid. Dividing the trapezoid into two triangles creates the basis for seeing how the area formula for the trapezoid is derived. Seeing the traditional formula requires one more step where the ½ is factored as a coefficient.

Triangles can play a role in helping students understand how to derive the area of any polygon. Figure 2.4 also shows how an irregular polygon like the pentagon can be divided into triangles in order to find its area. Regular polygons such as the hexagon allow students to use problem-solving strategies such as making a simpler version of the problem in order to find the area. In this case, the student might subdivide the hexagon into six equilateral triangles, measure the base and height of each one, and then multiply that area by six.

Finally, well-structured activities that allow students to investigate properties of circles enable students to understand the concept of pi as well as the formula for the area of a circle. As Figure 2.4 indicates, students can measure the diameter and circumference of a cylinder and compare the two measurements. Diameter divides circumference 3.14 times. Taking this kind of exploration a step further, if circles are systematically divided into small wedges or what appear to be small triangles and reassembled into a parallelogram, students can get an approximate sense of how the area formula πr^2 is derived.

This kind of foundation in two-dimensional objects lays the groundwork for studying properties of three-dimensional objects. Using the van Hiele system as a

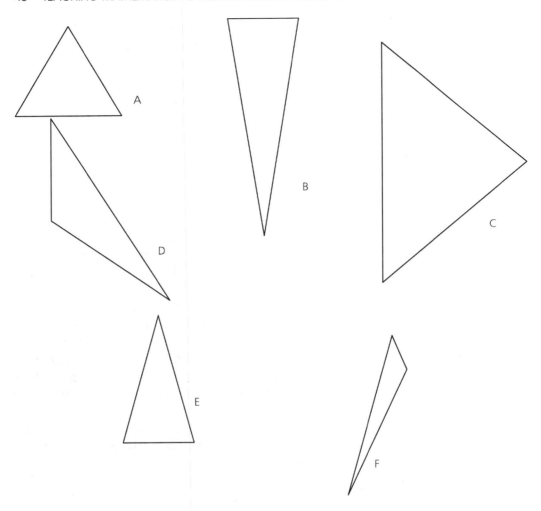

FIGURE 2.3. Identifying different types of triangles.

guide, an initial activity would be to compare properties of prisms and pyramids. Figure 2.5 shows that these comparisons entail considerations of cylinders and cones as respective members of the different categories of prisms and pyramids.

Figure 2.5 indicates how students can investigate the relationship between two- and three-dimensional objects, specifically prisms. For example, triangular prisms are composed of a stack of triangles in the same way that a cylinder is a stack of circles. Pyramids, particularly cones, present a different kind of conceptual challenge simply because rotating a right triangle 360° will be inadequate for understanding volume formula for a cone of ⅓ base • height. As with the volume of a sphere, there are no easy ways to link the formula with a robust visualization of how the formula is derived. However, a tactile way to prove the cone formula is simply to pour the contents (i.e., the volume) of a cone into a cylinder of the same diameter and height. As Figure 2.5 indicates, three cones fill the cylinder; hence the volume of the cone is one-third that of the cylinder.

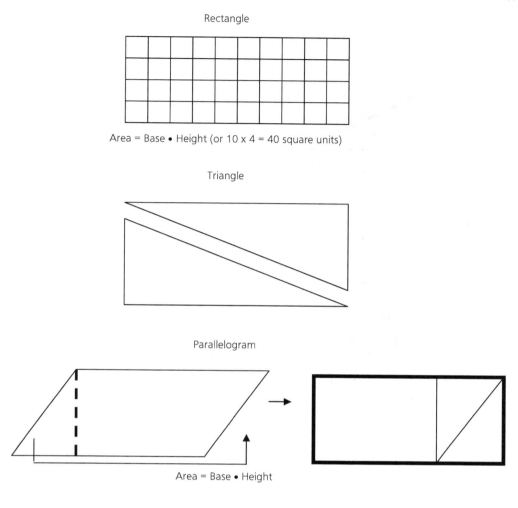

Rectangle

Area = Base • Height (or 10 x 4 = 40 square units)

Triangle

Parallelogram

Area = Base • Height

(cont.)

FIGURE 2.4. The role of triangles in various two-dimensional objects.

These examples of geometry thinking based on the van Hiele system indicate a shift in what is valued knowledge in mathematics instruction for students with learning disabilities. Hiebert (1999) has argued that the current shift in mathematics instruction in the United States—and arguably, at a global level (see *Journal of Learning Disabilities*, January/February 2004)—has to do with an emerging consensus on what students need to know in the world today and the near future. Clearly, the increasing role of technology has devalued the importance of computational fluency alone. Activities like the ones described above that promote conceptual understanding also provide opportunities for adaptive reasoning, logical thinking, and explanation as well as a productive disposition as described in *Adding It Up* (Kilpatrick et al., 2001).

Trapezoid

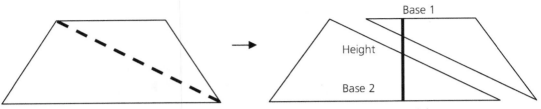

Area = ½ Base 1 • Height + ½ Base 2 • Height

Area = ½ (Base 1 + Base 2) • Height

Other Polygons

Irregular Pentagon

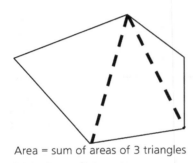

Area = sum of areas of 3 triangles

Regular Hexagon

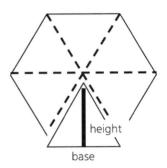

Area = 6 • (½ • base • height)

FIGURE 2.4. *(cont.)*

Problem Solving

For many years, problem solving for students with LD involved what some researchers have characterized as "end-of-the-chapter" problems (Goldman, Hasselbring, and the Cognition and Technology Group at Vanderbilt, 1997; Woodward, 2004). These problems typically are found in traditional math textbooks and special education curricula. Students answer a set of one- or two-step word problems that provide practice on an algorithm such as multiplication that was also part of the textbook chapter. The typical strategy is to search for a keyword (e.g., "more" means to add, "each or every" means multiply or divide) and use this information to directly translate the problem into its computational form.

Cognitive research conducted in the 1990s showed that this kind of instruction was not only limiting, but it was generally associated with *poor* problem solvers. Hegarty and her colleagues (Hegarty, Mayer, & Green, 1992; Hegarty, Mayer, & Monk, 1995) have demonstrated that students who search for keywords and do not

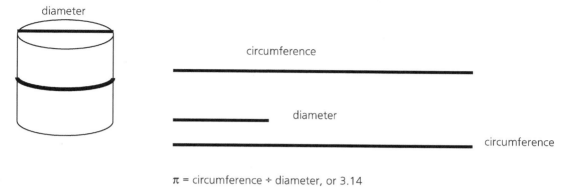

π = circumference ÷ diameter, or 3.14

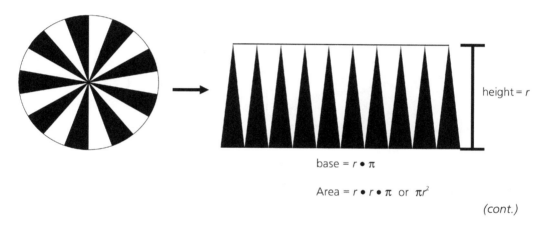

base = $r \bullet \pi$

Area = $r \bullet r \bullet \pi$ or πr^2

(cont.)

FIGURE 2.5. Properties of a circle and its area.

spend sufficient time representing the problem are prone to a significant number of errors when problems are presented in an inconsistent format (e.g., where the correct solution to a word problem with "more" required subtraction rather than addition).

Recent problem-solving research in special education indicates an important move away from direct translation methods toward strategy-based instruction, problem representation, and dialogue (Jitendra, 2002; Jitendra, DiPipi, & Perron-Jones, 2002; Montague & van Garderen, 2003; van Garderen & Montague, 2003). Work of this kind is critical because of the tendency on the part of so many students, particularly those with LD, to answer problems impulsively. These students need to learn how to *persist* when performing complex tasks (Kolligian & Sternberg, 1987). In fact, a striking characteristic of so many students in mathematics classes is captured by the mistaken belief that all math problems can (and should) be answered in five minutes or less (Doyle, 1988; Schoenfeld, 1988).

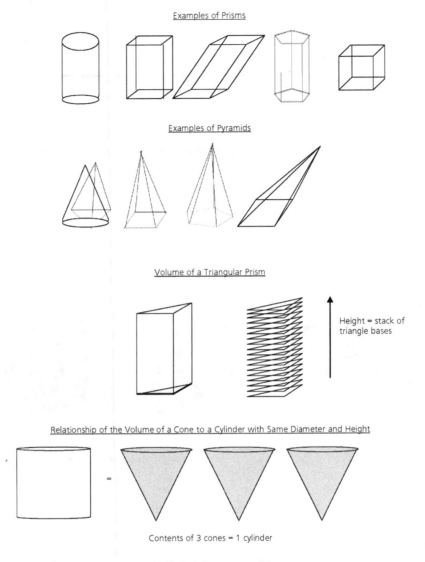

FIGURE 2.5. *(cont.)*

In an effort to assist students in developing strategic knowledge and persistence, I and my colleagues (Woodward, Monroe, & Baxter, 2001) created small-group contexts for problem solving. Groups consisted of no more than eight low-achieving students with LD who worked together in class once a week for approximately 30 minutes. This structure provided opportunities for all students to discuss one or two complex problems. It should be emphasized that students were encouraged to solve each problem collaboratively. Hence, they could observe and contribute based on their initiative or when asked by the teacher. This arrangement was in marked contrast to settings where students are expected to answer problems individually. Finally, the structure also facilitated the kind of fine-grained scaffolding that is infeasible in whole-class discussions (Stone, 1998).

Rather than memorize strategies, students were given laminated guides or "bookmarks" that prompted them through the steps of problem solving (i.e., read and reread, find out what the problem is asking for, select and execute a strategy, and evaluate the answer). Furthermore, the bookmark listed six of the most common domain-specific strategies for solving math problems (e.g., make a simpler problem, work backwards, guess and check, make a table or organized list). Pilot work for this research indicated that these were often more useful strategies than the commonly recommend strategy of "draw it."

Figure 2.6 presents a problem we used in a small-group context, as well as a portion of the teacher–student dialogue during the problem-solving session. The dialogue begins after the teacher and students have read the problem twice and talked about what the problem "was asking for." One of the most notable features of the dialogue is the varied participation. The teacher ensures that no single student or subset of students dominates all of the tasks. In addition to scaffolding student responses, the teacher often revoices student comments and, in doing so, inserts mathematical vocabulary into the discussion (O'Connor & Michaels, 1996).

Perhaps the most intriguing moment in this dialogue occurred when the teacher erred in recording student guesses on the whiteboard. Inadvertently, the teacher wrote 51 and corrected herself to write 52. The same mistake occurred on the next guess, when she wrote 50 instead of 55. Observational notes from this lesson indicated that Terrell had not made any contributions to the discussion up to this point in the lesson. Instead, he watched as others either answered a portion of the problem (e.g., Alicia's answer to the first question) or offered guesses. It was when the teacher made repeated errors recording student suggestions that he offered an alternative solution. A follow-up interview with Terrell indicated that he thought the way the teacher was doing it was "too messy" and that a list would make it easier to find the right answer. Observations over several months of problem solving suggested that "making a list" or "make a table" were powerful strategies that could be used to solve a range of problems.

Two other observations about problem solving arise from this example. First, this dialogue occurred early in the process of small-group problem solving. The goal at this point in the intervention was to create a working community where students felt comfortable sharing their ideas with others in a discussion. This kind of risk taking is not to be underestimated, given how often these students opt out of whole-class discussions (Baxter, Woodward, & Olson, 2001). This goal contrasts sharply with the typical emphasis on the need for individual accountability in math classrooms (Putnam & Borko, 2000). Over time researchers resolved this conflict between group and individual work by having students work a problem similar to the one used in the discussion individually after the small-group work concluded. Also, there were increasing occasions in whole-class settings when these students worked problems by themselves or with minimal teacher prompting.

A second consideration has to do with group participation. Explicit, verbal participation in group work is often considered to be the index of engagement and learning. However, Terrell's contribution, which occurred 15 minutes into the lesson, suggests that learning can occur through observation in well-constructed set-

Problem: Sara's father is 60 years old. Sara is ¼ her father's age. How many years older is Sara's father than Sara? At what age was Sara $\frac{1}{10}$ her father's age?

ALICIA: I know what ¼ is. It's .25. Let me have a calculator. I can figure it out. . . . One fourth of 60 is 15. So Sara is 15 years old.	[Alicia uses a calculator]
TEACHER: That's good. Does everyone agree? Did she figure out Sara's age correctly? . . . OK, what about the second question? Tony, what is the second question asking for?	
TONY: They want to know when Sara was $\frac{1}{10}$ her father's age.	
TEACHER: So does anyone have a way we can start to solve this problem? Does anyone have a strategy?	[Student consults the problem solving bookmark]
MICHA: We could guess a number.	
TEACHER: OK, so we could use the strategy Guess and Check. Do you want to start, Micha?	
MICHA: Well, what if Sara is 1? That would make her father 10.	
AARON: But that can't be because we just said that Sara was 15.	
MICHA: Yeah, but she could still be 1.	
AARON: But not if her father was 45 when she was 15. If she is 1 then that's 14 years ago. That means you'd take away 14 from 45. That wouldn't be 10.	
TEACHER: Jason, what do you think?	
JASON: Yeah, she couldn't be 1 and her dad's 10. I think Aaron's right. If you take 15 from 45, that's 30, so he couldn't be 10 and Sara is 1.	
TEACHER: Jason, so do you have a strategy for solving the problem? Let's use the whiteboard to write our numbers.	[Teacher writes current ages first]
JASON: I would guess she is 7 years younger than her father?	
TEACHER: OK, that would make Sara 8 and her father 51, I mean 52.	
ANGELA: That doesn't work because 7 times 10 isn't 52.	Sara Father 5 60
JASON: Then let's try 5 years younger?	8 7 5̶1̶ 52
TEACHER: OK, that would make Sara 10 and her father 50, I mean 55.	Sara Father 5 60
BRYAN: That doesn't work either because 10 times 10 is 100, not 55.	5 10 5̶0̶ 55
TERRELL: Let me try something. Can I do something [with the whiteboard]? So I think Sara's father was 50 and Sara was 5 because 5 times 10 is 50.	[Terrell takes whiteboard and writes the two columns below]
TEACHER: How did you figure that out? What strategy did you use?	
TERRELL: I saw you writing, so I thought a list would be easier.	Sara Father 15 60
TEACHER: Does everyone think that Terrell's answer is right? Is that what the question is asking for? Can you tell me how?	14 59 13 58
BRYAN: The question says that they want to know when Sara was $\frac{1}{10}$ her father's age.	12 57 11 56
TEACHER: And . . .	10 55 9 54
BRYAN: So, if Sara is 5 and her father is 50, then 5 times 10 is 50.	8 53 7 52
TEACHER: Or 5 is $\frac{1}{10}$ of 50, and 50 times $\frac{1}{10}$ is 5.	6 51 5 50
	[Students agree]

FIGURE 2.6. Teacher–student dialogue during problem solving.

tings. This point is consistent with Lave and Wenger's (1991) notion of practical peripheral participation. There is little research in the special education literature on the effects of environments that promote learning through observation accompanied by scaffolded verbal interactions.

IMPLICATIONS FOR INSTRUCTION

These kinds of approaches to instruction for late elementary and middle school students with LD—as well as those in remedial mathematics classes—cannot be accomplished without substantive changes in curriculum and instructional practices. Curricular change is essential because it can authorize different methods and instructional goals. All three topical examples described above make this clear. The development of number sense requires different kinds of instructional examples and different forms of practice. New curricula are also essential because teachers are in no position to develop and then validate new approaches by themselves. Conceptual frameworks and new methods that appear in the professional literature do not readily transfer to the classroom on a sustained basis. Finally, curricular materials that are consistent with the 2000 NCTM *Standards* need to be adapted for struggling students. There is no reason to believe that one set of curricular materials will serve the needs of all students in a heterogeneous middle school classroom. Our earlier work indicated that the pace of instruction as well as the complexity or cognitive load of the materials was too much for struggling students (Baxter et al., 2001; Woodward & Baxter, 1997).

These students need materials that make more explicit connections between topics (e.g., the development of number sense strategies such as approximation and their use in data analysis and problem-solving activities). They also need more opportunities to develop and apply strategies. The small-group problem solving described above exemplifies this. Finally, struggling students need intense practice on meaningful skills as well as distributive practice (e.g., systematic instruction in math facts that links to a wider set of number sense activities). Another significant problem with reform-based curricular materials is that they do not provide enough practice over time, and consequently some students do not master one concept before another one is introduced.

However, curricular change is not enough. A central theme in *Adding It Up* (Kilpatrick et al., 2001) is that students need to approach mathematics as a sense-making discipline, not one where the primary experience is drill on isolated procedures. Far too often students with LD and those in remedial classrooms spend their time completing worksheets or responding to low-level questions in a direct instruction context. Neither of these approaches helps students develop what *Adding It Up* (Kilpatrick et al., 2001) considers a *productive disposition* toward mathematics. These practices do little to help students approach the subject in a conceptually guided fashion or develop the persistence needed to solve complex problems.

What is needed at the level of instructional strategies is similar to many of the practices advocated by mathematics education today but, again, adapted for remedial and special education students. Particularly important is the concept of scaffolding, which, as Stone (1998) noted, is overused in special education. Often the term means little more than what process–product researchers called direct or explicit feedback decades ago.

A social constructivist view of scaffolding entails much more. Teachers are sensitive to the flow of a mathematical discussion and intervene judiciously. As the problem-solving example cited earlier indicates, they permit students to pursue a range of solutions because complex problems, by their very nature, do not have immediate answers. Scaffolding in this context also entails revoicing important terms and concepts. Whether it is multiplication, the concept of fractions, or a problem-solving strategy such as guess and check, teachers can formalize student understanding by rephrasing and refining the meaning of student talk. Ultimately, scaffolding entails the transfer of responsibility from the teacher to students.

One could argue that at the heart of mathematical proficiency is the development of productive dispositions. Unless remedial and special education students see mathematics as sense-making and useful, it is unlikely they will persevere as the topics become increasingly difficult and more abstract. For this reason alone, the field of special education needs to reconceptualize practices that were perhaps viable 20 years ago but are much less so today.

REFERENCES

Barrett, J., Clements, D., Klanderman, D., Pennisi, S., & Polaki, M. (2001, April). *Children's developing knowledge of perimeter measurement in elementary, middle, and high school.* Paper presented at the annual meeting of the American Educational Research Association, Seattle, WA.

Baxter, J., Woodward, J., & Olson, D. (2001). Effects of reform-based mathematics instruction in five third-grade classrooms. *Elementary School Journal, 101*(5), 529–548.

Becker, W. (1977). Teaching reading and writing to the disadvantaged: What we have learned from field research. *Harvard Educational Review, 47,* 506–521.

Brophy, J., & Good, T. (1986). Teacher behavior and student achievement. In M. Wittrock (Ed.), *The third handbook of research on teaching* (pp. 328–375). New York: Macmillan.

Carnine, D. (1997). Instructional design in mathematics for students with learning disabilities. *Journal of Learning Disabilities, 30*(2), 130–141.

Carnine, D. (2000). *Why education experts resist effective practices (and what it would take to make education more like medicine).* Washington, DC: Fordham Foundation. Retrieved November 15, 2002, from www.edexcellence.net/library/carnine.html

Carpenter, T., Fennema, E., & Romberg, T. (1993). *Rational numbers: An integration of research.* Hillsdale, NJ: Erlbaum.

Doyle, W. (1988). Work in mathematics classes: The context of students' thinking during instruction. *Educational Psychologist, 23*(2), 167–180.

Fuson, K. (1988). *Children's counting and concepts of number.* New York: Springer-Verlag.

Fuys, D., Geddes, D., & Tischler, R. (1988). *The van Hiele model of thinking in geometry among adolescents* (*Journal for Research in Mathematics Education Monograph 3*). Reston, VA: National Council of Teachers of Mathematics.

Geary, D. (1994). *Children's mathematical development*. Washington, DC: American Psychological Association.

Geary, D. (2001). A Darwinian perspective on mathematics and instruction. In T. Loveless (Ed.), *The great curriculum debate: How should we teach reading and math?* (pp. 85–107). Washington, DC: Brookings Institution Press.

Geary, D. (2004). Mathematics and learning disabilities. *Journal of Learning Disabilities, 37*(1), 4–15.

Gelman, R., & Gallistel, R. (1986). *The child's understanding of number*. Cambridge, MA : Harvard University Press.

Gersten, R., & Chard, D. (1999). Number sense: Rethinking arithmetic instruction for students with mathematical disabilities. *Journal of Special Education, 33*(1), 18–28.

Greeno, J. (1991). Number sense as situated knowing in a conceptual domain. *Journal for Research in Mathematics Education, 22*(3), 170–218.

Griffin, S., Case, R., & Siegler, R. (1994). Rightstart: Providing the central conceptual prerequisites for first formal learning of arithmetic to students at risk for school failure. In K. McGilly (Ed.), *Classroom lessons: Integrating cognitive theory and classroom practice* (pp. 25–49). Cambridge, MA: MIT Press.

Grouws, D. (1992). *Handbook of research on mathematics teaching and learning*. New York: Macmillan.

Hegarty, M., Mayer, R., & Green, C. (1992). Comprehension of arithmetic word problems: Evidence from students' eye fixations. *Journal of Educational Psychology, 87*(1), 76–84.

Hegarty, M., Mayer, R., & Monk, C. (1995). Comprehension of arithmetic word problems: A comparison of successful and unsuccessful problem solvers. *Journal of Educational Psychology, 87*(1), 18–32.

Hiebert, J. (1986). *Conceptual and procedural knowledge: The case of mathematics*. Hillsdale, NJ: Erlbaum.

Hiebert, J. (1999). Relationships between research and the NCTM Standards. *Journal of Research in Mathematics Education, 30*(1), 3–19.

Jitendra, A. (2002). Teaching students math problem-solving through graphic representations. *Teaching Exceptional Children, 34*(4), 34–38.

Jitendra, A., DiPipi, C., & Perron-Jones, N. (2002). An exploratory study of schema-based word-problem-solving instruction for middle school students with learning disabilities: An emphasis on conceptual and procedural understanding. *Journal of Special Education, 36*(1), 23–38.

Kilpatrick, J., Swafford, J., & Findell, B. (2001). *Adding it up: Helping children learn mathematics*. Washington, DC: National Academy Press.

Kolligian, J., & Sternberg, R. (1987). Intelligence, information processing, and specific learning disabilities: A triarchic synthesis. *Journal of Learning Disabilities, 20*(1), 8–17.

Lave, J., & Wenger, E. (1991). *Situated learning: Legitimate peripheral participation*. New York: Cambridge University Press.

Leinhardt, G., Putnam, R., & Hattrup, R. (1992). *Analysis of arithmetic for mathematics teaching*. Hillsdale, NJ: Erlbaum.

Loucks-Horsley, S., Love, N., Stiles, K., Mundry, S., & Hewson, P. (2003). *Designing professional development for teachers of science and mathematics*. Thousand Oaks, CA: Corwin Press.

Lyon, G. R., Fletcher, J., Shaywitz, S., Shaywitz, B., Torgesen, J., Wood, F., et al. (2001). Rethinking learning disabilities. In C. Finn, A. Rotherham, & C. Hokanson (Eds.),

Rethinking special education for a new century (pp. 259–288). Washington, DC: Thomas B. Fordham and Progressive Policy Institute.

Ma, L. (1999). *Knowing and teaching elementary mathematics: Teachers' understanding of fundamental mathematics in China and the United States.* Mahwah, NJ: Erlbaum.

Math Projects Journal. (2002). *TIMSS: A call for substance: An interview with Dr. William Schmidt.* Retrieved December 5, 2002, from www.mathprojects.com/scores/timss.asp#Link1

Montague, M., & van Garderen, D. (2003). A cross-sectional study of mathematics achievement, estimation skills, and academic self-perception in students of varying ability. *Journal of Learning Disabilities, 36*(5), 437–448.

National Council of Teachers of Mathematics. (2000). *Principles and standards for school mathematics.* Reston, VA: Author.

O'Connor, M., & Michaels, S. (1996). Shifting participant frameworks: Orchestrating thinking practices in group discussions. In D. Hicks (Ed.), *Discourse, learning, and schooling* (pp. 63–103). New York: Cambridge University Press.

Putnam, R., & Borko, H. (2000). What do new views of knowledge and thinking have to say about research on teacher learning? *Educational Researcher, 29*(1), 4–15.

Putnam, R., Lampert, M., & Peterson, P. (1990). Alternative perspectives on knowing mathematics in elementary schools. In C. Cazden (Ed.), *Review of research in education* (Vol. 16, pp. 57–149). Washington, DC: American Educational Research Association.

Reid, D. K., & Valle, J. (2004). The discursive practice of learning disability: Implications for instruction and parent–school relations. *Journal of Learning Disabilities, 37*(6), 466–481.

Schmidt, W., McKnight, C., & Raizen, S. (1997). *A splintered vision: An investigation of U.S. science and mathematics education.* Dordrecht, The Netherlands: Kluwer Academic.

Schoenfeld, A. (1988). When good teaching leads to bad results: The disaster of "well-taught" mathematics courses. *Educational Psychologist, 23*(2), 145–166.

Siegler, R. (1996). *Emerging minds: The process of change in children's thinking.* New York: Oxford University Press.

Stone, C. (1998). The metaphor of scaffolding: Its utility for the field of learning disabilities. *Journal of Learning Disabilities, 31*(4), 344–364.

Toumasis, C. (1994). When is a quadrilateral a parallelogram? *Mathematics Teacher, 87*(3), 208–211.

van Garderen, D., & Montague, M. (2003). Visual-spatial representation, mathematical problem solving, and students of varying abilities. *Learning Disabilities Research and Practice, 18*(4), 246–255.

Woodward, J. (2004). Mathematics reform in the U.S.: Past to present. *Journal of Learning Disabilities, 37*(1), 16–31.

Woodward, J., & Baxter, J. (1997). The effects of an innovative approach to mathematics on academically low-achieving students in mainstreamed settings. *Exceptional Children, 63*(3), 373–388.

Woodward, J., Monroe, K., & Baxter, J. (2001). Enhancing student achievement on performance assessments in mathematics. *Learning Disabilities Quarterly, 24*(1), 33–46.

Woodward, J., & Montague, M. (2002). Meeting the challenge of mathematics reform for students with learning disabilities. *Journal of Special Education, 36*(2), 89–101.

CHAPTER 3

Teaching Problem-Solving Skills to Middle School Students with Learning Difficulties

Schema-Based Strategy Instruction

YAN PING XIN and ASHA K. JITENDRA

Carolina, a seventh-grader with learning disabilities (LD) is included in a general education mathematics classroom. Mr. Shoemaker, the mathematics teacher, understands that some students need systematic, intensive instruction in word-problem solving. He has the approval of the school principal to initiate an after-school mathematics program for all students who are not meeting expectations and need intensive instruction. Mr. Shoemaker decides to test students on solving grade-level word problems to determine eligibility for the after-school program. Carolina is confident that she will be successful because she has been working with Ms. Guy, the special education teacher, to solve basic arithmetic problems using several problem-solving strategies. In fact, Carolina recently learned to use counters and the "draw a picture" strategy to solve fraction problems involving multiplication. She is ready to take the test, because she believes that she can apply some of the learned strategies to solve the problems on the test. Mr. Shoemaker directs students to show all their work on each item. Using the "draw a picture" strategy, Carolina completes the first item and is reinforced by her success. Then she reads the next problem, "Howard read 12 books in the summer reading program. He read ¾ as many books as his friend Tony. How many books did Tony read?" Carolina is excited that she can solve this problem because she learned last week how to use a picture to represent a fraction. She starts to draw a picture to represent ¾, and solves the problem (see the first problem in Figure 3.1). Georgia, another seventh-grader with LD, approaches the proportion problem slightly differently (see the second problem in Figure 3.1).

It seems obvious that both Carolina's and Georgia's problem solution processes are not unlike those of many middle school students struggling with

Howard read 12 books in the summer reading program. He read ¾ as many books as his friend Tony. How many books did Tony read?

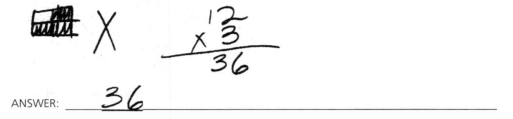

ANSWER: _____ 36

Lee and Sienna were responsible for making drinks for the party last weekend. They used 3 lemons for every 2 quarts of lemonade. If they bought 12 lemons, how many quarts of lemonade could they make?

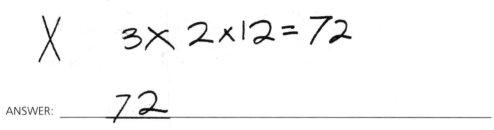

ANSWER: _____ 72

FIGURE 3.1. Sample of middle school students' independent work in solving word problems on a pretest before schema-based instruction (Xin, 2003).

word problems. When solving the multiplicative comparison problem, Carolina attempted to draw a picture to help with the solution process but was not successful. An examination of Georgia's work indicates that he grabbed all the numbers in the proportion problem and applied multiplication without an understanding of the problem. Interestingly, many other students with learning disabilities may not have any strategies to approach various arithmetic multiplication and division word problems. Clearly, we need to unpack students' failure to solve word problems and promote the application of evidence-based problem-solving strategies.

In this chapter, we begin by describing the importance of mathematical word-problem solving. Next, we provide a framework for understanding what schema-based strategy instruction entails followed by an application of the strategy to solve multiplication and division word problems. Finally, we provide implications for practice with regard to effective mathematical problem solving.

MATHEMATICAL PROBLEM SOLVING

Problem solving, a central theme in the *Principles and Standards for School Mathematics* developed by the National Council of Teachers of Mathematics (NCTM, 2000), is a process of moving from a "given state" to a "goal state" with "no obvious way" to progress from one state to the other state (Mayer & Hegarty, 1996, p. 31). Mathematical problem solving involves the application of knowledge, skills, and strategies to novel problems (e.g., Fuchs, Fuchs, Finelli, Courey, & Hamlett, 2004). Although the current emphasis is on complex authentic problems situated in everyday contexts, story problems that range from simple to complex problems represent "the most common form of problem solving" (Jonassen, 2003, p. 267) in school mathematics curricula, and learning how to solve story problems is the basis for solving more authentic real-world problems (Van de Walle, 2004).

Story problems pose difficulties for many students because of the complexity of the problem-solving process (Jonassen, 2003; Schurter, 2002). In fact, there is some evidence that "when IQ and reading are controlled, 'true' math deficits are specific to mathematical concepts and problem types" (Zentall & Ferkis, 1993, p. 6). Therefore, teaching for conceptual understanding of fundamental math concepts and principles by providing problem-solving opportunities that emphasize mathematical thinking and reasoning is critical. In addition, the following questions are important to answer when designing instruction: "What type of task and what task demands are involved?" "Who is the learner?" "How does he or she learn?" Understanding the variables related to problem difficulty, students' developmental and cognitive characteristics, and evidence-based problem-solving instruction provides a relevant context for developing the content of remedial instructional programs for students with mathematics disabilities. Specifically, instruction that explicitly focuses on the semantic structure of word problems is necessary to help students with mathematics disabilities to become better problem solvers (e.g., Fuchs et al.. 2004; Fuchs, Fuchs, Prentice, Burch, Hamlett, Owen, & Schroeter, 2003; Hutchinson, 1993; Jitendra, DiPipi, & Perron-Jones, 2002; Jitendra, Griffin, McGoey, Gardill, Bhat, & Riley, 1998; Xin, Jitendra, & Deatline-Buchman, 2005; Zawaiza & Gerber, 1993).

WHAT IS SCHEMA-BASED STRATEGY INSTRUCTION?

The goal of schema-based problem-solving instruction is to help students establish and expand domain knowledge in which *schemas* are the central focus. A schema is a general description of a group of problems that share a common underlying structure requiring similar solutions (Chen, 1999; Gick & Holyoak, 1983). According to Marshall (1995), schemas are the appropriate mechanism for the problem solver to "capture both the patterns of relationships as well as their linkages to operations" (Marshall, 1995, p. 67).

Schema-based instruction explicitly analyzes the problem schema (e.g., the part–part–whole problem structure) and the *links* pertaining to how different elements of the schema are related (e.g., parts make up the whole). These links, in turn, are critical in the selection of appropriate operations needed for problem solution. For example, if the whole in the problem is unknown, adding the parts is necessary to solve for the whole; if one of the parts is unknown, subtracting the part(s) from the whole is needed to solve for the unknown part. An important difference between schema-based instruction and other instructional approaches is that only the former emphasizes integrating the various pieces of factual information essential for problem solving, rather than focusing on isolated facts. While factual details are important, they should not be the central focus of instruction and learning. In short, a schema-based strategy allows students to approach the problem by focusing on the underlying semantic or problem structure, thus facilitating conceptual understanding and adequate word-problem solving skills (Marshall, 1995).

Building on the work of Marshall (1995), Mayer (1999), and Riley, Greeno, and Heller (1983), we describe below a problem-solving model that emphasizes explicit schema understanding. Essential elements of the model make up four separate but interrelated problem-solving procedural steps. The four steps are problem schema identification, representation, planning, and solution. The corresponding conceptual knowledge for each step includes schema knowledge, elaboration knowledge, strategic knowledge, and execution knowledge.

Schema Knowledge/Problem Schema Identification

The central function of schema-based instruction is pattern or schema recognition, which involves not only linguistic and factual knowledge during problem translation but also schematic knowledge for problem identification (Mayer, 1999). For example, take the following problem: "Jill has worked 3 times as many problems as Dave. If Jill has worked 36 problems, how many problems has Dave worked?" Solving this problem requires not only an understanding of what "3 times as many as" means (linguistic and factual knowledge) but also the ability to identify it as a comparison problem based on the knowledge that it compares the number of problems Jill worked to that Dave worked. Recognition of problem schemas (e.g., compare) is facilitated when the basic semantic relations (e.g., "Jill has worked 3 times as many problems as Dave") among the various problem features are evident. Different problem schemas have their own distinct core features (see the description of problem types in the next section of this chapter, "Multiplication and Division Word Problems").

Elaboration Knowledge/Representation

The second step involves developing a schematic diagram or template that corresponds with the representation of the problem identified in the first step. Specifically, this step entails the interpretation of information in a problem by elaborating on the main features of the schema, thus enabling a problem solver to create a template of the problem situation. For example, "A woman's car gets 22 miles to a gallon of gas. She drove her car for 2 weeks without getting gas. How many miles can she drive on 4 gallons of gas?" After identifying that the problem involves a proportion structure, the problem solver would need to further elaborate on the two dimensions that form the ratio (i.e., "miles" to "gallon of gas"). Based on this elaboration, the problem solver can then map out the two ratios that are proportional; that is, "22 miles" to "one gallon of gas" and "? miles" to "4 gallons of gas." Understanding is demonstrated by how the learner maps these details of the problem onto the schema diagram or template such that the diagram depicts the proportional relation (see illustrations in the section "Schema-Based Problem-Solving Instruction"). At this time, all irrelevant information in the problem is discarded and representation of the problem is based on available schema elaboration knowledge. As such, the information that "she drove her car for 2 weeks without getting gas" would be considered irrelevant to solving the problem, because it does not include information about the two dimensions ("miles" and "gallon of gas") that form the ratio and proportion. In sum, representation of the problem requires an understanding of the two dimensions that form the ratio and the fact that the two ratios are equivalent (i.e., proportional).

Strategic Knowledge/Planning

The third step refers to planning, which involves (1) setting up goals and subgoals, (2) selecting the appropriate operation (e.g., multiplication, division), and (3) writing the math sentence or equation. A problem solver may successfully identify and elaborate on a specific schema in a problem but may not demonstrate strategic knowledge to plan for the solution. For example, the problem solver may easily identify the following as a comparison problem: "Jill has worked 3 times as many problems as Dave. Wayne has worked 2 times as many as Dave. If Wayne has worked 28 problems, how many problems has Jill worked?" However, some students may have difficulty solving the problem even if they possess elaboration knowledge of the comparison schema (i.e., the number of problems Jill has worked is compared to the number of problems worked by Dave, and the number of problems Jill has worked is 3 times as many as the number Dave has worked). Because the number of problems Dave has worked is not given in the problem, the ability to accurately solve this problem may be a function of the problem solver's prior experience in solving two- or multistep problems. Specifically, to solve for the number of problems that Jill has worked (the primary goal), it is necessary to first solve for the number of problems Dave has worked (the subordinate goal).

Also critical to the planning step is the problem solver's understanding of mathematical situations that involve the use of arithmetic conceptual knowledge. For instance, if the multiple is unknown, multiplication would be the choice of operation; in contrast, division would be an appropriate operation if the referent unit is the unknown quantity. In sum, planning may not necessarily be straightforward.

Execution Knowledge/Solution

The last step of problem solving is to carry out the plan. Execution knowledge consists of techniques that lead to problem solution, such as performing a skill (e.g., multiplying, dividing) or following an algorithm. Such knowledge might be shared among many schemas. For instance, execution knowledge for arithmetic story problem schemas may have to do with carrying out the four operations. The difference between planning and solution is that the former focuses on a particular choice and order of operation, whereas the latter implements the plan.

MULTIPLICATION AND DIVISION WORD PROBLEMS

Basic arithmetic problem situations involving multiplication and division include *multiplicative compare*, *equal groups* (e.g., rate times a quantity, fair share or partition, measurement division), *proportion*, *Cartesian product (or combinations)*, and *rectangular area* (Greer, 1992; Schmidt & Weiser, 1995). Marshall (1995) classified the most basic and important problem types involving multiplication and division into two broad categories, *restate* (multiplicative compare [MC]) and *vary* (i.e., equal groups and proportion) problems (see Table 3.1 for examples of various problem types).

Restate or Multiplicative Compare Problems

According to Marshall (1995), a restate problem essentially entails a relational statement that describes a linkage between two subjects or objects, which is frequently expressed by phrases such as "four times as much as," "one half of," and so forth. For example, in the problem "Luann has 9 pictures to put in her photo album. Andrew has 3 times as many pictures as Luann. How many pictures does Andrew have?", the statement "Andrew has 3 times as many pictures as Luann" is a relational statement. In addition, the restate problem describes a restatement of the relationship by assigning numerical values to the two subjects (e.g., Luann and Andrew). Implicit in the restate problem situation is that the numerical relationship between the two values must also satisfy the relational statement. That is, both the relational statement "Andrew has 3 times as many pictures as Luann" and statements about Luann (i.e., 9 pictures) and Andrew (i.e., 27 pictures, which is the answer to the question "How many pictures does Andrew have?") are true.

Vary Problems

The vary situation exists when a specified relationship (e.g., rate or ratio) connecting two things is constant across other statements of the same relation. The two things "may be two different objects or one object and a measurable property associated with it" (Marshall, 1995, p. 73). In the following example, "In Mr. Smith's office, there are 4 bookshelves. On each bookshelf, there are 12 books. How many books are there on the bookshelves?", the two things in the problem are "books" and "bookshelves." The relationship connecting books and bookshelves is expressed as follows: "There are 12 books on each bookshelf." This relationship is preserved across two statements. Typically, one of the statements (e.g., "There are 12 books on each bookshelf") includes one as the basis for its ratio or declares a per unit value, and the other statement involves a scalar enlargement or decrement (i.e., between 1 and 12 or 4 and ?). Vary problem situations either explicitly or implicitly express an "if . . . then" relationship. Although it appears that there are only three quantities involved (12 books, 4 bookshelves, and ? total books), vary problems call for finding the unknown among four quantities (Vergnaud, 1984, cited in Nesher, 1992). The four quantities are embedded in two dimensions (bookshelf and book), with each containing two numbers (i.e., if 1 bookshelf has 12 books, then 4 bookshelves have ? books).

SCHEMA-BASED PROBLEM-SOLVING INSTRUCTION

When teaching students to solve problems such as those presented at the beginning of this chapter, it is necessary to first provide instruction in schema knowledge and problem schema identification (i.e., *problem schema instruction*). During the problem schema instruction phase, students learn to identify the problem structure and represent the features of the problem situation using schematic diagrams (see Figure 3.2). In this phase, story situations with no unknown information (see Table 3.1) are presented. The purpose of presenting story situations is to provide students with a complete representation of the problem structure of a specific prob-

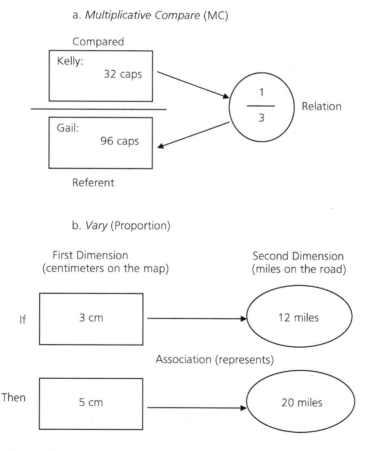

FIGURE 3.2. Schematic representations of (a) *multiplicative compare* and (b) *vary* (*proportion*) problems. Figure 3.2b adapted from Marshall (1995, p. 135). Copyright 1995 by Cambridge University Press. Adapted by permission.

TABLE 3.1. Sample Story Situations (Problems)

Problem types	Sample story situations (problems)
	Restate: Multiplicative comparison (MC) problems
MC compared–I	Luann has 9 pictures to put in her photo album. Andrew has 3 times as many pictures as Luann. Andrew has 27 pictures (How many pictures does Andrew have?).
MC compared–F	Julia made 28 cupcakes for celebrating the 100th school day. Patty made ¼ as many cupcakes as Julia did. Patty made 7 cupcakes (How many cupcakes did Patty make?).
MC referent–I	Liz has 8 Barbie dolls. She has 4 times as many Barbie dolls as her friend Beth. Beth has 2 Barbie dolls (How many Barbie dolls does Beth have?).
MC referent–F	Larry made 6 baskets in the basketball game last night. He made 1/3 as many baskets as Tom. Tom made 18 baskets (How many baskets did Tom make?).
MC scalar function	Ann has 5 green-color pencils and 30 red-color pencils. She has 6 times as many red-color pencils as green-color pencils (How many times as many red-color pencils as green-color pencils does Ann have?).
	Vary problems
Rate times a quantity	Ms. Penn bought 3 cases of candy bars for the PTA meeting held last week. Each case of candy bars contains 12 Kit Kat bars. Ms. Penn bought a total of 36 Kit Kat bars (How many Kit Kat candy bars did Ms. Penn buy in all?).
Fair share/partition	A building has a fire escape with a total of 90 steps across 6 floors. If each floor has the same number of steps, then there are 15 steps for each floor (How many steps are there for each floor?).
Measurement division	The Joy Company packs 48 cans of tomatoes in each crate. The company will need 15 crates in order to pack 720 cans of tomatoes (How many crates will the company need to pack 720 cans of tomatoes?).
Proportion	Lee and Sienna were responsible for making drinks for the party last weekend. They used 3 lemons for every 2 quarts of lemonade. If they bought 12 lemons, they could make 8 quarts of lemonade (How many quarts of lemonade could they make?).

Note. I, integer (the relational statement illustrates a multiple relation); F, fraction (the relational statement illustrates a partial relation).

lem type. The problem schema instruction phase is followed by *problem solution instruction*. During this phase, students learn to solve problems with unknowns (see Table 3.1). Below we describe in detail how to implement schema-based instruction to help students solve multiplication and division word problems.

Teaching Multiplicative Compare Problems

We developed a four-step strategy (FOPS) checklist to help anchor students' learning of the schema strategy in solving the MC problem type (see Figure 3.3).

To illustrate problem schema instruction, let's look at how a teacher can model problem schema identification with the following MC story situation: "Kelly has 32 bottle caps in her collection. She has ⅓ as many caps as Gail. Gail has 96 caps in her collection."

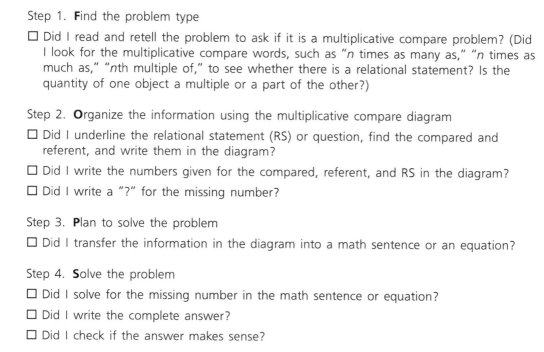

Step 1. **F**ind the problem type

☐ Did I read and retell the problem to ask if it is a multiplicative compare problem? (Did I look for the multiplicative compare words, such as "*n* times as many as," "*n* times as much as," "*n*th multiple of," to see whether there is a relational statement? Is the quantity of one object a multiple or a part of the other?)

Step 2. **O**rganize the information using the multiplicative compare diagram

☐ Did I underline the relational statement (RS) or question, find the compared and referent, and write them in the diagram?

☐ Did I write the numbers given for the compared, referent, and RS in the diagram?

☐ Did I write a "?" for the missing number?

Step 3. **P**lan to solve the problem

☐ Did I transfer the information in the diagram into a math sentence or an equation?

Step 4. **S**olve the problem

☐ Did I solve for the missing number in the math sentence or equation?

☐ Did I write the complete answer?

☐ Did I check if the answer makes sense?

FIGURE 3.3. Self-monitoring checklist for solving multiplicative compare problems.

"Step 1 asks me to identify the problem type. I will read the story and look for phrases such as ' . . . as many . . . as . . . ' to see whether the story involves a relational statement (RS). I read the story situation and found the RS, 'She has ⅓ as many caps as Gail.' This is the RS, because the number of bottle caps Kelly (*compared*) has is compared to that Gail (*referent*) has. As such, it is a compare problem situation. Also, in this story situation, the number of bottle caps Kelly has is a part (i.e., ⅓) of the number of bottle caps that Gail has. It is important to understand that the comparison in this story situation implies a *multiplicative* relationship rather than an *additive* compare situation (e.g., Kelly has 3 *more* caps than Gail). I am done with Step 1 and ready for Step 2.

"Step 2 tells me to use the MC diagram [point to Figure 3.2a] to organize or represent the information. To do that I must first identify the 'compared' and 'referent' by examining the RS, as well as map the corresponding information (e.g., numbers) onto the diagram. OK, I found the RS in Step 1 when I identified the problem type. I will underline the RS, because it provides information about the compared, the referent, and the relation. The RS, 'She has ⅓ as many caps as Gail,' indicates that 'She' (i.e., 'Kelly') is the compared and 'Gail' is the referent. Remember, a 'referent' is something that you compare against. I am now ready to write these names in the diagram for the compared and referent. I will also write '⅓' in the diagram to describe the *relation* between the compared and referent. Now, let's reread the problem to find the information given about the compared, Kelly, and the referent, Gail, to complete the diagram (solicit responses from students). The problem says that Kelly has 32 bottle caps and Gail has 96 caps in her collection, so we will write '32 caps' for Kelly, and '96 caps' for Gail in the diagram."

Upon completing the mapping of information onto the diagram, the teacher should lead students to summarize the information in the problem using the completed diagram and to check the accuracy of the representation by transforming the information in the diagram directly into a meaningful mathematics equation. It is important to note that a correct representation using the MC diagram should lead to a correct equation, $^{32}/_{96} = ⅓$, because the diagram reflects the schematic structure (i.e., specific mathematical relations) of the MC problem type. As such, if students' representation yields an incorrect equation (e.g., $^{96}/_{32} ≠ ⅓$), they should be prompted to check it by reviewing the information related to each component (i.e., the referent, compared, and relation). This checking serves to strengthen conceptual understanding of the problem structure and highlights the utility of using the schematic diagram. That is, when solving a real MC problem with an unknown quantity, the equation transformed from the schematic representation can be used to solve for the unknown.

During the problem-solving instruction phase, students learn to solve for the unknown quantity in word problems, and therefore, instruction addresses all four strategy steps (see sample script in Figure 3.4). Students are prompted to first identify and represent the problem (i.e., Steps 1 and 2 of the strategy) using the MC schematic diagram, as they were in the problem schema instruction phase. The only difference is that students are instructed to use a question mark (?) or a letter (e.g., x) to represent the unknown quantity in the diagram. Step 3 involves transforming the information in the diagram into a math sentence or equation. In Step 4, students are instructed to solve for the unknown in the math sentence or equation using their knowledge about equivalent fractions or cross-multiplication. After students solve for the unknown, they are prompted to write a complete answer and check the reasonableness of their answer. Finally, students are reminded to check the accuracy of both the representation and computation.

Teaching Vary Problems

Again, we developed a four-step strategy (FOPS) checklist to facilitate solving the vary problem type (see Figure 3.5).

To illustrate problem schema instruction, let's look at how a teacher can model problem schema identification with the following vary story situation: "If 3 centi-

Teacher: "We learned about the multiplicative compare problem type and how to use the multiplicative compare diagram to represent information in the story. Let's review what we learned about the multiplicative compare problem." Call on students to elicit the following information:

- The relational statement, which includes phrases such as "3 times as many as" and "one-fourth as many as" can help identify the multiplicative compare problem.
- The relational statement describes the two sets (compared and referent) that are compared and expresses the quantity of one object (compared) as a multiple or part of the other object (referent). (*Note:* The referent is something that you compare against.)

Indicate that students learned to use a multiplicative compare diagram to represent information in multiplicative compare stories that did not involve an unknown or missing quantity. That is, the numerical values associated with each of the three parts (i.e., the compared, the referent, and the RS) were all given. Today's lesson will focus on multiplicative compare problems in which the numerical value associated with one of the three components will be missing and will require using the multiplicative compare diagram to represent information in the problem and solve for the missing quantity. In addition, students will learn to use four steps to solve multiplicative compare problems. Review the four steps: F—Find the problem type; O—Organize the information using a diagram; P—Plan to solve the problem; S—Solve the problem. Indicate that when the first letters of each step are combined, the letters make a funny word, FOPS, and that remembering FOPS can help them recall the four steps.

Display the problem to the class: Kelly has 32 bottle caps in her collection. She has $\frac{1}{3}$ as many caps as Gail. How many bottle caps does Gail have? Call on a student to read the problem.

Problem Schema Identification and Representation

Given that this is the first day that this problem is introduced, the teacher models by thinking aloud how she or he would attempt to solve this problem. Here is a sample script:

Teacher: "The first step is to identify the problem type. To figure out whether this is a multiplicative compare problem, I will first read and retell it in my own words to understand what is given and what needs to be solved. OK, this problem compares the number of bottle caps that Kelly (compared) has to the number of bottle caps that Gail (referent) has. The relational statement (i.e., She has $\frac{1}{3}$ as many caps as Gail) tells me that this is a multiplicative compare problem, because it includes the phrase '$\frac{1}{3}$ as many as,' as well as describes the quantity of the compared (the number of bottle caps Kelly has) to be a part of the referent (the number of bottle caps Gail has).

"The second step is to represent and organize the information in the problem using the multiplicative compare diagram. OK, the relational statement is important, because it provides information about the compared and referent and describes the relation between the compared and referent. So, I will underline the relational statement. The relational statement in this problem indicates that Kelly is the compared and Gail is the referent. I will write their names in the diagram for the compared and referent. I will also write in '$\frac{1}{3}$' for the relation, because the relational statement indicates that the number of bottle caps Kelly has is a part of the number of bottle caps Gail has in her collection. Next, I will reread the problem to find out the information given about the compared, Kelly, and the referent, Gail. The problem says that Kelly has 32 bottle caps. So, I will write 32 bottle caps for Kelly. I don't know how many bottle caps Gail has from the problem. This is the missing number we are asked to solve for in this problem. So I will write '? bottle caps for Gail.'

(cont.)

FIGURE 3.4. Sample script for solving multiplicative compare problems.

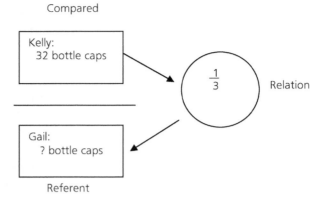

"Now, I will make sure that the information in the problem is accurately represented on the diagram. Kelly (compared) has 32 bottle caps. She has ⅓ as many bottle caps as Gail (referent). This is the relational statement that compares the two quantities (i.e., the number of bottle caps Kelly has to the number of bottle caps Gail has). I have to solve for the number of bottle caps Gail (referent) has in her collection."

Problem Planning and Solution
    Teacher: "The third step is to set up a math sentence or equation. Now I am ready to set up the math equation to solve the problem by transforming the information in the diagram directly into the following equation:

$$\frac{32}{?} = \frac{1}{3}$$

"The fourth step is to solve the problem by finding the unknown quantity in the math equation. I will use the multiplication rule for finding equivalent fractions to solve for the unknown; or I can directly use cross-multiplication to solve for the unknown. [*Note*. The teacher may demonstrate the calculation procedure using either the equivalent fraction strategy or cross-multiplication method]. That is, ? = 32 × 3 = 96. So, the complete answer to this problem is 'Gail has 96 bottle caps.' I will write 96 in the diagram for the bottle caps that Gail has. Now, I will check to see whether the answer makes sense. Based on the information given in the RS (Kelly has ⅓ as many bottle caps as Gail), Kelly has fewer bottle caps than Gail. So the answer 'Gail has 96 bottle caps' makes sense. I will also use the cross-multiplication method to check the accuracy of my calculation. Replace the '?' with the answer '96' in the equation. By using cross multiplication, I get 96 × 1 = 32 × 3, that is, 96 = 96. So my calculation is correct."

FIGURE 3.4. (*cont.*)

meters on the map represent 12 miles on the road, then 5 centimeters represent 20 miles on the road."

"Step 1 asks me to identify the problem type. To do that, I will read the story to figure out (1) whether the story is about an association (ratio or rate) between two things (or dimensions); and (2) whether there is an 'if . . . then' statement that makes up two pairs of associations. OK, I read this story situation, which involves an association (i.e., ratio) between two dimensions, 'centimeters' (cm) on the map and 'miles' on the road. The story also involves an 'if . . . then' relationship, in that if 3 cm on the map represent 12 miles on the road, then 5 cm represent 20 miles on the road. So it is a vary story situation. I am done with Step 1 and ready for Step 2.

"Step 2 tells me to use the vary diagram [point to Figure 3.2b] to organize or represent the information. To do that, I must identify the two dimensions (i.e., 'cm' and 'miles') and map the information about the two pairs of associations (numbers and label) onto the diagram. OK, I know that the story is about an association (i.e., ratio) between two dimensions, 'cm' on the map and 'miles' on the road. I will write 'cm on the map' to represent one dimension and 'miles on the road' as the other dimension in the vary diagram.

"Next, I have to find the information for the two pairs of associations. I will read the story again. The first statement says, 'If 3 centimeters on the map represent 12 miles on the road.' I will write '3 cm' for the 'cm' dimension and '12 miles' for the 'miles' dimension to represent the first pair of associations (i.e., the 'If' part of the vary diagram). Now I need to find the second pair of associations between the 'cm' and 'miles.' I will read the second statement in the story, which states 'then 5 centimeters represent 20 miles on the road.' So, I will write '5 cm' for the 'cm' dimension and '20 miles' for the 'miles' dimension in the 'Then' part of the *vary* diagram.

Step 1. **F**ind the problem type

☐ Did I read and retell the problem to ask if it is a vary problem? (Did I look for a "rate" or "ratio" type of association between two dimensions? Does the problem involve an "if . . . then" kind of statement that makes up two pairs of associations?)

Step 2. **O**rganize the information using the vary diagram

☐ Did I write the labels for the two dimensions in the diagram?
☐ Did I write the numbers given for the two pairs of associations in the diagram?
☐ Did I write a "?" for the missing number?

Step 3. **P**lan to solve the problem

☐ Did I transform the information in the diagram into a math sentence or an equation?

Step 4. **S**olve the problem

☐ Did I solve for the missing number in the math sentence or equation?
☐ Did I write the complete answer?
☐ Did I check if the answer makes sense?

FIGURE 3.5. Self-monitoring checklist for solving vary problems.

"OK, now I have mapped both pairs of associations ('cm' to 'miles') onto the diagram. I will check the accuracy of my representation by transforming the information in the diagram directly into a meaningful mathematics equation. Because the diagram reflects the proportion structure of the vary problem type, the direct transformation should lead to the following correct equation: $3\ cm/5\ cm = 12\ miles/20\ miles$. If my representation does not establish this equation, then I have a problem with my representation. For example, my equation (e.g., $3\ cm/20\ miles \neq 12\ miles/5\ cm$ or $3\ cm/5\ cm \neq 20\ miles/12\ miles$) is incorrect, because I either did not form a correct ratio between two dimensions or failed to make a correct alignment in my mapping when representing the information in the problem. I really need to reread the story and make sure the two numbers (e.g., 3 and 12) that form a given ratio (3 cm to 12 miles) are correctly paired and the two dimensions (i.e., 'cm' and 'miles') are corrected aligned across the two pairs of associations."

During the representation, it is essential that the teacher emphasize the correct alignment of the two dimensions (i.e., "cm" and "miles") across the two pairs of associations, because the notion of constant ratio or rate across two pairs of associations is an essential element in the vary problem schema and important to accurate problem solution. For instance, if the first pair is mapped such that "3 cm" is placed to the left and "12 miles" to the right of the vary diagram, then the second pair should also be mapped similarly with the "cm" dimension (i.e., "5 cm") to the left and the "miles" dimension (i.e., "20 miles") to the right (see Figure 3.2b), rather than "20 miles" to the left and "5 cm" to the right of the vary diagram.

In the problem-solving instruction phase, problems with unknown information are presented (see sample script for the vary problem in Figure 3.6). Students are instructed to first identify and represent the problem using the corresponding vary schematic diagram and flag the unknown with a "?" or "x." Step 3 requires students to transform the diagram into a math equation. In Step 4, students solve for the unknown in the math sentence or equation. After students solve for the unknown, they are prompted to write a complete answer and check the reasonableness of their answer.

When teaching students to solve multiplication and division word problems using the schema-based instructional strategy, only one type of word problem with the corresponding schema diagram should appear initially on student worksheets following the instruction of that word problem type (e.g., MC problem). After students learn how to solve both MC and vary problems, word problems with both types and diagrams should be presented, with an emphasis on identifying the problem type (the first step in the four-step strategy). This would entail a discussion of the sameness and difference between the MC and vary problems.

It must be noted that during the schema-based strategy instruction, the teacher first models the strategy with multiple examples. Explicit instruction is then followed by teacher-guided practice and finally independent student work. Correc-

Teacher: "We learned about the vary problem type and how to use the vary diagram to represent information in the story. Let's review what we learned about the vary problem." Call on students to elicit the following information:

- It describes an association (ratio or rate) between two things or dimensions.
- There are two pairs of associations (i.e., the "if" and "then" statement) that involve four quantities. The "if" statement declares a per unit value or unit ratio between two things or dimensions, and the "then" statement is the variation (enlargement or reduction) of the two quantities in the given ratio or rate.
- The unit ratio or rate remains constant across the two pairs of associations.

Indicate that students learned to use the vary diagram to represent information in vary stories that did not involve an unknown or missing quantity. That is, all four quantities in the two pairs of associations were given. Today's lesson will focus on vary problems in which one of the four quantities will be missing and will require using the vary diagram to represent the information in the problem and solve for the missing quantity. In addition, students will use the same four steps (FOPS) they used for solving multiplicative compare problems to solve vary problems.

Display the problem to the class: *If 3 centimeters on the map represent 12 miles on the road, then how many centimeters will represent 20 miles on the road?* Call on a student to read the problem.

Problem Schema Identification and Representation

Given that this is the first day that this problem is introduced, the teacher models by thinking aloud how she or he would attempt to solve this problem. Here is a sample dialog:

Teacher: "The first step is to identify the problem type. To figure out whether this is a vary problem, I will first read and retell it in my own words to understand what is given and what needs to be solved. OK, this problem talks about centimeters (cm) on the map and miles on the road. So, this problem is about an association between 'centimeters on the map' and 'miles on the road.' It also involves an 'if . . . then' relationship, in that if 3 cm represent 12 miles on the road, then '?' cm will represent 20 miles on the road.

"The second step is to represent and organize the information in the problem using the vary diagram. OK, I know this problem is about cm on the map and miles on the road. So, I will label 'cm on the map' to represent one dimension and 'miles on the road' as the other dimension and write them in the vary diagram. I will also write in the word *represent* to indicate the association between cm on the map and miles on the road (i.e., 3 cm represent 12 miles). Next, I will find the information for the two pairs of associations (i.e., the four quantities). If I reread the problem, it says that 3 cm represent 12 miles. So, I will write '3 cm' for the first dimension and '12 miles' for the second dimension in the 'If' part of the vary diagram. I need to find what information is given for the second pair of associations between the two dimensions. The problem asks, 'How many centimeters represent 20 miles on the road?' So, I will write '? cm' for the first dimension and '20 miles' for the second dimension in the 'Then' part of the vary diagram. I don't know the number of cm on the map that represents 20 miles on the road, which I need to solve for in this problem.

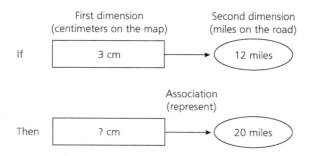

FIGURE 3.6. Sample script for solving vary problems.

"Now, I will make sure that the information in the problem is accurately represented on the diagram. If 3 cm on the map represent 12 miles on the road (first pair of associations), I need to solve for the number of cm on the map (first dimension), which represents 20 miles on the road (second dimension) in the second pair of associations."

Problem Planning and Solution
    Teacher: "The third step is to set up a math sentence or equation. Now I am ready to set up the math equation to solve the problem by transforming the information in the diagram directly into the following math equation, because the two pairs of associations are equivalent ratios:

$$\frac{3 \ cm}{? \ cm} = \frac{12 \ miles}{20 \ miles}$$

$$\frac{3}{?} = \frac{12}{20}$$

"The fourth step is to solve the problem by finding the unknown quantity in the math equation. I will use the multiplication rule for finding equivalent fractions to solve for the unknown; or I can directly use cross-multiplication to solve for the unknown (*Note.* The teacher may demonstrate the calculation procedure using either the equivalent fraction strategy or cross-multiplication method). That is, $? = (3 \times 20) \div 12 = 5$. So the complete answer to this problem is '5 cm on the map represent 20 miles on the road.' I will write 5 for centimeters on the map in the second pair of the vary diagram. Now, I will check to see whether the answer makes sense. Based on the information given in the problem, 5 cm seems correct, because 20 miles should be represented by more cm (5) on the map than 12 miles (which is represented by 3 cm). I will also use the cross-multiplication method to check the accuracy of my calculation. Replace the '?' with the answer '5' in the math equation. By using the cross-multiplication method, I get $5 \times 12 = 3 \times 20$, that is, $60 = 60$. So my calculation is correct."

FIGURE 3.6. *(cont.)*

tive feedback and additional modeling should be provided as needed during practice sessions. In addition, it is reasonable to allow students to use calculators in carrying out the algorithm based on their needs (e.g., accommodating for computation skill deficits). Finally, as students learn to internalize the schematic diagrams and the strategy steps, the diagrams and strategy checklists should be gradually faded. Let's revisit how Carolina and Georgia performed on a word-problem solving posttest following schema-based instruction they received in the after-school mathematics program. As seen in Figure 3.7, these students' solution process reflects conceptual understanding, which is evident by how they accurately represented the information in the problems using schematic diagrams that made explicit the mathematical relations involved. The problem schema representation and planning helped these students to experience success in problem solving.

SUMMARY

Overall, classroom instruction that emphasizes the mathematical structure of word problems and elaborative knowledge of problem schemas needed to coherently represent the information in the problem is essential to address the mathematical difficulties evidenced by students with LD. The effectiveness of such instruction is evident with middle school students with learning disabilities or difficulties. Students commented that "it made it easier for me to solve problems," "now I know what to do when I see those problems," and "it helped me learn something I could never learn before." Students stated that they enjoyed applying the strategy, and some students demonstrated generalization of the learned skill to complete unfamiliar word problems on a schoolwide standardized state test.

On the basis of the program of research on schema-based instruction, we present some guidelines regarding how to enhance the mathematical problem solving of students with LD. We first offer some guidelines for teacher implementation of schema-based strategy instruction. Then, we provide recommendations for effective instruction.

Guidelines for Teachers

It is important that the teacher has the relevant instructional materials needed to effectively implement the schema-based strategy instruction. First, it is beneficial to script the lessons so that teachers can emphasize specific behaviors (pointing to diagrams, presenting information, asking questions). Teaching procedures must be

Christi collected 24 bottle caps for the art class. She collected 2/3 as many caps as Lan. How many caps did Lan collect for the art class?

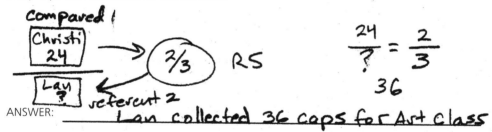

A recipe for chocolate cupcakes uses 3 eggs to make 20 cupcakes. If you want to make 80 cupcakes, how many eggs will you need?

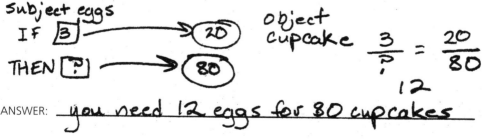

FIGURE 3.7. Sample of student work in solving MC and vary problems on a posttest following schema-based instruction (Xin, 2003).

carefully designed to include clear and consistent wording. The explanations must be explicit and emphasize key vocabulary (e.g., compared, referent) as a means to ensure that students easily understand the information presented. It is crucial that the instructor is familiar with the scripts, which should serve to anchor the instruction in teaching for understanding unique features and key components of the two problem types (i.e., MC, vary). Second, selecting or constructing a variety of story situations (with no unknown information) and problems (with unknown information) from appropriate grade level mathematics curriculum programs that involve MC and vary problem types (see sample story situations/problems in Table 3.1) is essential. Initial story situations and word-problem-solving worksheet sets should include only the taught problem type (e.g., MC, vary). For additional worksheet sets, include both problem types so that students can discriminate the different problem types and apply the schema-based problem-solving strategy. Third, posters or note cards with strategy checklists (see Figures 3.3 and 3.5) that highlight key elements and critical steps for solving specific problem types may be posted on classroom walls or bulletin boards, or placed on each student's desk or notebook. They can serve as visual prompts or scaffolds during initial strategy instruction. Fourth, it is important to emphasize instruction in schematic representations for MC and vary problems. Whether teacher-designed or student-generated diagrams are used, it is crucial that the diagrams illustrate the essential features and semantic relations in the problem.

Recommendations for Effective Problem-Solving Instruction

First, promoting mathematical problem solving for students with LD requires knowledge of problem types (or schemas) and elaborative knowledge of problem schemas. This means that students must be able to recognize and discern the two problem schemas (e.g., MC, vary) as well as identify the various features and semantic relations that make up the problem to coherently represent the information in the problem. Because students typically tend to grab numbers in the problems and start to compute without understanding the problem situation, initial tasks should include story situations with no unknown information to inhibit direct translation (e.g., translate the word *times* to an operation of multiplication). Given that accurate representation of a story problem requires integrating the information in the problem (e.g., mathematical relations), the focus of this instruction should be on critical thinking and reasoning to promote conceptual understanding. For example, when solving MC problems, students should read the whole problem situation to first find the two things compared in the problem in order to identify the compared and referent, which may not always be obvious in the problem. For example, in the following problem, "Michael sold 18 delta kites on Friday. He sold half as many kites on Saturday (as on Friday). How many delta kites did he sell on Saturday?" Michael is not the identity of either the referent or the compared. Instead, "kites sold on Saturday" and "kites sold on Friday" are the compared and referent, respectively. Similarly, it is important for students to first identify the two dimensions associated with each other that form a rate or ratio when solving vary problems, especially when the problem entails irrelevant information. For example, identifying the two dimensions associated in the following problem, is critical to successful problem solving: "Denzel got a job for the summer. He worked 20 hours per week, and his net pay each week was $120. How much will Denzel earn in 12 weeks?" Although it appears that there are three dimensions in the problem (i.e., hours per week, dollars paid each week, and weeks), one dimension (i.e., hours in the week) is irrelevant to what must be solved for in the problem (i.e., the amount Denzel will earn in 12 weeks). In sum, a sound understanding of the whole problem situation is a critical component of schema strategy instruction.

A second recommendation for enhancing mathematical problem solving involves the need for quality representations such as schematic representations that illustrate the mathematical relationships between objects and that facilitate the transformation of information from the diagram into an appropriate math equation (Hegarty & Kozhevnikov, 1999). Such representations are particularly beneficial for students with LD, who often have difficulties in generating complete and accurate mental problem representations critical for meaningful problem solving (Marshall, 1995; Lewis & Mayer, 1987; van Garderen & Montague, 2003). Because these students evidence attention, organizational, and working memory problems (Gonzalez & Espinel, 1999; Zentall & Ferkis, 1993), providing them with the schema diagrams as scaffolds during initial learning is important. Also necessary is the need to provide explicit instruction in mapping information in the problem onto the schematic diagrams using substantive and elaborated explanations. For example, aligning the two dimensions across two pairs of associations is critical when representing vary problems using the schema diagram. Thus, clearly articulated explanations during schema mapping are critical to ensure that students are placing numbers and labels into the diagram based not on the sequence of numbers appearing in the problem but on an understanding of the problem situation.

A third recommendation is the need for explicit instruction to check whether the answer makes sense or is reasonable, an essential component of schema strategy instruction. Checking the answer is designed to increase reasoning and critical thinking. As such, it goes beyond the notion of checking the computation to requiring students to check whether their diagram accurately represents the specific problem type.

REFERENCES

Chen, Z. (1999). Schema induction in children's analogical problem solving. *Journal of Educational Psychology, 91*, 703–715.

Fuchs, L. S., Fuchs, D., Finelli, R., Courey, S. J., & Hamlett, C. L. (2004). Expanding schema-based transfer instruction to help third graders solve real-life mathematical problems. *American Educational Research Journal, 41*, 419–445.

Fuchs, L. S., Fuchs, D., Prentice, K., Burch, M., Hamlett, C. L., Owen, R., & Schroeter, K. (2003). Enhancing third-grade students' mathematical problem solving with self-regulated learning strategies. *Journal of Educational Psychology, 95*, 306–315.

Gick, M. L., & Holyoak, K. J. (1983). Schema induction and analogical transfer. *Cognitive Psychology, 15*, 1–38.

Gonzalez, J. E. J., & Espinel, A. I. G. (1999). Is IQ–achievement discrepancy relevant in the definition of arithmetic learning disabilities? *Learning Disability Quarterly, 22*, 291–301.

Greer, B. (1992). Multiplication and division as models of situations. In D. Grouws (Ed.), *Handbook of research on mathematics teaching and learning* (pp. 276–295). New York: Macmillan.

Hegarty, M., & Kozhevnikov, M. (1999). Types of visual-spatial representations and mathematical problem solving. *Journal of Educational Psychology, 91*, 684–689.

Hutchinson, N. L. (1993). Effects of cognitive strategy instruction on algebra problem solving of adolescents with learning disabilities. *Learning Disabilities Quarterly, 16*, 34–63.

Jitendra, A., DiPipi, C. M., & Perron-Jones, N. (2002). An exploratory study of schema-based word-problem-solving instruction for middle school students with learning disabilities: An emphasis on conceptual and procedural understanding. *Journal of Special Education, 36*, 23–38.

Jitendra, A. K., Griffin, C. C., McGoey, K., Gardill, M. C., Bhat, P., & Riley, T. (1998). Effects of mathematical word problem solving by students at risk or with mild disabilities, *The Journal of Educational Research, 91*, 345–355.

Jonassen, D. H. (2003). Designing research-based instruction for story problems. *Educational Psychology Review, 15*, 267–296.

Lewis, A. B., & Mayer, R. E. (1987). Students' miscomprehension of relational statements in arithmetic word problems. *Journal of Educational Psychology, 79*, 361–371.

Marshall, S. P. (1995). *Schemas in problem solving*. New York: Cambridge University Press.

Mayer, R. E. (1999). *The promise of educational psychology: Vol. 1. Learning in the content areas.* Upper Saddle River, NJ: Merrill Prentice Hall.

Mayer, R. E., & Hegarty, M. (1996). The process of understanding mathematics problems. In R. J. Sternberg & T. Ben-Zeev (Eds.), *The nature of mathematical thinking* (pp. 29–53). Mahwah, NJ: Erlbaum.

National Council of Teachers of Mathematics. (2000). *Principles and standards for school mathematics.* Reston, VA: Author.

Nesher, P. (1992). Solving multiplication word problems. In G. Leinhardt & R. T. Putnam (Eds.), *Analysis of arithmetic for mathematics teaching* (pp. 189–219). Hillsdale, NJ: Erlbaum.

Riley, M. S., Greeno, J. G., & Heller, J. I. (1983). Development of children's problem-solving ability in arithmetic. In H. P. Ginsburg (Ed.), *The development of mathematical thinking* (pp. 153–196). New York: Academic Press.

Schmidt, S., & Weiser, W. (1995). Semantic structures of one-step word problems involving multiplication or division. *Educational Studies in Mathematics, 28*, 55–72.

Schurter, W. A. (2002). Comprehension monitoring: An aid to mathematical problem solving. *Journal of Developmental Education, 26*(2), 22–33.

Van de Walle, J. A. (2004). *Elementary and middle school mathematics: Teaching developmentally* (5th ed.). Boston: Allyn & Bacon.

van Garderen, D., & Montague, M. (2003). Visual-spatial representation, mathematical problem solving, and students of varying abilities. *Learning Disabilities Research and Practice, 18*, 246–254.

Xin, Y. P. (2003). *A comparison of two instructional approaches on mathematical word problem solving by students with learning problems.* Ann Arbor, MI: ProQuest Information and Learning Company.

Xin, Y. P., Jitendra, A. K., & Deatline-Buchman, A. (2005). Effects of mathematical word problem solving instruction on students with learning problems. *Journal of Special Education, 39,* 181–192.

Zawaiza, T. B. W., & Gerber, M. M. (1993). Effects of explicit instruction on community college students with learning disabilities. *Learning Disabilities Quarterly, 16,* 64–79.

Zentall, S. S., & Ferkis, M. A. (1993). Mathematical problem solving for youth with ADHD, with and without learning disabilities. *Learning Disabilities Quarterly, 16,* 6–18.

CHAPTER 4

Teaching Visual Representation for Mathematics Problem Solving

DELINDA VAN GARDEREN

Ms. Lilly placed a word problem on the Smartboard for her students to see. She then proceeded to model to the students how to solve the problem. She began by reading the problem out loud. After that she told the students that she was going to "draw a picture." She emphasized that it was an excellent strategy to use as a way to understand the problem in order to make it easier to solve the problem. After she had drawn her diagram, she used it to generate an equation, which she then calculated to solve the problem. Ms. Lilly gave all her students a worksheet containing problems similar to the one she had just modeled and instructed them to work on and solve them. As the students worked on the problems, she walked around monitoring what they were doing. To her disappointment, only a couple of students drew diagrams to solve the word problems. She also observed that some students who were not drawing diagrams were struggling. To help them, she reminded the students to "make a drawing." The next day, Ms. Lilly gave her students a math test that included several word problems. When grading the test she noted only a few students drew diagrams. A closer look at the diagrams also revealed that some of the diagrams were either missing important information from the word problem or incorrectly depicted the relationships among the parts of the diagram. As a result, some students who drew a diagram did not always get the problem correct.

A commonly recommended strategy for solving mathematical word problems is to "make a drawing" (Shigematsu & Sowder, 1994). Ms. Lilly, like many teachers, believed that drawing a diagram would make it easier to solve word problems. It is thought that drawing a diagram will make the relationships in the word problem clearer for students, thus laying the foundation for solving it (Diezmann & English, 2001; Nunokawa, 1994). However, this is not always the case, as Ms. Lilly found when grading her students' math test. While a diagram can have a positive role in mathematical word-problem solving, the pathway toward the flexible use of diagrams to solve word problems is challenging for students in general and, in particular, for students with mathematics disabilities (Diezmann & English, 2001; Pape & Tchoshanov, 2001). In this chapter, reasons for using diagrammatic instruction to solve word problems are given. Recommendations for developing diagrammatic ability, knowing about diagram use, and being able to use that knowledge to help students with mathematics disabilities solve word problems are presented. Suggestions on how to incorporate diagrammatic instruction as a part of daily instruction are provided. Finally, potential problems that students with mathematics disabilities may have when using diagrams to solve word problems are highlighted.

WHY INSTRUCT STUDENTS WITH MATHEMATICS DISABILITIES TO USE DIAGRAMS FOR SOLVING WORD PROBLEMS?

There are a number of compelling reasons for teaching students with mathematics disabilities how to generate and use their own diagrams to solve word problems. First, many students with mathematics disabilities have working memory problems that may interfere with their ability to keep track of the numerous demands of a word problem (Geary, 1996; Swanson, Cooney, & O'Shaughnessy, 1995). A diagram provides an important visual referent that students can use to help reduce and manage the memory demands of a problem (Diezmann & English, 2001). After all, as Polya (1957) noted, "a detail pictured in our imagination may be forgotten; but the detail traced on paper remains, and, when we come back to it, it reminds us of our previous remarks, [and] it saves us some of the trouble we have in recollecting our previous consideration" (pp. 103–104).

Second, a diagram, unlike a mental image or the spoken word (other ways to represent word problems), can be easily monitored by both teachers and students and, therefore, evaluated and improved upon (Kulm, 1994). Many students with mathematics disabilities lack the necessary self-regulation strategies that good problem solvers use to monitor what they are doing and what they have done (Montague, 1997). The "visibility" of a diagram provides a platform to teach students to monitor and examine their progress.

A third reason for using diagrams is their flexibility of use. Given the time constraints and the need to meet certain curricular demands, identifying strategies that can be used flexibly and in various situations is important. Diagrams can be used for solving routine and nonroutine word problems. They can be used for other mathematics subject areas such as geometry or number operations. Moreover, they may be used at all grade levels (Diezmann & English, 2001; Geary, 1996; Ives & Hoy, 2003; Kulm, 1994; Novick, Hurley, & Francis, 1999; van de Walle, 2004).

Finally, diagrams can be used as a strategy to increase the motivation of students with mathematics disabilities. Many such students have typically endured years of failure and frustration in mathematics. As a result, they often lack the motivation and interest to solve word problems (Jones, Wilson, & Bhojwani, 1998). Getting students to draw diagrams, an activity many consider fun to begin with, may increase interest and motivation.

DEVELOPING STUDENTS' ABILITY TO SOLVE WORD PROBLEMS USING DIAGRAMS

A major difference between successful and unsuccessful problems solvers is their ability to represent the problem (Parmar, 1992; Hutchinson, 1993; Montague & Applegate, 1993; van Garderen & Montague, 2003). Problem representation involves translating the problem from words into a meaningful representation on paper (e.g., diagram), with objects (e.g., base 10 blocks), or in one's mind (Janvier, 1987; Jitendra, 2002). This is a crucial step for coming to understand and be able to solve it (Mayer & Hegarty, 1996). However, students with mathematics disabilities typically generate fewer representations for solving word problems than their peers without disabilities. This reluctance to use a representation may be a result of a limited understanding of what a representation such as a diagram is, or uncertainty how to generate and use a representation in the process of solving a problem (Diezmann & English, 2001; van Garderen & Montague, 2003). Further, if a representation of the problem is generated, it is often poorer in quality and lacks important relational information needed to understand and, subsequently, to solve the problem (van Garderen & Montague, 2003).

Lack of pedagogical knowledge regarding how to teach students with mathematics disabilities to generate and use diagrams for solving word problems may be a further complication. Textbooks rarely provide sufficient information beyond the instruction to "draw a diagram," followed by an example. Yet, instruction clearly needs to move beyond simply getting students to "visualize" the problem (Hegarty & Kozhevnikov, 1999). Encouragement alone is insufficient (Dufour-Janvier, Bednarz, & Belanger, 1987).

The importance of developing widespread representational fluency in students with mathematics disabilities should not be underestimated. Generating a representation such as a diagram involves understanding the meaning of the text, translating that information into a representation that highlights the quantitative features of a problem, and finally developing an understanding of the important quantitative relationships among the individual statements (Geary, 1996). In general, diagrammatic instruction needs to focus on (1) conceptual understanding of diagrams, (2) how to generate diagrams, and (3) using diagrams to reason with (Diezmann & English, 2001).

Conceptual Understanding of Diagrams

For many students difficulties in using diagrams for solving problems may relate to what they understand a diagram to be and how they think it can help them. Diagrams are commonly portrayed as being either "a picture" or a "drawing." In the opening vignette, Ms. Lilly referred to a diagram as being both a picture and a drawing. However, this can be misleading, and students may generate diagrams that portray only surface details rather than the relational information. Additionally, attention to the production of a drawing may distract students from solving the problem (Diezmann & English, 2001; Dufour-Janvier, Bednarz, & Belanger, 1987).

A diagram is "a visual representation that displays information in a spatial layout" (Diezmann & English, 2001, p. 77). To circumvent possible confusion and misunderstanding, spend time defining what a diagram in mathematics is. The following definition may be used as an example: *A diagram is a representation that shows the parts of a math word problem and how they are related*. The following three points as to how diagrams can help solve word problems flow from this definition. They help us to (1) understand what the word problem is asking us to do, (2) keep track of what we are doing while we are solving the problem, and (3) check that our answer makes sense. Once the students understand what a diagram is and what its potential benefits are, instruction should focus on how to generate it.

Generating a Diagram

Generating an appropriate diagram for a word problem can be challenging. Over time most students, given exposure to and involvement in solving a variety of problems, become proficient and efficient in generating diagrams (Dufour-Janvier, Bednarz, & Belanger, 1987; Lesh, Post, & Behr, 1987). However, for some students diagram generation continues to be problematic (Diezmann & English, 2001; van Garderen & Montague, 2003). As Ms. Lilly saw, this results in varying levels of success. Some of her students had difficulty initiating the process of diagram generation, whereas others did so but had difficulty representing the relational information adequately. To help these students, specific instruction may include the following: (1) general principles for generating diagrams, (2) use of graphic codes (e.g., letters or numbers) and symbols (e.g., a stick figure for a person) in diagram generation, and (3) diagram types for different word problems.

General Principles

Time constraints, such as the need to be efficient in generating a diagram for a word problem within a set time period on a standardized test, have often been cited as an argument against encouraging students to use diagrams (Dufour-Janvier, Bednarz, & Belanger, 1987; Presmeg, 1986a). When starting instruction in diagram generation, it is helpful to provide students with general principles they should always follow while generating a diagram to avoid spending too much time on it. Ms. Lilly, for example, could provide her students with the following principles: (1) we do not always have to draw everything that is stated in the problem, (2) what we draw does not need to look realistic, and (3) we do not want to take too long drawing a diagram.

Using Graphic Codes and Symbols in Diagram Generation

Diagram generation does not relate to ability to draw. Rather, it is the capacity to develop graphic codes and symbols to represent the information in the problem that is important (Dufour-Janvier, Bednarz, & Belanger, 1987). The problem is that many students do not know what graphic codes and symbols they can use as they generate their diagrams. Therefore, instruction on what graphic codes and symbols are and how they relate to objects or people in a word problem may be required. Ms. Lilly could, for example, first inform the students that they can use graphic codes, such as a letter or numeral, or symbols such as a circle or star to represent different objects or people in a word problem. For example, instead of drawing a tree, it is possible to use the letter t to represent the tree. Or, instead of drawing a car, a circle can be drawn to represent the car. Second, Ms. Lilly could have the students generate a graphic code or symbol for a given object or person (e.g., fish $= f$ or ➤). Third, using a simple word problem, Ms. Lilly could demonstrate how to develop graphic codes or symbols for the various objects and/or persons in the problem. Fourth, she could ask the students to generate graphic codes or symbols to form a diagram of the information contained in a word problem, using a symbol, such as a question mark, to indicate the unknown. Thus, Judy (Figure 4.1), a student of Ms. Lilly, knew that Bill made four kinds of candy. She therefore drew four boxes to represent the four types of candy. For each type of candy, Judy knew that Bill made 13 pieces. She then wrote "13" under each candy type. For the unknown, how many pieces of candy Bill had all together, Judy drew a question mark. With this information in place, she realized that, to get the answer, he would have to add the pieces of candy together. She then wrote in the addition signs demonstrating how the various parts of the problem were related.

Bill made 4 kinds of candy for the party. If he made 13 pieces of each kind, how many pieces of candy did he have all together?

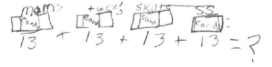

FIGURE 4.1. Judy's diagram representing what was known and unknown for the candy problem.

Diagram Types

As a part of diagram generation instruction, students can be taught about the different ways diagrams can be drawn to best represent relationships presented in the word problem. Teaching them the different ways problems can be diagrammed can contribute to establishing a schema (knowledge structure) that they can use as a basis for understanding and identifying the patterns of relationships contained in the word problem (Marshall, 1995). Four general-purpose diagrams for specific problem types have been identified (Diezmann & English, 2001; Novick, Hurley, & Francis, 1999) *networks, matrices, hierarchies,* and *part–whole* diagrams.[1]

1. *Networks,* sometimes referred to as *line diagrams,* consist of points linked together by lines. This type of diagram is best suited for word problems that require objects or things to be put into order as a way of organizing the various pieces of information found in the problem. Peter's diagram (Figure 4.2) for the tree problem is an example of a line diagram.

2. *Matrices* or *tables* can be used to represent relationships between two or more sets of information. This type of diagram is particularly useful for word problems that involve combining information and questions that require deductive thinking. Sam (Figure 4.3) used a table to solve the farm animal task. Sam used a table as a means of visually representing various combinations that could have been the solution to the problem.

3. *Hierarchies,* for example *tree diagrams* or *family trees,* can be used to display diverging or converging paths among a series of points. Reggie (Figure 4.4) used a tree diagram to display all the possible choices he had in completing a science project for class.

4. *Part–whole diagrams* are diagrams that have no readily recognizable form but can be used to demonstrate relationships between a part and a whole. These diagrams are essential for grouping things together. Lucy's diagram (Figure 4.5), unlike Sam's for the farm animal task, is an example of a part–whole diagram, in which the parts are the circles representing each animal and the whole is the total number of legs.

At each of the two ends of a straight path, a man planted a tree, and then every 5 feet along the path he planted another tree. The length of the path is 15 feet. How many trees were planted?

FIGURE 4.2. Peter's line diagram for the tree problem.

There are 8 animals on a farm. Some of them are hens and some are rabbits. Between them they have 22 legs. How many hens and how many rabbits are on the farm?

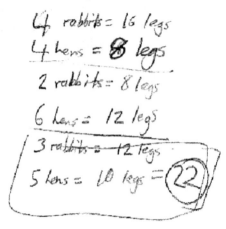

FIGURE 4.3. Sam's table for the animal farm problem.

Reggie had to do a science project for class. His teacher said the project could be in the form of either a poster or a booklet. The science project could be on frogs, bats, or iguanas. How many choices did Reggie have?

FIGURE 4.4. Reggie's tree diagram for the science project problem.

There are 8 animals on a farm. Some of them are hens and some are rabbits. Between them they have 22 legs. How many hens and how many rabbits are on the farm?

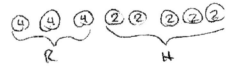

FIGURE 4.5. Lucy's part–whole diagram for the animal farm problem.

Reasoning with a Diagram

For any imagery to be useful it needs to be coupled with analysis and thought (Presmeg, 1986b). Once generated, the diagram needs to be used as a part of the reasoning process in order to reach a solution to the word problem (Diezmann & English, 2001). Teaching students how to use their diagrams to reason with them is important. To accomplish this, the students first need to be encouraged to think of their diagram as a tool to aid them in the process of solving the problem. Too often diagrams and other representational forms are seen as end products rather than as tools for explanation. This limits their usefulness as a means for identifying relationships (Pape & Tchoshanov, 2001).

Second, students should be taught to understand that a given diagram should yield consistent answers (Diezmann & English, 2001). To do this, a part of the instruction needs to focus on accuracy of information in the diagram. One problem is that in the process of translating the word problem into a diagram, numbers may be transposed or copied incorrectly. To prevent this, the students can be taught to check their diagrams against the problem. Instruction may also need to focus on how to use diagrams to track the solution, ideas, and inferences. Many students become "lost" when using their diagram during the solution of a problem. It is recommended that instruction be provided on precision in location and movement on a diagram (Diezmann & English, 2001). For example, Mary (Figure 4.6), after drawing a line with a clear beginning, middle, and end to mark the length of the trip, carefully marked the sections of the trip made by the hitchhiker when walking and when traveling by truck.

It is also recommended that students be taught how to use a suitable strategy for tracking and checking their work (Diezmann & English, 2001). Movement can be tracked using indicators such as lines, arrows, dots, or numbers. However, students should be encouraged to position any tracking indicators to the side of the diagram rather than on top of it to avoid confusion when attempting to check their work.

Finally, an important part of using any visual image as a part of the reasoning process is to be able to decompose and recombine the image when and where needed. In other words, be able to break down an image into smaller parts and then recombine those parts into a new image that is useful for solving the problem (Brown & Wheatley, 1997). This may also involve correcting the diagram. For example, to answer the tile problem Kim first drew a circle to represent a table (Figure 4.7). She then divided the table into sections. In the process of trying to solve

A hitchhiker set out on a journey of 60 miles. He walked the first 5 miles and then got a lift from a truck driver. When the driver dropped him off, he still had half of his journey to travel. How far had he traveled in the truck?

FIGURE 4.6. Mary's diagram for the hitchhiker problem.

Paul is covering a table with small tiles. It will take 10 rows of tiles with 5 tiles in each row to cover the table. How many tiles are needed in all to cover the table?

FIGURE 4.7. Kim's manipulation of her diagram to solve the tile problem.

the problem, she realized that her diagram was inadequate, as the number of rows of tiles and the number of tiles in each row were incorrect. She then erased her diagram and redrew it to better represent what the problem was asking, which enabled her to solve the problem. Unfortunately, some students may be reluctant to or find it challenging to rearrange or redraw their diagrams.

IMPLEMENTING DIAGRAMMATIC INSTRUCTION

Teachers play an important role in developing diagrammatic ability in students. However, researchers have found that most students rarely have opportunities to use diagrams in mathematics classes (Presmeg, 1986a; Wheatley, 1991). Factors such as textbooks, current teaching methods, timed tests, lack of time due to curricular demands, and educator disinterest in diagrams have been cited as working against their use (Presmeg, 1986a).

Given these concerns, selecting the best instructional approach is important. Of the various approaches, explicit instruction, in which concepts are presented in a clear, direct manner to promote student understanding and mastery, is recommended. Explicit instruction has been shown to be particularly effective for teaching students with mathematics disabilities (Montague, Warger, & Morgan, 2000). Such instruction incorporates several teaching practices that have been identified as essential for positive student outcomes. It is characterized by (1) identification of performance expectations, typically through the use of some advanced organizer, (2) description and teacher modeling of the strategy, (3) provision of guided practice either individually or sometimes involving students working together, (4) independent practice, (5) monitoring of achievement, and (6) reinforcement and corrective feedback (Jones, Wilson, & Bhojwani, 1998; Miller, 2002). An example of a lesson incorporating explicit instruction components can be found in Figure 4.8.

Instruction focused on developing diagrammatic ability in students with mathematics disabilities need not take up an inordinate amount of time during the lesson. A structured 10 to 15 minutes per day may be sufficient. The length of the instructional period depends on the needs of the students. However, the information should be presented systematically beginning with the development of conceptual knowledge of diagrams. This then can be followed by diagram generation

One strategy that good math problem solvers might use is to draw a diagram. Do you know what a diagram is? (*Students respond.*)

A diagram in mathematics is not a picture or a drawing like a piece of artwork. This is what I mean when I use the word *diagram*. (*Show definition, either on a chart or overhead. Read definition to students.*) A diagram is an image that shows the parts of a math problem and how they belong together.

What is a diagram? (*Students respond.*)

There are three good reasons why we should use a diagram when solving word problems. (*While reading to students write reasons on a chart or overhead. This chart can be used for review in another lesson.*)

First, we can use diagrams to help us *understand what the problem is asking us* to do.

Second, we can use diagrams to help us *keep track of what we are doing* while we are solving the problem.

Third, we can use diagrams to *check that our answer makes sense.*

Let's read together why we should use a diagram when solving word problems. (*Read together.*)

Why should we use diagrams? (*Students respond.*)

When we draw a diagram, there are several hints that can help us. (*While reading to students, write reasons on a chart or overhead. This chart can be used for review in another lesson.*)

First, we *do not always have to draw everything* in the problem.

Second, when we draw a diagram, all the things or people in the problem *do not need to look realistic.*

Third, we *don't want to take too long* drawing them.

What are the hints that can help us when we draw diagrams? (*Students respond.*)

We can use symbols, numbers, and letters to represent different things or people in word problems. For example, if my math problem has a dog in it, rather than drawing the dog, we can use the letter *d* to represent the dog. Let me show you. (*Demonstrate on a blank overhead transparency.*) We could also use a circle to represent the dog. Let me show you. (*Demonstrate.*) It does not matter what we draw, as long as we know and remember what it means.

Here is another example. If my math problem has a road in it, we could draw a line to show the road. Let me show you. (*Demonstrate.*)

Your diagram might be different from another person's diagram. That is fine. But, make sure that you can remember what the diagram represents.

Tell me what symbol, such as a number, letter, or image, would you use for:

A tree? (*Students respond.*) Draw that diagram. (*On a piece of paper, students draw chosen symbol for the tree.*)

A car? (*Students respond.*) Draw that diagram. (*Students draw.*)

A person? (*Students respond.*) Draw that diagram. (*Students draw.*)

Here is a word problem that you might be asked to solve. (*Put problem on overhead. Read the problem.*)

Richard and Susan's school was selling boxes of M&M's to raise money for new computers. Together Richard and Susan sold 240 boxes of M&M's. Susan sold 145 boxes of M&M's. How many boxes of M&M's did Richard sell?

I can use the information in the problem to draw a diagram. First, I am going to identify the different things or people in the problem. There are two people: Richard and Susan, and boxes of M&M's. Now that I know what is in the problem, I am going to use that information to draw a diagram that will help me solve the problem.

(cont.)

FIGURE 4.8. Sample lesson outline and script.

In this problem there are two people: Richard and Susan. I am going to use the first letter in their name to represent them. (*Draw an R and an S.*) I also know there are boxes of M&M's in this problem. I know that Susan sold 145 boxes. So under *S* for Susan I am going to draw a box and label it M&M's. Inside the box I am going to write 145 to remind me how many she sold. (*Draw boxes of M&M's.*) I am going to draw a box under the *R* for Richard and label it M&M's. Because I do not know how many Richard sold, I am going to draw a question mark here to let me know this is what I have to find out. Anything else?

Here is another word problem. (*Put problem on overhead.*) Let's read the problem together. (*Read together.*)

In one box there are 100 cans of tuna. If John ordered four boxes of tuna, how many cans of tuna are there altogether?

Tell me, what different things or people are in the problem? (*Students respond.*) Using the information from the problem, let's draw a diagram together. (*Draw with students.*) In this problem there is one person, John. I am going to use the first letter in his name to represent him. (*All draw a J.*) There are also four boxes of tuna that John ordered. I am going to draw four boxes. (*Draw four boxes.*) I know that each box contained 100 cans of tuna. So in each box I am going to write *100* to remind me of how many cans are in each box. (*Write 100 in each box.*) I am going to draw a circle around the four boxes because I know I have to find out how many I have altogether. Now I am going to put a question mark on top of the circle because I do not know how many there are altogether and this is what I have to find out. Anything else?

Here are three problems. (*Give students a worksheet with three word problems on it.*) Let's read the first problem together. (*Read the problem.*) Tell me what different things or people are in the problem. (*Students respond.*) Using this information, tell me the diagram you would draw to represent the problem. (*Students direct you to draw diagram.*)

For the next two problems, I would like you to read them and then identify the things or people in the problem. Using that information, draw a diagram that represents the word problem. I will help you with the words if you need help. When you have finished, we will compare what we did. (*Students work on problems. Provide help as needed. After the students have completed their diagrams, compare what has been done.*)

FIGURE 4.8. (*cont.*)

and using the diagram as a part of the reasoning process to reach a solution. Other instructional considerations could include:

- Using problems that the students can read without much difficulty. This means starting with problems that they can solve with some ease. Initially the instruction should focus on strategy development and use. Once the students are capable of generating simple diagrams and using them as a part of the problem-solving process, gradually increase their difficulty.
- Focusing on one diagram type at a time. To reinforce the utility of the diagram type, provide the students with sets of problems that can be represented using that diagram type (Diezmann & English, 2001).
- Providing opportunities for the students to compare their diagrams in order to highlight similarities and differences in their approaches to the same word problem (Diezmann & English, 2001).
- Providing the strategy instruction toward the beginning of the academic year. This provides the students with the time to develop and practice using diagrams.

A CAUTION

Developing diagrammatic ability in students with mathematics disabilities may take more time than expected. Also, it is important to realize that *knowledge of and ability to generate and use diagrams does not necessarily ensure improvement in word-problem solving performance.* Consider the following three illustrations.

Isabelle was capable and confident in her ability to generate a diagram for a word problem. Her diagram (Figure 4.9) represented the various parts of the word problem. She knew the problem would take two steps to solve. She knew she would have to calculate how much the book and the poster cost. The total amount spent would then be subtracted from the $5.00 in order to get the change. She wrote the first algorithm and correctly computed the answer. However, she failed to set up the second algorithm correctly and, as a result, ended up with an incorrect answer to the problem.

Levi was taught what a diagram was. After receiving instruction, he spent several days practicing how to generate diagrams. He was then taught two different ways to draw diagrams and, given word problems for each diagram type, drew a representation pertinent to each word problem. Levi was capable and confident in generating diagrams. Despite the instruction, when asked to solve several word problems, at no point did he generate a diagram that helped him solve the word problem (Figure 4.10).

Trudy was given the newspaper word problem to solve. After reading it to herself she proceeded to draw a diagram of the various parts of the problem. She drew a line to represent a week. The days relevant to the word problem were marked off and labeled. She then wrote the number of newspapers printed for Monday to Wednesday and for Thursday to Saturday. From her reading of the problem she knew that what was unknown was the number of copies printed on Sunday. To demonstrate this she drew a question mark. Using her calculator, she added 172,767 and 230,357. Not really knowing what to do next, Trudy stated that she was going to add 633,924 to the total already calculated. In addition, she entered the number incorrectly. As shown in Figure 4.11, her solution to the problem was incorrect.

Alice bought a book about birds for $1.85 and a poster for $1.25. She gave the clerk $5.00. How much change did she receive?

FIGURE 4.9. Isabelle's solution to the bird problem.

The bakers want to bake a total of 170 cookies for a bake sale on Saturday. If they bake 48 cookies on Tuesday and 62 cookies on Thursday, how many more cookies do they need to bake?

280 cookies

In one week, 633,924 copies of the daily paper were printed. From Monday to Wednesday a total of 172,767 papers were printed. From Thursday to Saturday 230,357 were printed. How many copies of the Sunday paper were printed?

1037048 copies

Jenny rents her computer for $50 per day. If she rented it out for 20 days last month, how much money did she pay?

1000 for 20 days

Alice bought a book about birds for $1.85 and a poster for $1.25. She gave the clerk $5.00. How much change did she receive?

$1.90

FIGURE 4.10. Levi's solutions for four word problems.

Solving mathematical word problems is a highly complex process requiring students to use various cognitive processes (e.g., estimation, computation) and metacognitive strategies (e.g., self-checking) (Kilpatrick, 1985; Montague, 1997). The ability to use and generate diagrams (a visualization strategy) is one cognitive strategy of the many needed. Therefore, to assume that diagrammatic instruction alone is sufficient is unwise, as was evident in Isabelle's situation. Her difficulty was with setting up an algorithm and with her inability to compute the answer—that is, her use of cognitive processes. Furthermore, she failed to check if her answer made sense and was calculated correctly—use of metacognitive strategies. This demonstrates that explicit instruction in other cognitive and metacognitive strategies for solving word problems should also be provided.

Failure by students with mathematics disabilities to connect use of a strategy to the process of solving mathematical word problems is also common (Walker &

In one week, 633,924 copies of the daily paper were printed. From Monday to Wednesday a total of 172,767 papers were printed. From Thursday to Saturday 230,357 were printed. How many copies of the Sunday paper were printed?

FIGURE 4.11. Trudy's diagram and solution for the newspaper problem.

Poteet, 1989–1990). In spite of the instruction, Levi failed to connect the use of the strategy to the process of solving the word problem. This highlights how the use of diagrams as a part of the problem-solving performance needs to be clearly demonstrated. A word-problem-solving cognitive strategy such as Visualize (Figure 4.12) could be used to accomplish this.

A diagram can also be used as a way of coming to understand the various quantitative relationships in a word problem. However, despite the ability to generate a diagram that shows the various parts of the word problem, some students may struggle to identify and diagram the relationships among the various parts. For example, Trudy, in spite of being able to display the information in the word problem, misinterpreted the quantitative relationships found among the statements. Solving word problems is, in part, dependent on conceptual knowledge of the mathematical domain involved (Geary, 2004; Montague, 1997). Many students

SAY: READ the problem for understanding.

ASK: "Do I understand the problem?" If not, reread the problem.

CHECK: For understanding as I solve the problem.

SAY: VISUALIZE the problem.

STEP 1: DRAW: Ask: "What type of diagram should I draw?"
                       Draw: A diagram of what I know and a symbol for what I do not know.
                       Check: That I have drawn the diagram correctly.

STEP 2: ARRANGE:
                       Ask: "Does my diagram show how the parts of the problem are related?"
                       Rearrange: The diagram if needed.
                       Check: That my diagram matches what the problem is asking.

STEP 3: OPERATION(S):
                       Ask: "What operations and how many steps are needed to solve the problem?"
                       Write: An algorithm to solve the problem.
                       Check: That my algorithm matches my diagram.

SAY: COMPUTE the answer.

ASK: "Have I correctly computed the answer?"

CHECK: That all the operations were done in the right order.

SAY: CHECK the answer.

ASK: "Does my answer make sense?"

CHECK: That everything is right. If not, go back. Then ask for help if I need it.

FIGURE 4.12. Visualize, a four-part cognitive strategy for solving word problems that incorporates the use of diagrams. Based on Montague's (1997) cognitive–metacognitive model of mathematical problem solving.

---

with mathematics disabilities have poor conceptual understanding of number operations and poor number sense in general (Geary, 2004; Miller & Mercer, 1997). These deficits may interfere with diagram generation and word-problem solving in general. A part of the mathematics instruction may therefore need to be focused on developing number sense, mathematical reasoning, and conceptual knowledge in children (Gersten & Chard, 1999). Interestingly, there is a relationship between conceptual understanding and the consistent use of strategies for problem solving (Rittle-Johnson & Alibali, 1999). Gains in conceptual and strategic knowledge may develop interactively with strategic knowledge influencing conceptual understanding and vice versa. For example, a number line may be used as a visualization strategy to calculate an answer to a word problem. However, a number line may also be used to introduce or reinforce conceptual understanding of number operations (Gersten & Chard, 1999). Therefore, use of diagrams may also be considered as a part of instruction for developing conceptual understanding. Use of diagrams can lead to both an improvement of students' mathematical abilities and development of their advanced problem solving and reasoning (Presmeg, 1992). After all, diagrams can be thought of as "models for thinking" (Denis, 1991, p. 104).

CONCLUSION

Flexible use of representations such as diagrams is critical to becoming a better word problem solver. Use of diagrams supports NCTM expectations in that "students are expected to (a) use and create representations to organize, record, and communicate mathematical ideas; (b) select, apply, and translate among mathematical representations, and (c) use representation(s) to model and interpret physical, social, and mathematical phenomena" (NCTM, 2000, p. 67). However, it should not be assumed that students with math disabilities know what a diagram is and how to generate and use one to their advantage for solving word problems. Provision of explicit instruction to develop diagrammatic ability may be required. This instruction may have to focus on conceptual understanding of a diagram, diagram generation, and how to use that diagram to reason with as a part of the problem-solving process. The use of diagrams as a problem-solving strategy will only be effective for a student who has learned to use them in a flexible manner during the problem-solving process (Dreyfus & Eisenberg, 1996). Finally, it should not be assumed that even this instruction, is sufficient for improving problem-solving performance. It may be necessary to instruct the students further on how to use a diagram as a part of the process for solving word problems.

REFERENCES

Brown, D. L., & Wheatley, G. H. (1997). Components of imagery and mathematical understanding. *Focus on Learning Problems in Mathematics, 19*, 45–70.

Denis, M. (1991). Imagery and thinking. In C. Cornoldi & M. A. McDaniel (Eds.), *Imagery and cognition* (pp. 103–131). New York: Springer-Verlag.

Diezmann, C. M., & English, L. D. (2001). Promoting the use of diagrams as tools for thinking. In A. A. Cuoco & F. R. Curcio (Eds.), *The roles of representation in school mathematics: 2001 yearbook* (pp. 77–89). Reston, VA: National Council of Teachers of Mathematics.

Dreyfus, T., & Eisenberg, T. (1996). On different facts of mathematical thinking. In R. J. Sternberg & T. Ben-Zeev (Eds.), *The nature of mathematical thinking* (pp. 253–284). Mahwah, NJ: Erlbaum.

Dufour-Janvier, B., Bednarz, N., & Belanger, M. (1987). Pedagogical considerations concerning the problem of representation. In C. Janvier (Ed.), *Problems of representation in the teaching and learning of mathematics* (pp. 109–122). Hillsdale, NJ: Erlbaum.

Geary, D. C. (1996). *Children's mathematical development: Research and practical applications.* Washington, DC: American Psychological Association.

Geary, D. C. (2004). Mathematics and learning disabilities. *Journal of Learning Disabilities, 37,* 4–15.

Gersten, R., & Chard, D. (1999). Number sense: Rethinking arithmetic instruction for students with mathematical disabilities. *Journal of Special Education, 44,* 18–28.

Hegarty, M., & Kozhevnikov, M. (1999). Types of visual–spatial representations and mathematical problem solving. *Journal of Educational Psychology, 91,* 684–689.

Hutchinson, N. L. (1993). Effects of cognitive strategy instruction on algebra problem solving with adolescents. *Learning Disability Quarterly, 16,* 34–63.

Ives, B., & Hoy, C. (2003). Graphic organizers applied to higher-level secondary mathematics. *Learning Disabilities Research and Practice, 18,* 36–51.

Janvier, C. (1987). Representation and understanding: The notion of function as an example. In C. Janvier (Ed.), *Problems of representation in the teaching and learning of mathematics* (pp. 67–71). Hillsdale, NJ: Erlbaum.

Jitendra, A. (2002). Teaching students math problem-solving through graphic representations. *Teaching Exceptional Children, 34,* 34–38.

Jones, E. D., Wilson, R., & Bhojwani, S. (1998). Mathematics instruction for secondary students with learning disabilities. In D. P. Rivera (Ed.), *Mathematics education for students with learning disabilities: Theory to practice* (pp. 155–176). Austin, TX: PRO-ED.

Kilpatrick, J. (1985). A retrospective account of the past 25 years of research on teaching mathematical problem solving. In E. A. Silver (Ed.), *Teaching and learning mathematical problem solving: Multiple research perspectives* (pp. 1–15). Hillsdale, NJ: Erlbaum.

Kulm, G. (1994). *Mathematics assessment: What works in the classroom.* San Francisco: Jossey-Bass.

Lesh, R., Post, T., & Behr, M. (1987). Representations and translations among representations in mathematics learning and problem solving. In Claude Janvier (Ed.), *Problems of representation in the teaching and learning of mathematics* (pp. 33–40). Hillsdale, NJ: Erlbaum.

Marshall, S. P. (1995). *Schemas in problem solving.* New York: Cambridge University Press.

Mayer, R. E., & Hegarty, M. (1996). The process of understanding mathematical problems. In R. J. Sternberg & T. Ben-Zeev (Eds.), *The nature of mathematical thinking* (pp. 29–53). Mahwah, NJ: Erlbaum.

Miller, S. P., & Mercer, C. D. (1997). Educational aspects of mathematics disabilities. In D. P. Rivera (Ed.), *Mathematics education for students with learning disabilities: Theory to practice* (pp. 81–96). Austin, TX: PRO-ED.

Montague, M. (1997). Cognitive strategy instruction in mathematics for students with learning disabilities. *Journal of Learning Disabilities, 30,* 164–177.

Montague, M., & Applegate, B. (1993). Mathematical problem-solving characteristics of middle school students with learning disabilities. *Journal of Special Education, 27,* 175–201.

Montague, M., Warger, C., & Morgan, T. H. (2000). Solve It: Strategy instruction to improve mathematical problem solving. *Learning Disabilities Research and Practice, 15,* 110–116.

National Council of Teachers of Mathematics. (2000). *Principles and standards for school mathematics.* Reston, VA: Author.

Novick, L. R., Hurley, S. M., & Francis, M. (1999). Evidence for abstract, schematic knowledge of three spatial diagram representations. *Memory and Cognition, 27,* 288–308.

Nunokawa, K. (1994). Improving diagrams gradually: One approach to using diagrams in problem solving. *For the Learning of Mathematics, 14,* 34–38.

Pape, S. J., & Tchoshanov, M. A. (2001). The role of representation(s) in developing mathematical understanding. *Theory into Practice, 40,* 118–127.

Parmar, R. S. (1992). Protocol analysis of strategies used by students with mild disabilities when solving arithmetic word problems. *Diagnostique, 17,* 227–243.

Polya, G. (1957). *How to solve it: A new aspect of mathematical method* (2nd ed.). Garden City, NY: Doubleday.

Presmeg, N. C. (1986a). Visualization and mathematical giftedness. *Educational Studies in Mathematics, 17,* 297–311.

Presmeg, N. C. (1986b). Visualization in high school mathematics. *For the Learning of Mathematics, 6,* 42–46.

Presmeg, N. C. (1992). Prototypes, metaphors, metonymies, and imaginative rationality in high school mathematics. *Educational Studies in Mathematics, 23,* 595–610.

Rittle-Johnson, B., & Alibali, M. W. (1999). Conceptual and procedural knowledge of mathematics: Does one lead to the other? *Journal of Educational Psychology, 91,* 175–190.

Shigematsu, K., & Sowder, L. (1994). Drawings for story problems: Practices in Japan and the United States. *Arithmetic Teachers, 41,* 544–547.

Swanson, H. L., Cooney, J. B., & O'Shaughnessy, T. E. (1995). Learning disabilities and memory. In B. Wong (Ed.), *Learning about learning disabilities* (2nd ed., pp. 107–152). San Diego: Academic Press.

van Garderen, D., & Montague, M. (2003). Visual-spatial representation, mathematical problem solving, and students of varying abilities. *Learning Disabilities Research and Practice, 18,* 246–254.

Van de Walle, J. A. (2004). *Elementary and middle school mathematics: Teaching developmentally* (4th ed.). New York: Longman.

Walker, D. W., & Poteet, J. A. (1989–1990). A comparison of two methods of teaching mathematics story problem-solving with learning disabled students. *National Forum of Special Education Journal, 1,* 44–51.

Wheatley, G. H. (1991). Enhancing mathematics learning through imagery. *Arithmetic Teacher, 39,* 34–36.

CHAPTER 5

Self-Regulation Strategies for Better Math Performance in Middle School

MARJORIE MONTAGUE

M r. Sosa teaches four classes of seventh-grade general mathematics and one remedial math class. The students in these classes represent diverse abilities and achievement levels. In addition to the remedial class, he has many students in the general education classes who have considerable difficulty in mathematics, especially in solving mathematical word problems. Many of the students in his classes have identified learning disabilities, a few have been identified with attention-deficit/hyperactivity disorder, and still others are second-language learners. Other students of Mr. Sosa's, however, can solve typical textbook problems like the following because they have mastered the problem-solving strategies needed to be successful. As important, they have developed a variety of self-regulation strategies that help them monitor and evaluate their problem solving. The challenge for Mr. Sosa is to teach the students who are having difficulty solving problems the strategies that the other students use effectively and efficiently.

These are typical textbook math problems Mr. Sosa's good problem solvers are able to solve with relative ease:

A train going to New York travels 75 miles per hour for 1 hour. Then, because of weather problems, it slows to 35 miles per hour for the rest of the trip. If the trip takes 8 hours, how many miles has the train traveled when it gets to New York?

> Mr. Hanson bought a used car for $5,000. His monthly payment was $173.32 for 3 years. What is the amount of interest he was charged?

Many students, especially those with learning disabilities (LD), have considerable difficulty solving problems like these. They may have the basic computational and procedural knowledge and skills needed but still cannot solve them. The purpose of this chapter is to explain why students have so much difficulty and what teachers like Mr. Sosa can do to help students become better math problem solvers. The following three questions frame the chapter.

- Why are students with LD such poor mathematical problem solvers?
- What do good problem solvers do to solve math problems?
- How can we teach students with LD to be better math problem solvers?

Examples of students' problem-solving and instructional vignettes are provided to guide teachers. Additionally, Solve It!, a math-problem-solving instructional program validated with middle school students with LD, is described (Montague, 2003).

WHY ARE STUDENTS WITH LEARNING DISABILITIES SUCH POOR MATHEMATICAL PROBLEM SOLVERS?

Many students with LD have serious perceptual, memory, language, and/or reasoning problems that interfere with mathematical problem solving (Bley & Thornton, 1995). That is, students may have trouble reading and understanding the problem, attending to the information in the problem, identifying important information and representing that information, developing a plan to solve the problem, and computing (e.g., recalling math facts and remembering algorithmic procedures). Even though students may have acquired the basic knowledge and skills in reading and mathematics and, therefore, should be able to carry out these cognitive activities, they often do not because of these problems. Additionally, these students often experience significant self-regulation problems that interfere with problem solving.

Students with LD characteristically are deficient in the ability to select appropriate strategies to use and to regulate themselves during academic tasks (Wong, Harris, Graham, & Butler, 2003). That is, they have self-regulation problems that prevent successful completion of tasks. These students are typically disorganized, do not know where or how to begin, lack enabling strategies, and do not evaluate what they do. The ability to regulate one's cognitive activities underlies the executive processes associated with metacognition (Flavell, 1976). Metacognition consists of both *knowledge and awareness* of one's cognitive strengths and weaknesses and *self-regulation*, the ability to coordinate that awareness with appropriate action (Wong, 1999). Metacognition develops in young children from an early age and matures during early adolescence, sometime between the ages of 11 and 14. Meta-cognitive ability is essential for successful academic performance across domains (Montague, 1998).

For mathematical problem solving, students need to be able to determine if they understand the problem after they read it, recognize the important information, develop a visual representation of the problem that reflects the important information, make a logical plan to solve the problem, think about a reasonable solution and answer, compute with confidence, and verify their solution as accurate. They need to be able to guide themselves through the process as they execute the solution by using self-regulation strategies. These strategies include self-verbalization, self-questioning, and self-evaluation. In other words, students need to be able to tell themselves what to do, ask themselves questions to determine if they have acted appropriately, monitor their performance as they solve the problem, and, finally, check and verify that what they have done is correct.

To illustrate, take a moment to solve the following problem.

> Caroline owns a dog kennel. She usually has 15 dogs to care for every week. Each dog eats about 10 pounds of food per week. She pays $1.60 per pound for the food. How much does Caroline pay to feed 15 dogs each week?

Now, stop and make a list of the cognitive processes and metacognitive strategies you used to solve the problems. Most people engage in some or all of the following activities, depending on the difficulty level of the problem:

- Rereading the problem or parts of the problem
- Identifying the important information
- Asking themselves questions
- Putting the problem into their own words
- Visualizing or drawing a picture or diagram of the problem
- Telling themselves what to do
- Making a plan
- Estimating the outcome
- Working backward and forward
- Checking that the process and the product are correct

To reiterate, students with LD generally are poor problem solvers due to strategy deficits or differences that impede effective and efficient problem solving. They may have a repertoire of strategies and yet have difficulty selecting appropriate strategies and organizing and executing them. They also are inefficient in abandoning and replacing ineffective strategies, do not readily adapt previously used strategies, and do not generalize strategy use. Students with LD need help in acquiring and applying cognitive processes and self-regulation strategies that underlie effective and efficient problem solving. For math problem solving, they need to learn how to understand the mathematical problems, analyze the information presented, develop logical plans to solve problems, and evaluate their solutions.

HOW DO GOOD PROBLEM SOLVERS SOLVE MATH PROBLEMS?

We know that good problem solvers are good strategic learners and that students with LD are poor strategic learners. There are several other characteristics that differentiate good and poor problem solvers. Good problem solvers usually are highly motivated and persist in their effort. They control their emotions and are appropriately confident. They focus their attention appropriately and are self-directed and self-regulating. Poor problem solvers, on the other hand, have low motivation and give up easily. They lack strategies or have a limited repertoire, and if they have acquired strategies, they experience difficulty selecting, organizing, and using them appropriately. They are poor self-regulators and are unable to detect and correct errors. Table 5.1 lists the salient differences between good and poor problem solvers.

We investigated the math problem-solving processes and strategies of middle school students by having students "think aloud" while they solved problems (Montague & Applegate, 1993). The example below shows how Ana, an average-achieving eighth-grade student, used self-regulation strategies to guide her as she solved the following problem.

> Four friends have decided they want to go to the movies on Saturday. Tickets are $2.75 for students. Altogether they have $8.40. How much more do they need?

Ana's Think-Aloud

"OK, first I am going to read it to make sure. [She reads the problem.] I will read it twice to make sure that I understand it. [She reads the problem again.] Then I am going to pick out the numbers and see if they are neces-

TABLE 5.1. Differences between Good and Poor Problem Solving and Strategic Learning

Good	Poor
• Repertoire of strategies	• Limited strategies
• Metacognitive approach	• Immature metacognitive abilities
• Motivated	• Low motivation
• Memory capacity	• Attention, memory, language problems
• Developed language	• Impulsive
• Appropriately confident	• Uncertain approach to problems
• Attentional focus	• Inability to detect and correct errors
• Self-directed and self-regulating	• Problem representation difficulties
• Ability to generalize learning	• Poor generalizers

sary. Four friends have decided they want to go to the movies on Saturday. Tickets are $2.75 for students. So, we have two numbers already, 4 and $2.75, so I am multiplying to get the answer of how much money all the tickets are going to cost for all the friends—$2.75 times 4. [She computes.] So, then you already have your answer. Now it says altogether they have $8.40. So now you have to subtract to see how much more money they need—11 minus 8.40. Oh, let's see. [She computes.] I always check my work by going back and adding to see if it's right, the subtraction, because sometimes I have a bit of trouble so I go back. [She checks her computation.] That's it. I'm done."

Ana clearly uses self-regulation strategies. She tells herself what to do as she progresses through the problem, breaks the problem into parts, identifies the important information, notes the question, and assures herself that she understands it by reading and rereading and making a plan. She monitors her performance by talking herself through the problem and checking that she completes each step correctly. Eric is another average-achieving student. Let's look at his solution to a different problem.

A group bought 52 airline tickets. Each ticket was $26 less than the $280 regular-price ticket. How much did the group spend for the tickets?

Eric's Think-Aloud

"[He reads the problem.] Somewhat easy. A group bought 52 tickets. I am going to write 52. Each ticket was $26 less than the $280 regular price ticket. How much did the group spend on tickets? So, I am going to look back at the problem and so I am going to multiply 52 times 26. [He computes.] Then it's no less than . . . OK, I don't know what I just did. I really don't know. OK, each ticket is $26 less than the regular-price ticket. Why is it a $280 regular-price ticket? OK, I am going to do this one over again. A group bought 52 tickets. Each ticket was $26 less than the $280 regular-price ticket. So the tickets used to cost $280. OK. So, how much did the group spend for tickets? Oh, OK, that's easy. First I need to subtract 26 from 280. Then I multiply that number by 52. [He computes.] Now I understand what I did."

Like Ana, Eric uses self-regulation strategies to guide himself as he solves the problem. First, he evaluates the difficulty level and decides the problem is "somewhat easy." He tells himself what to do and asks himself questions. He monitors his performance and realizes that he does not understand what he did about halfway through and decides to start over by reading the problem again. He makes sure he understands the problem and clearly sets a plan. When he finishes, he acknowledges his understanding and is satisfied. Now look at Greg's think-aloud for the same problem. Greg, an eighth-grader, was placed in a learning disabilities program when he was in the fourth grade.

Greg's Think-Aloud

"[He reads the problem.] 280 take away 26 is 6, 8 take away 2 is 6, and 2 is 266."

Greg seemingly has no strategies in place for solving the problem. Presumably, he sees the word *less* and subtracts without any clear understanding of the problem. Greg is typical of most students with LD who have no resources for problem solving. He needs explicit instruction in how to read, understand, analyze, and evaluate math problems and, most notably, needs instruction in self-regulation strategies. The primary self-regulation strategies throughout the process of math problem solving are self-instruction, or telling yourself what to do, self-questioning, or asking yourself questions, and self-monitoring, or checking yourself. Self-regulation strategies help students gain access to the content of problem solving (i.e., the cognitive processes and strategies that good problem solvers use), apply those processes and strategies, and regulate their use of processes and strategies as well as their overall performance as they solve problems.

Good problem solvers use a variety of processes and strategies as they read and represent the problem before they make a plan to solve it. First, they *read* the problem for understanding. As they read, they use comprehension strategies to translate the linguistic and numerical information in the problem into mathematical notations. For example, good problem solvers may read the problem more than once and may reread parts of the problem as they progress and think through it. They use self-regulation strategies by asking themselves if they understood the problem and by monitoring their performance as they solve the problem.

They *paraphrase* the problem by putting it into their own words. They identify the important information and may even underline parts of the problem. Good problem solvers ask themselves what the question is and what they are looking for. They check the information against the problem and the question. *Visualizing* or drawing a picture or diagram means developing a schematic representation of the problem so that the picture or image reflects the relationships among all the important problem parts. Using both verbal translation and visual representation, good problem solvers not only are guided toward understanding the problem, but they are also guided toward developing a plan to solve the problem. Here is the point at which students decide what to do to solve the problem. They tell themselves to make a drawing or develop a visual representation that shows the relationships among the problem parts. They check the "picture" against the problem information. They have represented the problem and they are now ready to develop a solution path.

They *hypothesize* by thinking about logical solutions and the types of operations and number of steps needed to solve the problem. They may write the operation symbols as they decide on the most appropriate solution path and the algorithms they need to carry out the plan. They tell themselves to decide what steps and operations are needed. They ask themselves if the plan makes sense given the information they have and monitor themselves to ensure that the plan is a good one as they continue. Good problem solvers usually *estimate* or predict the answer using mental calculations or even may quickly use paper and pencil as they round the numbers up and down to get a "ballpark" idea. They tell themselves to round the numbers both up and down and ask themselves if they did. They check that they used all the important information.

They are now ready to *compute*. So they tell themselves to do the arithmetic and then compare their answer with their estimate. They also ask themselves if the answer makes sense and if they have used all the necessary symbols and labels such as dollar signs and decimals. They check to make sure that all the operations were done in the right order and that they followed their plan. Finally, they *check* to make sure they used the correct procedures and that their answer is correct. They check the plan and the computation. They ask themselves if they have checked every step and if they computed correctly. They ask if their answer is accurate, and, if they are unsure, they ask for help.

Students who are poor mathematical problem solvers, as most students with LD are, do not process problem information effectively or efficiently. They lack or do not apply the resources needed to complete this complex cognitive activity. These students also lack the self-regulation strategies that good problem solvers use. To help students with LD to become good problem solvers, teachers must understand and teach the cognitive processes and self-regulation strategies that good problem solvers use. That is, they must teach the content of math-problem-solving instruction. To do this, they must use instructional procedures that are research based and have proven effectiveness. These procedures are the basis of cognitive strategy instruction, which has been demonstrated to be one of the most powerful interventions for students with LD (Swanson & Hoskyn, 2001). Cognitive strategy instruction is characterized by an instructional routine that emphasizes guided discussion and interactive activities, verbal rehearsal of processes and self-regulation strategies, active engagement in the learning process, student commitment to performance goals, acquisition and application of cognitive processes and strategies, practice and mastery, progress monitoring, and immediate success.

The content of math-problem-solving instruction is the host of cognitive processes and self-regulation strategies that good problem solvers use to solve mathematical problems. Students must learn how to use these processes and strategies not only effectively but efficiently as well. Figure 5.1 lists the processes and their accompanying self-regulation strategies that facilitate application of the processes (Montague, 2003).

Teaching self-regulation strategies as a component of cognitive strategy instruction helps students to take control of their actions, make appropriate decisions, and become independent problem solvers. These strategies facilitate math problem solving by having students tell themselves what to do (self-instruction), ask themselves questions as they go about solving problems (self-questioning), and

READ (for understanding)

Say: Read the problem. If I don't understand, read it again.

Ask: Have I read and understood the problem?

Check: For understanding as I solve the problem.

PARAPHRASE (your own words)

Say: Underline the important information. Put the problem in my own words.

Ask: Have I underlined the important information? What is the question? What am I looking for?

Check: That the information goes with the question.

VISUALIZE (a picture or a diagram)

Say: Make a drawing or a diagram. Show the relationships among the problem parts.

Ask: Does the picture fit the problem? Did I show the relationships?

Check: The picture against the problem information.

HYPOTHESIZE (a plan to solve the problem)

Say: Decide how many steps and operations are needed. Write the operation symbols (+, −, ×, and /).

Ask: If I . . ., what will I get? If I . . ., then what do I need to do next? How many steps are needed?

Check: That the plan makes sense.

ESTIMATE (predict the answer)

Say: Round the numbers, do the problem in my head, and write the estimate.

Ask: Did I round up and down? Did I write the estimate?

Check: That I used the important information.

COMPUTE (do the arithmetic)

Say: Do the operations in the right order.

Ask: How does my answer compare with my estimate? Does my answer make sense? Are the decimals or money signs in the right places?

Check: That all the operations were done in the right order.

CHECK (make sure everything is right)

Say: Check the plan to make sure it is right. Check the computation.

Ask: Have I checked every step? Have I checked the computation? Is my answer right?

Check: That everything is right. If not, go back. Ask for help if I need it.

FIGURE 5.1. Math problem-solving processes and strategies. From Montague, Warger, and Morgan (2006). Copyright 2006 by Exceptional Innovations. Reprinted by permission.

check themselves throughout the problem-solving process (self-checking). Self-instruction involves providing one's own prompts and talking oneself through the problem-solving routine. Students may initially have difficulty using self-instruction because they may have difficulty verbalizing and remembering sequences of behaviors or activities. Self-instruction combined with self-questioning can be even more effective. Self-questioning is a form of cognitive cueing that helps remind students to use certain processes, skills, and behaviors. Students need to be taught which questions to ask and how to ask those questions as they solve problems. For example, after paraphrasing the problem, they should ask themselves, "Have I underlined the important information? What is the question? What am I looking for?"

Self-checking is used to help students reflect on the problem to make sure they selected an appropriate solution path and that they did not make any computational or procedural mistakes. The cognitive processes dictate the self-checking responses. Students learn to check:

- That they understand the problem
- That the information goes with the problem
- That the schematic representation reflects the problem information and shows the relationships among the problem parts
- That the plan makes sense
- That they used all the important information
- That the operations were completed in the right order
- That the answer is accurate. If not, they tell themselves to return to the problem and, if they still experience difficulty, to ask for help. Students need to be taught how to determine if they need help, whom to ask, and how to ask for it.

HOW CAN WE TEACH STUDENTS WITH LEARNING DISABILITIES TO BE BETTER MATH PROBLEM SOLVERS?

The cornerstone of cognitive strategy instruction is explicit instruction (for the application for mathematical problem solving, see Montague, Warger, & Morgan, 2000). Explicit instruction incorporates research-based practices and instructional procedures such as cueing, modeling, verbal rehearsal, and feedback. The lessons are highly organized and structured. Appropriate cues and prompts are given as students learn and practice the cognitive processes and self-regulation strategies. Students are given individualized, immediate, corrective, and positive feedback on performance. Instruction stresses overlearning, mastery, and automaticity. Students are active participants as they learn and practice math-problem-solving processes and strategies and interact with other students and their teachers.

A guided discussion technique is used to promote active teaching and learning. Students are engaged from the outset, beginning with a discussion about why mathematical problem solving is important. Students take a baseline measure to determine their individual performance level. This baseline provides the foundation for setting individual performance goals. With the teacher, students set individual performance goals and make a commitment to becoming better problem solvers. The problem-solving activities embedded in cognitive strategy instruction are described next. The sample lesson at the end of the chapter is an actual problem-solving demonstration by a mathematics teacher. The teacher "thinks aloud" while solving a problem to demonstrate how good problem solvers approach and solve a problem. The lesson illustrates how problem solving is modeled for students when the cognitive processes and metacognitive strategies are introduced.

Verbal Rehearsal

Before students begin to solve math problems, they must first memorize the cognitive processes and self-regulation strategies necessary for math problem solving. This content is introduced and demonstrated by the teacher to provide a context for application of the processes and strategies. Verbal rehearsal is a mnemonic strategy that enables students to memorize and recall automatically the labels and definitions of the math-problem-solving processes and strategies (Smith, 1998). Frequently, acronyms are created to help students remember as they verbally rehearse and internalize the labels and definitions for the processes and strategies. For math problem solving, the acronym RPV-HECC was created:

- **R** = Read for understanding
- **P** = Paraphrase—in your own words
- **V** = Visualize—draw a picture or diagram
- **H** = Hypothesize—make a plan
- **E** = Estimate—predict the answer
- **C** = Compute—do the arithmetic
- **C** = Check—make sure everything is right.

Cues and prompts are used initially to help students as they memorize the processes and their definitions. The goal is for students to recite from memory all processes and name the corresponding self-regulation strategies (the say, ask, check sequence for each process). When students have memorized the processes and are familiar with the self-regulation strategies for math problem solving, they can cue other students and the teacher as they begin to use the processes and strategies to solve problems.

Process Modeling

Process modeling, sometimes referred to as cognitive modeling, is simply thinking aloud while demonstrating an activity. Process modeling has been shown to enhance reading comprehension, computation skills, question asking and answering behavior, problem solving, and other academic and social behaviors (e.g., Montague, Applegate, & Marquard, 1993). For mathematical problem solving, this means that the problem solver says everything he or she is thinking and doing while solving a math problem. When students are first learning how to apply the processes and strategies, the teacher demonstrates and models what good problem solvers do as they solve problems. Students have the opportunity to observe and hear how good problem solvers solve mathematical problems. Both correct and incorrect problem-solving behaviors are modeled. Modeling of correct behaviors helps students understand how good problem solvers use the processes and strategies appropriately. Modeling of incorrect behaviors allows students to learn how to use self-regulation strategies to monitor their performance and locate and correct errors. Self-regulation strategies are learned and practiced in the actual context of problem solving. When students learn the problem-solving routine and can apply it, they then exchange places with the teacher and become models for their peers.

Initially, students will need plenty of prompting and reinforcement as they become more comfortable with the problem-solving routine. However, they soon become proficient and independent in demonstrating how good problem solvers solve math problems. One of the instructional goals is to gradually move students from overt to covert verbalization. As students become more effective problem solvers, they will begin to verbalize covertly and then internally. In this way, they not only become more effective problem solvers, but they also become more efficient problem solvers. As students become more adept at problem solving, they will begin to adapt and modify the processes and strategies and "make them their own." That is, they become better at evaluating the difficulty level of problems and, as a result, become more efficient, or "faster and better."

Visualization

Visualization, critical to problem representation, is the basis for understanding the problem (van Garderen & Montague, 2003). Visualization enables students to construct an image of the problem mentally or on paper . Students with LD are notoriously poor at visualization and, therefore, must be shown how to select the important information in the problem and develop a schematic representation. A schematic representation shows the relationships among the problem parts. Teachers must model how to draw a picture or make a diagram that shows the relationships among the problem parts using both the linguistic and numerical information in the problem. Visual representations can take many forms and will vary from student to student. Students may use a variety of visual representations such as pictures, tables, graphs, or other graphic displays. However, simply drawing a picture is insufficient. The graphic display or mental image must reflect the relationships among the pieces of information in the problem. Initially, students must be told to use paper and pencil because this is a new way of approaching math problems; later, as they become more proficient problem solvers, they will progress to mental images. Interestingly, if good problem solvers decide the problem is novel or challenging, they typically return to conscious application of processes and strategies.

Role Reversal

Students with LD tend to be dependent rather than independent learners. One instructional procedure that promotes independent learning is role reversal. As students become comfortable with the math-problem-solving routine, they can "change places" with the teacher; that is, they can assume the role of the teacher as model and expert. An overhead projector is preferable to chalkboards for demonstrations because it allows the problem solver to face the group and interact more directly. The students can then engage in process modeling just as the teacher did to demonstrate that they can apply effectively the cognitive processes and self-regulation strategies they have learned. Other students can prompt or ask questions for clarification. In this way, students learn to think about, explain, and justify their visual representations and their solution paths. Teachers may also take the role of the student who then guides the "student as teacher" through the process. This interaction allows students to appreciate that there is usually more than one correct solution path for a math problem; that is, problems can be solved in a variety of ways.

Peer Coaching

Peer coaching (i.e., peer partners, teams, and small problem-solving groups) gives students opportunities to see how other students approach mathematical problems differently, how they use cognitive processes and self-regulation strategies differently, and how they represent and solve problems differently. Peer coaching is a very effective instructional practice (Jenkins & O'Connor, 2003). Students gain a broader perspective on the problem-solving process and begin to realize that there is more than one way to solve a problem. As a result, they become more flexible and tolerant as thinkers. With partners or as a member of a group, students are supported and encouraged as they discuss the problems. They work cooperatively toward common solutions while appreciating the differences in approaches to each problem. They have ample opportunity to explain and clarify their choices. When students reach their performance goals and demonstrate mastery, novel or "real-life" problems like the following can be introduced for the partners, teams, or small groups (Montague, 2003).

Novel Mathematical Problem for Partner, Team, or Group Problem Solving

Your parents want to buy new school clothes for you, and they said you could spend $150. Make a list of items you would like to buy. Use newspaper ads to find prices. Then, decide which items you will actually purchase. Work with your group to complete your list. Compare your final purchases with the purchases of the other group members.

Performance Feedback

One of the most important instructional procedures is performance feedback (Swanson, 1999). It is critical to the success of the instructional program. Teachers should be aware of the importance of providing immediate, corrective, and positive feedback. Students' performance on regular progress checks, given throughout instruction, determines their level of mastery in terms of both their knowledge of the cognitive processes and self-regulation strategies and their application or performance on math problem-solving tests. Students graph their progress to visually display their performance, an activity that is very reinforcing for students as they can actually see their improvement over time. Careful analysis of performance during practice sessions and in mastery checks provides each student with honest feedback. Appropriate use of processes and strategies is reinforced continuously until students become proficient problem solvers. They need to know the specific behaviors for which they are praised so they can repeat these behaviors. Praise and reinforcement should be honest. Students should be taught how to give reinforcement to others and receive reinforcement from others. They need to have plenty of opportunities to practice giving and receiving reinforcement. The ultimate goal is to teach students how to monitor, evaluate, and reinforce themselves as problem solvers.

Distributed Practice

Distributed practice is vital if students are to maintain what they have learned (Swanson, 1999). To become good math problem solvers, students learn to use the processes and strategies that successful problem solvers use. As a result, their math-problem-solving skills and performance levels improve. To achieve high performance levels, students must have many and varied opportunities to practice initially as they learn the math-problem-solving routine, and then, to maintain high performance, they must continue to practice intermittently over time. Practice can be individual or students can work in teams or small groups. Problems ranging from textbook to real-life problems should be included. Novel problems like the "school clothes" problem may take several problem-solving sessions. Following practice sessions, discussion about strategies, error monitoring, and alternative solutions is essential.

Mastery Learning

A pretest is given before starting instruction to determine baseline performance levels of individual students. Then, throughout instruction, periodic mastery checks are given to monitor student progress over time and to determine the effectiveness of the program. If some students are not making sufficient progress, teachers must make modifications for these students to ensure success. Following instruction, periodic maintenance checks are provided. If students begin to slide in performance to the extent that they do not meet the required criteria on maintenance checks, booster sessions must be provided to return performance levels to mastery. These booster sessions are brief lessons consisting of review, practice, and a mastery check to refresh what students have previously learned and mastered.

SOLVE IT!: A VALIDATED MATH PROBLEM-SOLVING PROGRAM

Solve It! (Montague, 2003) is a program specifically designed to teach students the cognitive processes and self-regulation strategies for math problem solving. It was designed to improve the problem solving of middle and secondary school students who have adequate reading and computational skills but still have difficulty solving math problems. Solve It! teaches students how good problem solvers solve math problems. The processes and strategies were identified through an extensive review of literature and a process–task analysis of problem solving. A math-problem-solving routine was developed and tested in a series of studies with middle and secondary students with learning disabilities (Montague, 1992; Montague et al., 1993; Montague & Bos, 1986). These studies demonstrated the effectiveness of the program with individual students and groups of between 8 and 12 students. Following instruction, the students with learning disabilities were compared with average-achieving peers and performed as well. Students appeared to maintain strategy use and improved performance for several weeks following instruction. Performance did decline over time for some students, but brief booster sessions consisting of review and practice helped them return to mastery level. The research-based program was designed to be easily embedded in a standard mathematics curriculum. Poor math problem solvers experience success at the outset and rapidly improve in problem-solving performance. In the studies, students developed a more positive attitude toward problem solving, a greater interest in mathematics and problem solving, independence as learners, and confidence in their ability to solve math problems.

To facilitate instruction, Solve It! provides sequenced and scripted lessons to ensure that the content is covered, and research-based instructional procedures are used. These scripts are meant to be adapted by teachers, if desired, to reflect teaching style and students' needs. The program explicitly teaches students how to apply the cognitive processes and self-regulation strategies in the context of math problem solving. Prior to implementation, students are given pretests to determine baseline performance level. Additionally, an informal assessment tool, the Math Problem Solving Assessment—Short Form (MPSA-SF), is included to analyze students' knowledge and use of problem-solving processes and strategies (Montague, 1996).

Initial assessment and ongoing monitoring of students' math problem solving enables teachers to measure individual students' performance before, during, and following instruction and ascertain each student's knowledge and use of processes and strategies. Assessment procedures like the MPSA-SF are designed to be student-centered, process-oriented, and directly relevant to the instructional program. Results give teachers an understanding of a student's knowledge base, skill level, learning style, information-processing strengths and weaknesses, strategic activity, attitude, and motivation for learning in a particular domain, like mathematics. They enable teachers to make judgments and informed decisions about both individual and group instructional needs.

A SAMPLE SOLVE IT! LESSON

Solve It! lessons have instructional goals and behavioral objectives that are reflected in the content of the lesson. Each lesson lists the materials needed including instructional charts, practice problems, activities, and cue cards. Explicit instructional cues help the teacher pace the lesson by indicating which procedures to use and when to use them. The lesson script is divided into several steps. During Lessons 1–5, students learn the problem-solving routine (see Figure 5.1) and practice applying it. Practice sessions ensure that students' performance improves to a predetermined level (e.g., at least 70% correct on math-problem-solving mastery checks). Reinforcement and review are emphasized to help students maintain strategy use and improved performance over time. The criteria for moving to Lesson 6 are that all students in the group meet the mastery criterion (100%) for recitation of the cognitive processes from memory, that all students understand and are able to use the say, ask, check strategies, and that all students are able to work through practice problems with relative comfort and confidence. Students who do not meet criteria repeat Lessons 3–5. Practice sessions and progress checks are alternated until students meet the criteria for mastery. The following vignette illustrates how Solve It! is implemented in a general education math class.

Mr. Sosa's Remedial Math Class

Mr. Sosa has 18 students in his seventh-grade remedial math class. Six students have identified learning disabilities and receive resource room support. All of the students have difficulty solving mathematical word problems. Mr. Sosa has been using Solve It! with these students. During Lessons 1–3, students were introduced to the processes and strategies, and they observed Mr. Sosa as he solved math problems. By Lesson 4, all students reached 100% of the criteria in recitation of the cognitive processes from memory. They also were comfortable with the say, ask, check procedures and were less reliant on the wall charts and their study booklets. Mr. Sosa had modeled problem solving for the students several times during the previous lessons. On occasion, individual students "guided" him through the process.

Mr. Sosa is beginning Lesson 4. He plans to model a solution one more time before students solve problems on their own.

He places a transparency of the math problem on the projector.

"Watch me say everything I am thinking and doing as I solve this problem.

There are eight boxes of Krispy Kreme donuts on the shelf. Each box holds 15 donuts. Artie comes in to pick up 45 donuts for his class party. How many donuts are left?

First, I am going to read the problem for understanding.

"SAY: Read the problem. OK, I will do that. [He reads the problem.] If I don't understand it, I will read it again. Hmm, I think I understand it, but let me just read it again to make sure. [He reads the problem again.]

"ASK: Have I read and understood the problem? Yes, definitely.

"CHECK: For understanding as I solve the problem. OK, I understand it.

"Next, I am going to paraphrase by putting the problem into my own words.

"SAY: Put the problem into my own words. This kid picks up 45 donuts. There are 8 boxes. Each box has 15 donuts. How many are left? Underline the important information. I will underline 8 boxes and Each box holds 15 and pick up 45.

"ASK: Have I underlined the important information? Let's see, yes I did. What is the question? The question is 'How many donuts are left?' What am I looking for? I am looking for the number of donuts left.

"CHECK: That the information goes with the question. I have the number of boxes, the number of donuts in each box, and the number that the kid took. I need to find how many are left.

"Then I will visualize by making a drawing or a diagram.

"SAY: Make a drawing or a diagram. Hmm, I will draw 8 boxes and write 15 in each box. Then, to the right I will write 'take away 45.'

"ASK: Does the picture fit the problem? Yes, I believe it does tell the story.

"CHECK: The picture against the problem information. Let me make sure I wrote the correct numbers: 8 boxes, 15, and 45. Yes, I did.

"Now I will hypothesize by making a plan to solve the problem.

"SAY: Decide how many steps and operations are needed. Let me see. First I need to get the total number of donuts in the boxes. Then I need to subtract the 45 that the kid took. OK, 8×15, and then subtract 45. OK. So, multiply and then subtract. Now I will write the operation symbols: $\times$, $-$.

"ASK: If I multiply 8×15, I will get the total number of donuts, and then I will subtract 45 from the total number and get the number of donuts left. How many steps are needed? 2 steps.

"CHECK: That the plan makes sense. If not, ask for help. It makes sense. Next I need to estimate by predicting the answer.

"SAY: Round the numbers, do the problem in my head, and write the estimate. Round 8 to 10 and then multiply by 15. That's easy: 150. Round 45 to 50 and subtract from 150, which is 100. There should be about 100 donuts left. Write 100.

"ASK: Did I round up and down? I rounded only up, but that's OK. Did I write the estimate? Yes.

"CHECK: That I used all the important information. Two steps. OK. Now I compute by doing the arithmetic.

"SAY: Do the operations in the right order. Okay, first multiply: 8×15. OK [does the arithmetic thinking aloud], 120. Then subtract: $120 - 45$ [does the arithmetic thinking aloud]. That equals 75, my answer.

"ASK: How does my answer compare with my estimate? Hmm, not bad. I rounded up so my estimate would be more. Does my answer make sense? Yes, 75 donuts left. Are the decimals or money signs in the right places? None needed.

"CHECK: That all the operations were done in the right order. $\times$, $-$. Yes, they were. OK, now I really get to check to see if the answer is correct.

"SAY: Check the computation. Let's see. I will reverse the order to multiply and then check the subtraction by adding [demonstrates checking the computation].

"ASK: Have I checked every step? Yes. Have I used the right numbers [returns to the problem and checks the numbers again]. Yes, I have used the right numbers. Have I checked the computation? Yes, it's right. Is my answer right? Yes, the answer is right.

"CHECK: Now I will check myself again. I did everything correctly. The answer is right. I do not need to go back to the problem, and I do not need help."

Following the demonstration, students solve a problem on their own. They are told to use the processes and strategies and to think out loud just as the teacher did. They are also told to use their cue cards or refer to the Master Class Charts if they forget what to say and do. Mr. Sosa then selects a student to model the solution. He provides cues and prompts as needed to assist the student.

Like Mr. Sosa, teachers often ask how and when explicit strategy instruction should be provided for students with LD and also who should provide it. Research indicates that optimally, strategy instruction should be provided by expert remedial teachers who understand the characteristics of students with LD (Montague et al., 2000). Ideally, it should be provided to small groups of students (around 8 to 10), who have been assessed to determine that they will benefit from instruction. Grouping by need is important because some students may already be good problem solvers and may not need strategy instruction. Instruction is intense and time limited, so teachers may wish to remove students from the classroom for strategy instruction. Collaboration between general and special education teachers is essential if students are going to maintain and generalize what they have learned. Distributed practice and ongoing reinforcement are essential for long-term success.

These recommendations present several concerns surrounding the feasibility and practicality of providing cognitive strategy instruction. For instance, assessing students individually may not be possible with large groups of students. Individualizing instruction may be difficult, given the large numbers of students enrolled in most middle school teachers' math classes. Class size can range from 25 to 40 students, and teachers usually teach at least five classes. Enlisting the aid of the resource teacher to assist with instruction may be necessary. Identifying the students who need instruction and then grouping for instruction based on the various levels in the class can be a challenge for a math teacher. General education math teachers often feel unprepared to teach students who are in special programs. They may not feel confident that students can learn how to think differently and become good problem solvers. Finding time to talk with the resource teacher for students in special education can be difficult. Also, teachers often do not coordinate resource room instruction with the general education math curriculum. Communication between teachers sometimes can be difficult. Teachers may need to develop the knowledge and skills to implement cognitive strategy instruction successfully. Because the program is intense and highly interactive, teachers may need professional development to learn the instructional procedures that are the foundation of cognitive strategy instruction. Teachers may not be familiar with the research that supports cognitive strategy instruction and its components as well as the instructional procedures and, therefore, may not be convinced of its effectiveness.

CONCLUSION

Solve It! is a research-based program that makes the cognitive processes and self-regulation strategies needed for mathematical problem solving easy to teach. Students are provided with the processes and strategies that make math problem solving easy to learn. With Solve It!, students learn how to self-regulate and become successful and efficient problem solvers. The ability to regulate one's performance is essential to success. As students become more successful, they gain a better attitude toward problem solving and develop the confidence to persevere. Moving from textbook problems to real-life math situations creates a challenge for students, and they begin to understand why they need to be good problem solvers. Research-based programs like Solve It! provide problem solving instruction that gives students the cognitive and self-regulation resources to solve authentic, complex mathematical problems they encounter in everyday life. Teachers who are knowledgeable about the research in cognitive strategy instruction will be able to justify the instructional time spent in their classes on programs like Solve It! They will also be able to explain how the program complements and builds on the mathematics curriculum.

REFERENCES

Bley, N. S., & Thornton, C. A. (1995). *Teaching mathematics to students with learning disabilities* (3rd ed.). Austin, TX: PRO-ED.

Flavell, J. H. (1976). Metacognitive aspects of problem solving. In L. B. Resnick (Ed.), *The nature of intelligence* (pp. 231–245). Mahwah, NJ: Erlbaum.

Jenkins, J. R., & O'Connor, R. E. (2003). Cooperative learning for students with learning disabilities: Evidence from experiments, observations, and interviews. In H. L. Swanson, K. R. Harris, & S. Graham (Eds.), *Handbook of learning disabilities* (pp. 417–430). New York: Guilford Press.

Montague, M. (1992). The effects of cognitive and metacognitive strategy instruction on mathematical problem solving of middle school students with learning disabilities. *Journal of Learning Disabilities, 25,* 230–248.

Montague, M. (1996). Assessing mathematical problem solving. *Learning Disabilities Research and Practice, 11,* 228–238.

Montague, M. (1998). Research on metacognition in special education. In T. Scruggs & M. Mastropieri (Eds.), *Advances in learning and behavioral disabilities* (Vol. 12, pp. 151–183), Greenwich, CT: JAI Press.

Montague, M. (2003). *Solve it: A mathematical problem-solving instructional program.* Reston, VA: Exceptional Innovations.

Montague, M., & Applegate, B. (1993). Middle school students' mathematical problem solving: An analysis of think-aloud protocols. *Learning Disability Quarterly, 16,* 19–32.

Montague, M., Applegate, B., & Marquard, K. (1993). Cognitive strategy instruction and mathematical problem-solving performance of students with learning disabilities. *Learning Disabilities Research and Practice, 29,* 251–261.

Montague, M., & Bos, C. (1986). The effect of cognitive strategy training on verbal math problem solving performance of learning disabled adolescents. *Journal of Learning Disabilities, 19,* 26–33.

Montague, M., Warger, C., & Morgan, H. (2000). Solve it!: Strategy instruction to improve mathematical problem solving. *Learning Disabilities Research and Practice, 15,* 110–116.

Smith, C. R. (1998). *Learning disabilities: The interaction of learner, task, and setting* (3rd ed.). Boston: Allyn & Bacon.

Swanson, H. L. (1999). Instructional components that predict treatment outcomes for students with learning disabilities: Support for a combined strategy and direct instruction model. *Learning Disabilities Research and Practice, 14,* 129–140.

Swanson, H. L., & Hoskyn, M. (2001). Instructing adolescents with learning disabilities: A component and composite analysis. *Learning Disabilities Research and Practice, 16,* 109–119.

van Garderen, D., & Montague, M. (2003). Visual-spatial representations and mathematical problem solving. *Learning Disabilities Research and Practice, 18,* 246–254.

Wong, B. Y. L. (1999). Metacognition in writing. In R. Gallimore, L. P. Bernheimer, D. L. MacMillan, D. L. Speece, & S. Vaughn (Eds.), *Developmental perspectives on children with high-incidence disabilities* (pp. 183–198). Mahwah, NJ: Erlbaum.

Wong, B. Y. L., Harris, K. R., Graham, S., & Butler, D. (2003). Cognitive strategies instruction research in learning disabilities. In H. L. Swanson, K. R. Harris, & S. Graham (Eds.), *Handbook of learning disabilities* (pp. 383–402). New York: Guilford Press.

CHAPTER 6

Evaluating Instructional Effectiveness

Tools and Strategies
for Monitoring Student Progress

ANNE FOEGEN

Lilly Zheng is a special education teacher at Sullivan Middle School. She coteaches a math class for eighth-grade students with her general education colleague, Kate Thomas. Their class includes 4 students with individualized education plans (IEPs) who are on Lilly's caseload and 20 students who do not receive special education services. In October, Lilly and Kate began discussing their concerns about 3 students in the class who did not seem to be learning the important mathematics concepts and skills that they, as teachers, were trying to develop. Two of the students were on Lilly's caseload and 1 was not currently receiving any special education services. As Kate and Lilly discussed their concerns, they had several questions: Why is our instruction working well for many of the students in the class but not for these 3? What kinds of changes might we make to better meet the needs of these students? How can we evaluate the effectiveness of our instructional changes? Is there a way to track the learning of all the students so we can catch problems like these earlier, before they become major concerns?

PROGRESS MONITORING: A TOOL FOR EVALUATING
INSTRUCTIONAL EFFECTIVENESS

Kate's and Lilly's experiences illustrate the reality that despite teachers' best intentions and careful planning, even the most effective instructional interventions are not guaranteed to work with all students. Progress monitoring is one assessment tool that can assist teachers as they strive to provide the most effective instructional programs for their students. The term "progress monitoring" refers to an approach to formative assessment in which teachers regularly gather data on their students' academic or behavioral performance and use these data to inform their instructional decisions. Although progress monitoring can take many forms, the two that are most common are curriculum-based assessment and curriculum-based measurement (CBM). In this chapter, I will focus on CBM, an approach to progress monitoring that has an extensive research base supporting its efficacy for increasing student achievement. My goals in this chapter are to familiarize readers with the basic concepts of CBM and to explore tools and strategies for monitoring student progress in middle school mathematics.

The Foundations of CBM: History and Essential Concepts

CBM (Deno, 1985) involves using data from brief measures of academic performance administered on a regular basis to support formative evaluation of instructional effectiveness. The initial development of CBM focused on the areas of reading, written expression, and spelling, with some limited work in mathematics (Marston, 1989). A classic example of a CBM measure for elementary reading is the number of words a student can read correctly from a passage in one minute. Deno (1985) identified four essential characteristics for this and other CBM measures. The measures must be (1) reliable and valid, (2) simple and efficient, (3) easily understood, and (4) inexpensive. This combination of features guided the initial research and development work completed by Deno and his colleagues at the University of Minnesota in the early 1980s as part of the federally funded Institute for Research in Learning Disabilities (Deno, 2003). These features are important because they recognize the necessary balance between the technical, or psychometric, characteristics of the measures and the pragmatic need for a system that is both useful and efficient. While the reliability and validity of the measurement process is essential for insuring that accurate and appropriate decisions can be made from the data, technical adequacy alone is not sufficient for establishing an assessment system that is viable in school settings. The remaining features acknowledge the importance of considering the contextual constraints teachers face in their profession. By including these features, the CBM tasks and their use in a formative evaluation system are not only technically sound but also feasible for teachers to implement and sustain over time.

To use CBM measures for instructional decision making, teachers gather data on a student's initial performance level and use this information to set a goal for instruction. A graph is used to efficiently represent the student's initial performance level and the long-term goal for instruction. The teacher then begins instruction, regularly administering the brief CBM tasks and graphing the data to compare the student's progress to the rate of growth necessary to achieve the goal in the desired period of time. If a student's graph shows that the child is not making sufficient progress, the teacher can make an instructional change and continue gathering data.

Differentiating CBM from Other Forms of Progress Monitoring

It is important to differentiate CBM from other forms of progress monitoring involving mastery measurement, such as specific skill measurement (Shapiro, 1989) and precision teaching (Lindsley, 1990). The critical features that distinguish CBM relate to the types of tasks that are used, the procedures for administration and scoring, and the empirical evidence for the measurement procedures. The tasks commonly used in CBM are brief (often 1–5 minutes in length), enabling teachers to gather student performance data on the tasks regularly without sacrificing valuable instructional time. Traditionally, the tasks are drawn directly from the school's curriculum, although recent research has shown that similar results can be obtained using more generic materials drawn from other sources (Fuchs & Deno, 1994). Terms used to reflect this expansion of approaches to developing CBM tasks include "general outcome measurement" (Fuchs & Deno, 1991) and Dynamic Indicators of Basic Skills (Shinn, 1998). Another important distinction is that CBM tasks are typically selected to reflect long-term goals for instruction rather than more immediate instructional goals. In other types of progress monitoring, such as curriculum-based assessment, the materials used for assessment are more specific to the skills targeted for instruction and relevant to short-term instructional goals.

The procedures for administering and scoring CBM tasks also differentiate CBM from other forms of progress monitoring. Standardized procedures are used to administer CBM tasks, including the instructions that are given and the convention that CBM tasks are timed. Standardized administration procedures allow teachers to make direct comparisons between a student's scores from one data collection session and those from another. In addition, standardization permits the opportunity to combine and/or compare scores from students in multiple classes, schools, or districts. CBM scoring procedures are also standardized and emphasize the counting of directly observable aspects of student performance. These procedures limit the degree of inference required to determine a student's score and promote consistency across scorers.

Finally, CBM differs from other forms of progress monitoring because the research base for CBM is extensive. Fuchs (2004) described the research base for CBM as consisting of three stages in which measures are established and validated. In Stage 1, researchers explore whether the measures are reliable and valid for reflecting student performance at a single point in time. In other words, do the measures provide an accurate "snapshot" of student performance? In Stage 2, the research moves into examining whether the measures can be used to monitor student progress reliably and validly. In other words, can repeated measurement with the tasks be used to create an accurate "movie" of student performance over time? Finally, in Stage 3, researchers investigate the use of the measures to inform teachers' instructional decision making. In this stage, the primary question asked is

"Can the measures be used to support improved instructional decision making and student achievement?" The current research base for CBM includes studies representing all three of the stages. The research base is most complete in the area of elementary reading, with less available in the area of mathematics.

Contemporary Applications of CBM

As research has progressed on the use of CBM, the work has extended to include a more diverse set of applications. Current research activities are exploring the use of CBM at the secondary level in reading, writing, mathematics, and content-area instruction (e.g., Busch & Espin, 2003). In addition, researchers are examining the applicability of CBM for students who are second-language learners (e.g., Baker & Good, 1995) and the extension of CBM to develop measures for early childhood (e.g., McConnell, McEvoy, & Priest, 2002). Considerable work continues to be completed in which CBM is applied as a means of evaluating students' progress within a particular intervention. A widely used example of this application of CBM occurs within the Peer-Assisted Learning Strategies (PALS) programs for elementary reading and mathematics that have been developed by Lynn and Doug Fuchs and their colleagues (e.g., Fuchs, Fuchs, Hamlett, Phillips, & Bentz, 1994).

Using CBM to Evaluate Instruction: The Case of Joseph

An important aspect of CBM is that the measures are useful not only as static indicators of student proficiency in a content area, but that they can also serve as indicators of growth, providing a record of how a student's proficiency in a content area changes over time. This second aspect is vital in teachers' efforts to use CBM to evaluate their instruction. Deno and Fuchs (1987) described the procedures for developing CBM systems, including a framework that examines "what to measure," "how to measure," and "how to use the data." In addition, they emphasized the application of CBM as a tool for data-based problem solving. Within this context, CBM data provide the means for evaluating the effectiveness of solutions that education professionals develop for students who are experiencing learning problems. Let us return to our case study to illustrate this application of CBM from a teacher's perspective.

> As Lilly Zheng continued to mull over the challenges she and Kate were facing, she recalled that in a previous position at an elementary school, she had been facing similar difficulties meeting the instructional needs of a third-grade boy named Joseph. Lilly described her experiences with Joseph to Kate, in the hope that they might draw some insights that would assist with their current situation.
>
> Joseph was receiving special education services for reading, but not for math at the time that he was a student in Lilly's resource room. The third-grade teacher had commented that Joseph was having difficulty keeping up

with his peers in math, and that his problems did not seem specific to any particular aspect of mathematics, such as computation or problem solving. After consulting Joseph's parents, Lilly convened the IEP team and discussed implementing a short-term intervention to address Joseph's problems in mathematics. The team agreed that an eight-week intervention should be implemented and that data would be gathered to monitor Joseph's progress. The team agreed to meet again at the conclusion of the intervention to determine their next steps.

Lilly conducted several assessment sessions with Joseph to better understand which skills and concepts he understood and to identify some of his areas of difficulty. Based on these results, she designed a supplemental mathematics instructional plan that she would use to work with Joseph for 20 minutes each day. Lilly wanted to use CBM to evaluate the effectiveness of her instruction and considered two different types of math probes (one involving computation and one involving concepts and applications) available to monitor Joseph's progress (Fuchs, Hamlett, & Fuchs, 1998, 1999). Examples of each of these types of probes (although for sixth- vs. third-grade students) are provided in Figures 6.1 and 6.2. Lilly chose the concepts and applications probes because the school's curriculum and learning standards emphasized mathematical concepts to a greater extent than computation.

Lilly began the CBM process by administering three initial probes to determine Joseph's baseline level on the concepts and applications probes. Joseph obtained scores of about 6 problems correct on the concepts and applications probes. Next, Lilly repeated the same process with two boys in Joseph's class who were performing at about the middle of the class. These typical third-grade peers obtained scores of about 15 on the same probes. Lilly knew that the performance level of these peers could guide her decision about selecting a goal to work toward with Joseph. She created a graph that showed Joseph's baseline level of performance, the level of his peers' performance, and a goal line that connected Joseph's baseline level with the goal that Lilly set for him (see Figure 6.3). She hoped to help Joseph increase his score from 6 to 14 over the 8-week period of the intervention.

The data on the graph show Joseph's scores on the probes for the first 4 weeks that Lilly worked with him. Lilly was able to use the CBM data to determine that her current instructional plan was not successful in meeting Joseph's needs. Because the data points were consistently below the goal line (which shows the rate of progress Joseph needed to reach his goal in 8 weeks), Lilly decided to change her instruction for Joseph. She examined Joseph's work on the CBM probes and his recent class work to identify skills and concepts needing additional instruction and altered her instructional planning to meet these topics.

It is important to note that CBM data will not necessarily tell teachers *which* instructional changes to make. Although the probes that Lilly was using (Fuchs et al., 1999) included a computer program that offers analysis of content strands and suggests particular areas of instructional focus for teachers, not all forms of CBM include this level of support. If we return to the example of using the number of

Sheet #1   Computation 6

Password: ARM

Name: _____ Date: _____

A $\frac{3}{5} - \frac{1}{3} =$	B $\begin{array}{r} 2.66 \\ \times\ 5.4 \\ \hline \end{array}$	C $5\frac{3}{5} - 3\frac{4}{5} =$	D $\begin{array}{r} 15961 \\ +\ 92307 \\ \hline \end{array}$	E $\begin{array}{r} 23281 \\ -\ 16754 \\ \hline \end{array}$
F $\begin{array}{r} 2.591 \\ +\ 7.6588 \\ \hline \end{array}$	G $\begin{array}{r} 65983 \\ +\ 56937 \\ \hline \end{array}$	H $.13\overline{)884}$	I $122\overline{)8614}$	J $3 \times \frac{1}{2} =$
K $\begin{array}{r} 5952 \\ \times\ 246 \\ \hline \end{array}$	L $7\frac{4}{7} + 1\frac{2}{3} =$	M $45\overline{)65}$	N $3\frac{1}{3} + 8\frac{2}{3} =$	O $\begin{array}{r} 3.4423 \\ -\ 1.33 \\ \hline \end{array}$
P $\frac{2}{5} \times \frac{2}{5} =$	Q $81\overline{)9301}$	R $\begin{array}{r} 1.292 \\ \times\ 1.7 \\ \hline \end{array}$	S $1.3\overline{).598}$	T $\frac{7}{9} + \frac{2}{3} =$
U $\begin{array}{r} 3596 \\ \times\ 168 \\ \hline \end{array}$	V $7 \div \frac{1}{5} =$	W $\frac{3}{4} \div \frac{7}{9} =$	X $9\frac{3}{10} - 3\frac{3}{5} =$	Y $\begin{array}{r} 55867 \\ -\ 32719 \\ \hline \end{array}$

FIGURE 6.1. Sample computation probe. From Fuchs, Hamlett, and Fuchs (1998). Copyright 1998 by PRO-ED, Inc. Reprinted by permission.

Name _____ Date _____ Test 1 Page 1

Applications 6

Column A   Column B

(1)

Write **P** if the number is a prime number and **C** if the number is a composite number.

_____ 2   _____ 94

(2)

$7^2 =$ _____

(3)

When Emily woke up, the temperature was 42° F. By how many degrees did the temperature fall?

last night's temperature

_____ ° F

(4) Which expression matches the phrase:

The difference between y and 19?

(A) y - 19

(B) $\dfrac{19}{y}$

_____ (C) y + 19

If y = 25, then the value of the expression is

_____

A

(5)

Rename if necessary.

3 m 92 cm
+ 7 m 15 cm
_____
___m ___cm

(6)

15 girls wore pink dresses, 25 wore blue dresses, 7 wore purple dresses and 2 wore green dresses. Write the ratio of green dresses to purple dresses, using the word "to."

_____

(7)

(A) acute

(B) obtuse

(C) right

What kind of triangle? _____

(8)

Express 7% as:

a decimal _____

a fraction with denominator of 100 _____

(9)

2:5 is the same as ___:15

FIGURE 6.2. Sample concepts and applications probe (first page). From Fuchs, Hamlett, and Fuchs (1999). Copyright 1999 by PRO-ED, Inc. Reprinted by permission.

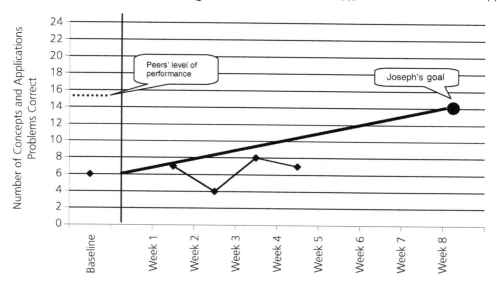

FIGURE 6.3. Graph of Joseph's math performance.

words a child can read in one minute as a CBM measure, a graph of these data for a particular student will tell a teacher if the child is not making sufficient progress, but the measures themselves do not provide direct guidance on how to alter instruction. One analogy that is often used (Deno, 1985) is that CBM data points act as educational "vital signs," serving a function similar to temperature or blood pressure for a physician. While a temperature of 104° signals a problem with a patient's health, it does not, in and of itself, suggest a specific course of treatment. Likewise, many CBM measures serve as indicators of students' general growth and academic "health." Because most forms of CBM do not provide direct guidance on changing instruction, teachers typically pair CBM with other forms of assessment. As an example, a teacher might use an analysis of student work samples or conduct a diagnostic interview to inform his or her decisions about the type of change to make in a student's instructional program.

MONITORING STUDENT PROGRESS IN MIDDLE SCHOOL MATHEMATICS

As Lilly shared her experience with Kate, she reflected on what she knew about CBM measures in mathematics for elementary students. She also realized that she wasn't aware of any measures specifically developed for middle school mathematics.

Although research on middle school mathematics progress monitoring is at an early stage, substantially more empirical support exists for mathematics measures at the elementary level. In this section of the chapter, I briefly review CBM measures for elementary mathematics progress monitoring and then introduce readers to emerging measures developed specifically for middle school mathematics. Then I provide specific information about administration and scoring for the middle school measures.

Existing Measures for Monitoring Mathematics Progress

Fuchs (2004) noted that researchers seeking to develop CBM measures have typically pursued one of two paths. One path is characterized by efforts to analyze the instructional curriculum and create tasks that serve as representative samples of a year's curriculum. This approach (used to create the probes illustrated in Figures 6.1 and 6.2) can be described as "curriculum sampling"; it allows analysis of specific skills within the curriculum and supports the identification of instructional recommendations. The disadvantage associated with this approach is that the probes are more time intensive to develop and often require a longer administration period so that students have time to complete a broader range of problem types. Fuchs described the second approach as one of identifying "robust indicators." These measures (the number of words read correctly in 1 minute would be an example) have strong correlations with other indicators of proficiency in a content area. Often these tasks represent complex abilities that require students to integrate a range of skills that are taught in the curriculum in order to complete the task successfully. The tasks serve as global indicators of proficiency in a broad content area. The disadvantage of this approach is that the probes are less helpful in identifying specific instructional recommendations.

Elementary Mathematics Measures

Existing CBM measures in mathematics for the elementary grades fall into both of the categories identified by Fuchs (2004). The "robust indicators" approach is represented in work that has examined basic arithmetic facts as indicators of proficiency in elementary mathematics. Early studies (e.g., Shinn & Marston, 1985) examined the use of single-operation tasks. As an example, a second-grade student might complete a task that involves all addition facts. Other researchers have studied the use of CBM probes that sample across all four operations (Espin, Deno, Maruyama, & Cohen, 1989). Some of the advantages associated with the fact measures are their simplicity and efficiency, as well as the ability to use a common task across multiple grade levels. One question that arises is the extent to which these research findings (obtained in the 1980s) correspond to present-day results. Given the dramatic changes in mathematics curriculum and instructional practices advocated by the National Council of Teachers of Mathematics (NCTM, 2000), and the extent to which these curricular guidelines have been adopted in curriculum materials and state standards, it is possible that current school mathematics curricula have less of an emphasis on computation, and therefore these indicators may be less effective in the present day.

The "curriculum sampling" approach is evident in elementary math tasks developed by Fuchs, Fuchs, and their colleagues (Fuchs, Hamlett, & Fuchs, 1990, 1998, 1999; Fuchs, Fuchs, Hamlett, Thompson, et al., 1994) and researcher-developed tasks created by sampling the computation problems taught in a particular grade level (Thurber, Shinn, & Smolkowski, 2002). The CBM tasks developed by Fuchs, Hamlett, and Fuchs (1990, 1998, 1999) are the most widely implemented example of this approach to CBM mathematics measures. These measures were developed through an analysis of the Tennessee state curriculum. The computation probes reflect the range of computational skills that are the focus of instruction in grades 1–6. The concepts and applications probes reflect noncomputational areas of instruction in grades 2–6. More specifically, the concepts and applications probes address specific strands of skills, such as counting and names of numbers in grade 2 and proportions, ratio and probability, and variables in grade 6.

The CBM packages developed by Fuchs, Hamlett, and Fuchs include blackline masters of the probes (30 equivalent forms are included for each grade level) and Macintosh-based software that automates the scoring and graphing of probe results. The software package also facilitates instructional decision making by prompting teachers to make instructional changes when a student's data indicate he or she will not meet the teacher-established goal and offering "expert system" data summarizing the strengths and needs of the class as a whole, as well as those of individual students (Fuchs, Fuchs, & Hamlett, 1994).

Middle School Mathematics Measures

In contrast to the volume of professional literature on CBM measures in mathematics for the elementary level, the development of mathematics measures appropriate for middle school students and content is in its infancy. Three options, discussed below, currently exist for practitioners seeking to monitor the progress of their middle school students in mathematics. The first two represent CBM measures developed specifically for middle school students by my colleagues and me (Foegen, 2000; Foegen & Deno, 2001) and by Helwig, Tindal, and their colleagues (Helwig, Anderson, & Tindal, 2002; Helwig & Tindal, 2002). The third option involves "stretching" the existing elementary measures to the middle school level.

My work (Foegen, 2000; Foegen & Deno, 2001) centers on an estimation task that is consistent with the "robust indicator" approach. This task (see Figure 6.4) includes both computation problems and contextual, or word problems. In either case, students are instructed to choose which one of three alternatives represents the best estimate of the answer. Students are urged to rely on mental math, rather than exact computation, to make their selections. To further encourage the use of mental math, the three alternatives from which students can choose an answer differ by a factor of 10. As an example, for the problem "Chandra paid $18.75 for a haircut and $49.25 for a perm. About how much did she spend on both items?", the answer alternatives are $7, $70, and $700. The intent of this structure is encourage students to rely on their estimation abilities, and on their more intuitive "number

Problem	Choices
A large pizza has 16 slices. 5 kids will share the pizza. About how many slices will each kid get?	0.3 3 30
22×59 is about	12 120 1,200
It takes 2½ yards of fabric to make a costume for the play. Mom has 11 yards of fabric. About how many costumes can she make?	0.4 4 40
$8\overline{)555}$ is about	0.7 7 70
The gym shoes cost $82. They are on sale for 25% off. About how much will you save?	$20 $200 $2,000
4×9.3 is about	0.36 3.6 36
Edward makes $4 per hour doing odd jobs. If he works 11 hours, about how much will he earn?	$4 $40 $400
$0.45 - 0.14$ is about	0.3 3 30
Luis wants to buy 6 new books. If each one costs $12, about how much will Luis pay for the 6?	$0.60 $6 $60
$8\overline{)0.19}$ is about	0.02 0.2 2
$97.7 - 21.4$ is about	27 270 2,700
Christine's car went 300 miles on 11 gallons of gas. About how many miles per gallon did the car go?	0.8 8 80
There are 30 students in the class. Each student paid $3.50 for the bus. About how much money do they have for a bus?	$10 $100 $1,000
$73 - 18$ is about	5 50 500
Joel earns $4.25 per hour stacking shelves at the grocery store. About how much will he earn in 20 hours?	$0.80 $8 $80
$78 + 17$ is about	10 100 1,000
The car's gas tank holds 14 gallons. You just pumped in 11.75 gallons to make the tank full. About how many gallons were already in the tank?	2 20 200
$219 + 879$ is about	10 100 1,000
For her birthday, Sue received $19 from Grandpa and $32 from Aunt Sue. About how much did she receive from these two people?	$5 $50 $500
$82\overline{)713}$ is about	1 10 100

FIGURE 6.4. Sample estimation probe.

sense" (Sowder, 1992), to rapidly make judgments as to which alternative is reasonable. Each task consists of 40 items (evenly split between computational and contextual estimation), and students are allowed 3 minutes to complete as many items as they can.

My work has also included a 1-minute basic facts task. This measure (Figure 6.5) includes 80 items evenly divided among the four operations. Single-digit combinations (0–9) form the pool from which the problems were randomly selected within each operation. While this measure is less representative of the middle school mathematics curriculum than is the estimation task, I hypothesized (Foegen & Deno, 2001) that fluency with basic facts might represent an important tool skill that would facilitate students' development of proficiency with more advanced mathematics concepts and skills.

Helwig, Tindal, and their colleagues (Helwig et al., 2002; Helwig & Tindal, 2002) have taken a slightly different approach to the development of a middle school CBM math measure. The problems on their concept-based tasks emphasize conceptual understanding rather than computation skill or application of mathe-

$1 - 1 =$	$8 \times 1 =$	$5 \times 5 =$	$1 \times 7 =$
$4 \times 7 =$	$5 \times 7 =$	$4 + 6 =$	$9 \times 5 =$
$3 + 0 =$	$3 \overline{)12} =$	$2 \overline{)14} =$	$6 \overline{)6} =$
$12 - 9 =$	$7 + 4 =$	$0 \times 7 =$	$7 - 4 =$
$5 \overline{)10} =$	$8 \overline{)48} =$	$11 - 7 =$	$4 \overline{)12} =$
$8 - 2 =$	$9 + 6 =$	$6 + 6 =$	$1 \times 2 =$
$8 + 7 =$	$0 \times 0 =$	$11 - 2 =$	$8 - 5 =$
$6 - 2 =$	$7 + 0 =$	$3 + 3 =$	$17 - 9 =$
$10 - 4 =$	$9 \times 9 =$	$4 \overline{)4} =$	$1 \overline{)5} =$
$1 \overline{)1} =$	$2 - 2 =$	$5 + 9 =$	$7 \times 8 =$
$6 \overline{)54} =$	$9 - 3 =$	$4 \overline{)32} =$	$16 - 7 =$
$4 + 5 =$	$14 - 9 =$	$7 + 6 =$	$2 \times 6 =$
$8 + 8 =$	$13 - 6 =$	$2 \times 4 =$	$5 \overline{)0} =$
$1 + 0 =$	$6 \times 2 =$	$2 + 8 =$	$1 + 8 =$
$9 \overline{)63} =$	$3 \overline{)27} =$	$3 \overline{)15} =$	$9 \overline{)36} =$
$0 + 0 =$	$8 \times 3 =$	$8 + 5 =$	$3 \overline{)12} =$
$13 - 8 =$	$6 \overline{)24} =$	$2 \times 2 =$	$2 - 0 =$
$9 + 1 =$	$6 - 3 =$	$0 + 7 =$	$3 \times 5 =$
$8 \overline{)8} =$	$4 \times 9 =$	$9 - 7 =$	$5 \overline{)40} =$
$5 + 2 =$	$7 - 0 =$	$1 \times 6 =$	$8 + 0 =$

FIGURE 6.5. Sample facts probe.

matics to contextual situations. Helwig and his colleagues drew from Hiebert and Lefevre's (1986) work to define conceptual understanding as organized schemas that link and integrate interrelated information. In other words, when students have strong conceptual understanding in mathematics, they are able to make connections and identify relationships between individual pieces of information, as well as building links between mathematical domains, such as geometry, algebra, and fractions. Figure 6.6 illustrates the types of items Helwig and his colleagues have included on their probes.

Helwig et al.'s measures differ from traditional approaches to CBM in that the tasks are administered in an untimed format (though the authors noted that most students have completed an 11-item task in about 10 minutes). Another difference is that the use of the measures as a sensitive gauge of student progress was not a driving consideration in the design process. While the research conducted to date on the concept-based measures has revealed strong relationships with state

---

13. If a city's normal yearly rainfall is 40 inches, what would the rainfall be if it rained 120% of normal? _____

21. Write a fraction between 1/7 and 1/8. _____

22. A can of paint holds enough paint to cover 15 square feet. You need to paint a wall that is 9 feet high and 10 feet long. How many cans of paint will you need?
_____

24. If you start with a number and multiply it by 6 and then subtract 4 from the answer, you end up with 38. What number did you start with? _____

25. Put these numbers in order from smallest to largest:

$$\frac{3}{8} \qquad \frac{3}{11} \qquad \frac{5}{11} \qquad \frac{1}{2}$$

____   ____   ____   ____

26. One piece of wood is 15 inches long. A second piece is only 3/5 as long. How long is the second piece? _____

30. Write a number between 6.4 and 6.5. _____

33. There are 2 pizzas left over from a birthday party. If 3 people want to share the pizzas equally, how much would each person get? _____

40. Every time the class put a quarter in a jar, their teacher put 3 quarters in. At the end of the year there were 96 quarters in the jar. How many did the teacher put in?
_____

41. Put these numbers in order from smallest to largest.

   .3   .27   .096   0.32   .256

____   ____   ____   ____   ____

45. A recipe calls for 4 teaspoons of baking powder for every 6 cups of flour. How many teaspoons of baking powder do you need if you use 15 cups of flour?
_____

FIGURE 6.6. Sample concept-based probe. From Helwig, Anderson, and Tindal (2002). Copyright 2002 by PRO-ED, Inc. Reprinted by permission.

achievement tests and potential for use in assessing adequate yearly progress (AYP), Helwig et al. (2002) found that average scores in a general population of eighth-grade students increased only 1.34 points across an academic year. Furthermore, many low-performing students were unable to answer any of the questions correctly. Until further research is conducted to increase the ability of the concept-based measures to monitor student progress, they will have limited utility for teachers who are seeking tools for progress monitoring. As a result of these limitations, I do not provide further detail regarding the administration and scoring of the concept-based measures.

The final option currently available to middle school teachers who wish to monitor the progress of their students in mathematics is to consider the extension of existing measures developed to reflect the elementary curriculum. If middle school students are performing at levels significantly below their peers, teachers may find that an elementary probe that corresponds to the students' instructional level provides a viable option for monitoring progress. In particular, the computation and concepts and applications measures developed by Fuchs et al. (1998, 1999) may prove to be useful for middle school students performing below grade level. Table 6.1 provides a summary of the measures available for use in monitoring the mathematics progress of middle school students.

Implementation Guidelines: Putting Progress Monitoring into Practice

In this section of the chapter, I review the procedures used for putting a middle school progress-monitoring program in place. I include guidelines for administration and scoring of the probes, as well as development of student graphs and options for instructional decision making.

Administration

As teachers prepare to administer CBM probes to students, they need to keep in mind the earlier discussion about standardized administration and exact timing, two characteristics that differentiate CBM from many other forms of classroom assessment. When CBM probes are administered to students, it is important that the conditions be consistent from one administration to the next. As a result, many forms of probes include a script teachers can use to be confident they will give consistent directions each time the probe is administered. Typically, the first administration of any type of progress monitoring probe is preceded by a brief instructional session in which the teacher familiarizes students with the types of problems they will be completing, the way in which students will be recording their responses on the probe, and the purpose for completing the probes. Subsequent administration scripts are more brief, often including a reminder as to the task that students are going to complete, the amount of time they will have available to work, and specific procedures for completing the task (i.e., the order in which to do

TABLE 6.1. Measures for Monitoring Middle School Mathematics Progress

Measure	Type of measure	Grade levels	Duration of task	Number of problems	Content
Basic facts	Robust indicator	1–8	1–2 minutes	Varies; usually 40–80	Single operation or mixed operation; no differences in probes by grade level
Computation	Curriculum sampling	1–6	2–6 minutes	25	Mixed computation problems representative of the computation skills taught at each grade level; different probes for each grade level
Concepts and applications	Curriculum sampling	2–6	6–8 minutes	24	Problems representative of concepts and applied mathematics skills taught at each grade level (e.g., numeration, reading charts and graphs, problem solving, understanding fractions and decimals); different probes for each grade level
Estimation	Robust indicator	6–8	3 minutes	40	Computation and contextual estimation problems; multiple choice answer alternatives differ by a factor of 10; no differences in probes by grade levels
Concept based	Robust indicator	8	Untimed	10–15	Problems that reflect conceptual understanding of number relationships (e.g., proportional thinking, relative sizes of fractions and decimal numbers); single grade level

122

the problems), as well as encouragement to students to do their best work and complete as many problems as possible in the time allowed.

Exact timing of the probes is important because it holds constant the amount of time students have to work on the probes from one administration to the next. Many teachers are reluctant to limit the time students have to work on an assessment. Some note that if time were unlimited students would be better able to demonstrate the range of their skills; others note that timing places unnecessary pressure on students. Within the context of a CBM model for assessment, timing the probes is critical because it allows teachers to make direct comparisons between a student's performance one day on Probe 5 and another day on Probe 6. Let's consider an example in which a teacher is not timing the probes. Assume Mr. Smith administers Probe 5 to Bill the first week of October. Bill works on the probe for 15 minutes and earns a score of 20 points. The third week of October, Mr. Smith administers Probe 6 to Bill, who works on the task for 12 minutes and earns 18 points. How should Mr. Smith interpret Bill's performance? Has it improved because he completed the task in less time? Has Bill lost ground because he earned a lower score? By holding constant the time Bill has to work on the probe, Mr. Smith would be able to make direct comparisons between Bill's scores from one administration to the next. In addition to enabling accurate interpretation of the data, exact time limits also ensure that excessive amounts of instructional time are not lost to assessment. Teachers can use kitchen timers, stopwatches, and audio recordings to facilitate exact timing of CBM probes.

Scoring

Once students have completed the probes, the next task is to score them. To score the facts probes, count the number of problems completed correctly in 1 minute. These probes are extremely quick and simple to score. For the estimation probes, a two-step process is required. Teachers must first count the number of correct *and* incorrect responses given by a student. If a problem is skipped, it is counted as neither correct nor incorrect. Next, the final score is computed by applying a correction for guessing (Foegen, 2000). This method, which is also used in many common multiple choice college entrance exams, applies a penalty for choosing an incorrect response. For the estimation probes, the penalty that is applied is equal to one-half the number of incorrect responses. This figure is subtracted from the number of problems correct. Let's consider an example. Maureen obtains 33 correct responses and 6 incorrect responses on her estimation probe. Her score on the probe would be 33 minus the penalty for guessing, which would be half of 6 (the number of incorrect responses). In other words, Maureen's total score would be determined in the following manner: $33 - 6(.5) = 33 - 3 = 30$. Likewise, Max's score on a probe on which he obtained 28 correct responses and 5 incorrect responses would be 25.5 [$28 - 5(.5) = 28 - 2.5 = 25.5$].

Scoring for the computation and concepts and applications probes is more complex. The computation probes are scored using a "digits correct" process in which each digit of the answer is compared to the digit expected in the correct answer. This process provides a means for awarding partial credit to a student's answer rather than requiring (as the facts and estimation probes do) that an answer be scored as either correct or incorrect. The concepts and applications probes are not scored using digits correct, but the manual (Fuchs et al., 1999) notes that some problem types are awarded more points than others. The software programs for both probe types provide automatic scoring once the student's scores are entered into the program. The National Center on Student Progress Monitoring recently published guidelines for hand scoring the computation and concepts and applications probes. Teachers can access these materials on the training page of the Center's website (www.studentprogress.org).

Graphing

The final aspect of implementation is the graphic display of student data. For teachers who opt to use the computation and concepts and applications probes, the computer software automatically completes the graphing component, providing teachers with individual graphs for each student and support in interpreting the data in the form of suggestions for teaching decisions. In this section I outline general guidelines for teachers who wish to construct their own graphs. Joseph's graph from Lilly's student teaching project (Figure 6.3) illustrates many of these conventions.

Several conventions are used when creating CBM graphs to facilitate common understanding and interpretation of the data. The horizontal axis represents time. The unit of time might be instructional sessions, school days, or months, depending on how often a teacher is administering CBM probes and the duration of time over which the probes will be administered. The vertical axis represents the unit of measurement for the probes, or whatever is being counted to determine the student's score on the probe. For a sixth-grade computation probe, this could be Number of Digits Correct in 6 Minutes; for an estimation probe, the axis could be labeled Number of Points Earned in 3 Minutes. The heading for the graph typically identifies the student and the content area, as well as any other descriptive information the teacher deems necessary, such as the grade level, the period of time covered by the graph, or the student's instructional goal.

Once the general structure of the graph has been created and appropriate labels have been added, the teacher is ready to begin gathering data. The first step is to gather baseline data. Teachers can do this by administering probes to the student over several days to determine the student's initial, or baseline, level of performance. In my experience, teachers commonly administer three different probes to students to obtain a reasonable estimate of the initial level. The student's scores on these probes are graphed, and a solid vertical line is drawn to separate these data points (representing the baseline phase) from the data points gathered after an intervention has begun. To obtain a single numerical estimate of the student's initial level of performance, the median (middle number when the scores are in rank order) of the baseline data points is used. This number is graphed on the solid black line to indicate the student's starting point prior to intervention and serves as the beginning point of the goal line.

The next step is to set an instructional goal. To determine the endpoint, or instructional goal, teachers can use several methods. In some districts, normative data are available reflecting the expected levels of performance in each grade level. Another option is to gather peer comparison data. To do this, a teacher identifies several (three to five) students in the same grade level who are performing at an average, but successful, level in comparison to teacher and district expectations. The teacher has these same students complete the baseline probes and averages their performance to estimate the scores typical peers would obtain. This level can then be used as a goal to be achieved through the instructional intervention. As teachers make decisions about establishing goals, it is important that they set ambitious goals for their students. Research on goal setting has determined that student performance can be enhanced when goals are clear, challenging, and within the student's reach (Fuchs, Bahr, & Rieth, 1989; Fuchs, Fuchs, & Deno, 1985). The goals also need to be realistic. If a middle school student is several years behind his or her peers in mathematics, it may be unreasonable to expect that a teacher could close this gap in a single academic year. Careful professional judgment should be used to balance competing demands and set goals that are both ambitious and realistic.

After the teacher selects an instructional goal level, he or she needs to record this on the graph by plotting the goal in reference to the time period. If the goal is being set for an academic year (as may be the case with an IEP goal), the teacher will need to create a progress-monitoring graph that spans 9 months. If the goal is being set for a shorter duration, the placement of the goal point on the graph should reflect this. Finally, the teacher connects the median of the baseline point with the goal point to create a goal line (also called an aim line by some). It is important to note that the goal line is not the goal itself. When I teach my undergraduate students about progress monitoring and trendlines, a common misconception is that if the student's data point (i.e., the score on the probe) is plotted and falls above the goal line, the goal has been achieved. This is inaccurate, because the goal line merely represents the rate of progress necessary to achieve the goal in the expected amount of time. It is the endpoint of the goal line, or the final level, that is the true goal the teacher is striving to achieve.

As the teacher begins working with the student and implements an instructional program, progress-monitoring probes are administered regularly to track the student's growth in mathematics. Although there are not agreed-upon guidelines for the frequency of measurement, many teachers administer CBM probes twice a week, weekly, or every two weeks. The frequency of measurement should be related to the level of concern about the student's performance in mathematics. For students who are experiencing great difficulty, more frequent measurement once or twice a week will allow teachers to quickly adjust instructional programs that are not proving successful. For students who are less discrepant from their peers, alternate-week or monthly monitoring may be sufficient. In the area of elementary reading, a common practice is to administer screening probes to all students in a school at three points during the year (fall, winter, spring) to identify students who may be at risk for low performance levels. For students who are progressing as expected, no additional progress monitoring may be necessary.

Making Data-Based Instructional Decisions

The final aspect of progress-monitoring implementation is the collection of ongoing data and the use of these data to evaluate instruction. Two common approaches to evaluating CBM data are the application of decision rules and the use of trendlines. In the decision rules approach, a teacher establishes rules for making instructional decisions before beginning the intervention. For example, Mr. Culbertson might decide that he will make an instructional change anytime that his student's data points fall below the goal line for three consecutive weekly probes. Likewise, he may decide that if the student's data points are above the goal line for six consecutive weekly probes, he will set a new and more ambitious goal. The numbers of consecutive probes used in these scenarios are just examples; in choosing their decision rules, teachers should consider the frequency of measurement and the length of time they are willing to wait to determine if a program is ineffective. The same professional judgment applied to setting a goal level will also be needed to establish decision rules.

A second approach to evaluating instructional effectiveness involves the use of trendlines. A trendline is a straight line that is drawn through the student's data points to provide an estimate of the level and rate of progress. Trendlines provide a visual means of incorporating all the data points into a single estimate, similar to using a mean to summarize the scores of a class of students on a test. The steps for drawing a trendline using the quarter-intersect method (Taylor, 2004; White & Haring, 1980) are illustrated in Figure 6.7. Once a trendline has been drawn, a teacher can project out the current rate of progress and determine if the student will reach the goal if that current rate of growth is maintained. If the projection shows the goal will be met, the teacher can continue the current instructional program. If the projection shows the student will not meet the goal or is not making adequate progress, the teacher can make an instructional change, continue monitoring progress, and then reevaluate the data. This process of data-based decision making is illustrated in the case study that follows.

Middle School Progress Monitoring in Action: The Case of Maria

One of the students about whom Lilly and Kate are concerned is Maria Jimenez, an eighth-grade student whose parents moved to the United States from Mexico. Maria speaks Spanish in her home, and although she was designated as an English-language learner in elementary school, she has been exited from services and no longer receives any additional support for language development. Maria has not been identified as a student with a disability who

Step 1.   Divide the points in half from right to left with a solid vertical line. If there is an even number of points, the line will be midway between the two "middle" points. If the number of data points is odd, the line will go through the middle point, which will not be considered in any of the subsequent steps.

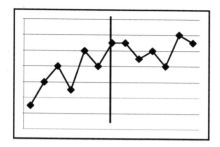

Step 2.   Divide each half of the data in half with a dashed line. This subdivides the data points into quarters. If the number of points is odd, the "quarter line" will go through a point, but this point WILL be used in subsequent steps (therefore a dashed rather than a solid line is used).

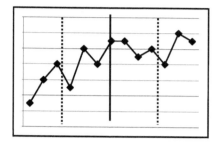

Step 3.   Find the median of each half of the data by numbering the points from the lowest to the highest value (moving from the bottom to the top of the graph, rather than from left to right). If data points have the same value, the order in which they are numbered does not matter. Mark the median level for the set of points on the quarter line for that half of the data.

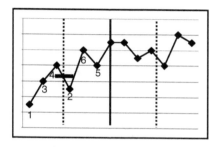

Step 4.   Repeat this process with the other half of the data points and mark the obtained value on the quarter line for that half of the data.

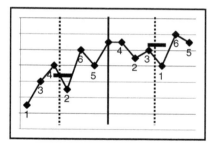

Step 5.   Connect the two median points marked on the quarter lines. This is your quarter-intersect trendline!

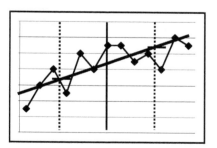

FIGURE 6.7. Steps for drawing a trendline.

is in need of special education services. Kate and Lilly are concerned because as the mathematics concepts are becoming more complex in eighth grade, Maria is having great difficulty keeping pace with her classmates and her grades in math are dropping. Maria is very conscientious about doing her homework but often completes the problems incorrectly. She has a very positive attitude and a supportive home environment. At fall parent–teacher conferences, Lilly and Kate discussed Maria's mathematics performance with her mother. Mrs. Jimenez is anxious to find a way to help Maria be more successful in mathematics, but when she's tried to help Maria with her homework, it has led to arguments and disagreements between parent and child. Because Maria is in the cotaught class, Lilly offered to design an instructional intervention to see if that would help Maria acquire new math concepts and skills. Mrs. Jimenez was eager to pursue this option and offered to provide any supports at home that the teachers felt might be helpful.

The following week, Lilly asked Maria to complete three estimation probes on different days during the week. Her scores were 4, 8, and 6. When three other average-performing female students in the class completed the same three probes, their scores were 20, 18, and 22. Lilly used Maria's median score as her baseline level and chose the average peer performance (20) as her goal for Maria's intervention for the next 12-week period. Lilly then set up a graph for Maria and decided with Kate that they would have Maria complete an estimation probe weekly to monitor the success of the intervention. The graphs in Figure 6.8 reflect the baseline data, the peer comparison level, and the goal line in the graph that Lilly created.

As Kate and Lilly discussed their concerns about Maria, they noted that several other students seemed to be struggling somewhat in mathematics, though not to the same degree as Maria. These students seemed to be following along and participating during class discussions and activities but had continuous questions during independent work time. This group of four or five students often spent much of their work time waiting for their turn to have a teacher answer their questions. As an initial intervention, Kate suggested that Lilly might work with this small group to provide some initial guided practice on the first few homework problems. In this way, the students would be in a more intimate setting, have more complete teacher attention, and be able to begin the assignment with careful supervision to ensure that they understood the problems they were completing. Lilly and Kate agreed that they would implement this plan for six weeks and then evaluate its effects. The first graph in Figure 6.8 shows Maria's scores on the estimation probes over the 6-week period and the trendline that Lilly drew based on the data. In evaluating the effects of the intervention, Lilly and Kate determined that although Maria was showing improvement, she was not making progress at a fast enough rate to achieve the goal they had set for her. The slope of Maria's trendline was positive and increasing, but when they projected out that same rate of improvement to the end of the 12-week period, they determined that she was not improving at a rate that would allow her to meet the goal. Together, they began investigating ways in which they could modify their instructional intervention to try and meet Maria's learning needs.

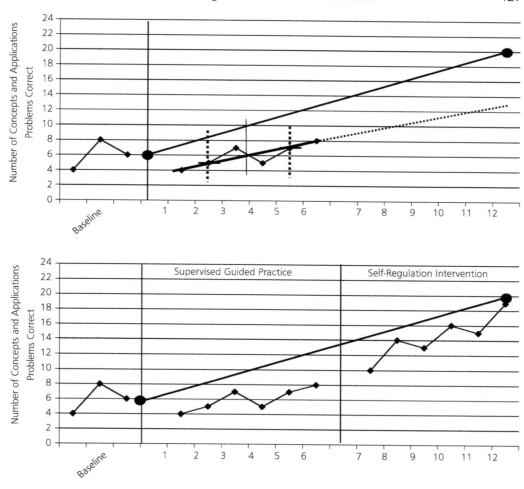

FIGURE 6.8. Maria's graphs for Intervention 1 and Intervention 2.

Lilly and Kate devoted a portion of their joint planning time to considering Maria's situation. Lilly noted that Maria was often careless in the work that she was doing and didn't seem to monitor her thinking as she completed the math work. The three students with mathematical disabilities in the class were experiencing similar difficulties. Lilly suggested that an explicit instructional strategy for self-regulation would be an appropriate intervention. Lilly had recently seen a program called Solve It! (see Chapter 5, this volume) that combined math-problem-solving instruction with explicit instruction in self-regulation strategies.

While Kate supported Lilly's recommendation, she expressed her concerns that the students might fall farther behind in math if they missed class time to receive instruction in the self-regulation strategy. Lilly commented that the three special education students all came to her resource room during Period 4. After further investigation, they learned that Maria had study hall

Period 4 and (after receiving permission from her mother) could join the group at that time. Lilly began working with the students on the Solve It! program during Period 4. The students continued to participate fully in Kate's general education math class. When Kate's activities involved problem solving, Lilly prompted the students to transfer their self-regulation skills to their general education assignments.

Lilly used the Solve It! assessments to track the students' progress specifically in the self-regulation program. At the same time, she continued weekly estimation probes with Maria and the three other students so she could track their growth in overall math proficiency. Maria's graph is shown at the bottom of Figure 6.8. The data on the graph show that Maria's rate of growth has increased over her growth rate for the first intervention. Maria's score on the 12th week of the intervention was within one point of the level Kate and Lilly had set as her goal.

As teachers face increasing pressures to demonstrate the effectiveness of their instruction by documenting student outcomes, there is a growing need for assessment tools that can be used to track the progress of students about whom teachers are most concerned. The development of progress monitoring measures in middle school mathematics is an emerging area of research that is grounded in a rich tradition of empirical support for curriculum-based measurement. Although many questions remain to be answered, the information in this chapter can provide guidance for teachers about potential tools and strategies that can be used to track student progress in middle school mathematics.

REFERENCES

Baker, S. K., & Good, R. H. (1995). Curriculum-based measurement of English reading with bilingual Hispanic students: A validation study with second-grade students. *School Psychology Review, 24*, 561–578.

Busch, T. W., & Espin, C. A. (2003). Using curriculum-based measurement to prevent failure and assess learning in the content areas. *Assessment for Effective Intervention, 28*(3–4), 49–58.

Deno, S. L. (1985). Curriculum-based measurement: The emerging alternative. *Exceptional Children, 52*, 219–232.

Deno, S. L. (2003). Developments in curriculum-based measurement. *Journal of Special Education, 37*, 184–192.

Deno, S. L., & Fuchs, L. S. (1987). Developing curriculum-based measurement systems for data-based special education problem solving. *Focus on Exceptional Children, 19*(8), 1–16.

Espin, C., Deno, S., Maruyama, G., & Cohen, C. (1989). *The Basic Academic Skills Samples (BASS): An instrument for the screening and identification of children at risk for failure in regular education classrooms.* Paper presented at the annual meeting of the American Educational Research Association, San Francisco, CA.

Foegen, A. (2000). Technical adequacy of general outcome measures for middle school mathematics. *Diagnostique, 25*, 175–203.

Foegen, A., & Deno, S. L. (2001). Identifying growth indicators for low-achieving students in middle school mathematics. *Journal of Special Education, 35*, 4–16.

Fuchs, L. S. (2004). The past, present, and future of curriculum-based measurement research. *School Psychology Review, 33*, 188–192.

Fuchs, L. S., Bahr, C. M., & Rieth, H. J. (1989). Effects of goal structures and performance contingencies on the math performance of adolescents with learning disabilities. *Journal of Learning Disabilities, 22*, 554–560.

Fuchs, L. S., & Deno, S. L. (1991). Paradigmatic distinctions between instructionally relevant measurement models. *Exceptional Children, 57*, 488–501.

Fuchs, L. S., & Deno, S. L. (1994). Must instructionally relevant performance assessment be based in the curriculum? *Exceptional Children, 61*, 15–24.

Fuchs, L. S., Fuchs, D., & Deno, S. L. (1985). The importance of goal ambitiousness and mastery to student achievement. *Exceptional Children, 52*, 63–71.

Fuchs, L. S., Fuchs, D., & Hamlett, C. L. (1994). Strengthening the connection between assessment and instructional planning with expert systems. *Exceptional Children, 61*, 138–146.

Fuchs, L. S., Fuchs, D., Hamlett, C. L., Phillips, N. B., & Bentz, J. (1994). Classwide curriculum-based measurement: Helping general educators meet the challenge of student diversity. *Exceptional Children, 60*, 518–537.

Fuchs, L. S., Fuchs, D., Hamlett, C. L., Thompson, A., Roberts, P. H., Kubek, P., & Stecker, P. M. (1994). Technical features of a mathematics concepts and applications curriculum-based measurement system. *Diagnostique, 19*(4), 23–49.

Fuchs, L. S., Hamlett, C. L., & Fuchs, D. (1990). *Monitoring basic skills progress: Basic math computation.* Austin, TX: PRO-ED.

Fuchs, L. S., Hamlett, C. L., & Fuchs, D. (1998). *Monitoring basic skills progress: Basic math computation* (2nd ed.). Austin, TX: PRO-ED.

Fuchs, L. S., Hamlett, C. L., & Fuchs, D. (1999). *Monitoring basic skills progress: Basic math concepts and applications.* Austin, TX: PRO-ED.

Helwig, R., Anderson, L., & Tindal, G. (2002). Using a concept-grounded, curriculum-based measure in mathematics to predict statewide test scores for middle school students with LD. *Journal of Special Education, 36*, 102–112.

Helwig, R., & Tindal, G. (2002). Using general outcome measures in mathematics to measure adequate yearly progress as mandated by Title I. *Assessment for Effective Intervention, 28*, 9–18.

Hiebert, J., & Lefevre, P. (1986). Conceptual and procedural knowledge in mathematics: An introductory analysis. In J. Hiebert (Ed.), *Conceptual and procedural knowledge: The case of mathematics* (pp. 199–223). Hillsdale, NJ: Erlbaum.

Lindsley, O. R. (1990). Precision teaching: By teachers for children. *Teaching Exceptional Children, 22*(3), 10–15.

Marston, D. (1989). Curriculum-based measurement: What it is and why do it. In M. R. Shinn (Ed.), *Curriculum-based measurement: Assessing special children* (pp. 18–78). New York: Guilford Press.

McConnell, S. R., McEvoy, M. A., & Priest, J. S. (2002). "Growing" measures for monitoring progress in early childhood education: A research and development process for individual growth and development indicators. *Assessment for Effective Intervention, 27*(4), 3–14.

National Council of Teachers of Mathematics. (2000). *Principles and standards for school mathematics.* Reston, VA: Author.

Shapiro, E. S. (Ed.). (1989). *Academic skills problems: Direct assessment and intervention.* New York: Guilford Press.

Shinn, M. R. (Ed.). (1998). *Advanced applications of curriculum-based measurement.* New York: Guilford Press.

Shinn, M., & Marston, D. (1985). Differentiating mildly handicapped, low-achieving, and regular education students: A curriculum-based approach. *Remedial and Special Education, 6*(2), 31–38.

Sowder, J. (1992). Estimation and number sense. In D. A. Grouws (Ed.), *Handbook of research on mathematics teaching and learning* (pp. 371–389). New York: Macmillan.

Taylor, R. L. (2004). *Assessment of exceptional students: Educational and psychological procedures* (6th ed.). Boston: Allyn & Bacon.

Thurber, R. S., Shinn, M. R., & Smolkowski, K. (2002). What is measured in mathematics tests? Construct validity of curriculum-based mathematics measures. *School Psychology Review, 30,* 363–382.

White, O. W., & Haring, N. G. (1980). *Exceptional teaching* (2nd ed). Columbus, OH: Merrill.

CHAPTER 7

Quality Mathematics Programs
for Students with Disabilities

DIANE KINDER and MARCY STEIN

Ms. Divet is a middle school resource teacher in a large urban district. Her fifth-period math intervention class consists of 13 sixth-graders with mathematical learning disabilities (MLD). While the performance of these students varies considerably, Ms. Divet has noticed some common problems. Notably, all of her students failed the fractions subtest from a diagnostic mathematics test.

In the past, Ms. Divet tried to use the general education mathematics materials to remedy her students' deficits. However, she realized the materials were not adequate when her students continued to struggle in math.

This year, when visiting the special education curriculum library, she found three math intervention programs. She decided to examine the fractions instruction in each to determine which program would be most helpful. She found distinct differences among the programs. For example, Program A contained individual units including one unit on fractions. Program B contained fractions instruction, in addition to other math skills, dispersed throughout the entire level. Program C consisted primarily of self-guided worksheet practice on fractions. Ms. Divet also found striking differences in the teacher directions and student activities in each program. Some programs consisted of student-directed activities with manipulatives, while others gave precise directions to the teacher for how to teach fraction strategies.

Although Ms. Divet was pleased to find a variety of materials, she did not feel confident in her ability to evaluate each program and find the appropriate curriculum for her students.

This scenario illustrates the all-too-common frustration faced by special education teachers trying to find appropriate materials for students who struggle with learning mathematics. In this chapter, after providing a context for improving mathematics achievement that includes available research on current student performance and evidence-based instructional practices, we provide a framework for evaluating commercial programs that is designed to help teachers such as Ms. Divet.

In the Introduction to this book, Montague and Jitendra describe characteristics of middle school students with MLD. Research regarding the prevalence and achievement of students with MLD is far more limited than similar research in reading (Geary & Hoard, 2003). However, considerable research on the mathematics performance of United States students on international and national assessments of mathematics such as the Trends in International Mathematics and Science Study (TIMSS), the Programme for International Student Assessment (PISA), and the National Assessment of Educational Progress (NAEP) is available. Although the results of these tests are not disaggregated for students with MLD, examining the results provides some insight into understanding how poorly students with MLD may be performing.

Recently reported results from the 2003 TIMSS indicated that only 7% of U.S. eighth-grade students scored at the advanced level compared to about one-third of students from the highest-performing (A+) countries—Singapore, Chinese Taipai, Korea, and Hong Kong SAR (Mullis, Martin, Gonzalez, & Chrostowski, 2004). While the performance of U.S. eighth-graders in mathematics improved between 1995 and 2003, most of this progress occurred between 1995 and 1999.

Another recent international assessment, PISA, provided even less positive results (Organisation for Economic Cooperation and Development, 2004). PISA is a standardized assessment developed jointly by 41 participating countries. The assessment includes areas of mathematics that 15-year-olds need for life skills and for further study of mathematics. In this assessment, the performance of U.S. students in overall mathematics literacy and problem solving was lower than the average performance of students for most countries. As in the 2000 PISA, the recent study reported that about two-thirds of the students in participating countries outperformed the U.S. students. In 2003, more U.S. students scored at or below the lowest level of proficiency in problem solving than the international average.

On the 2003 National Assessment of Educational Progress, only 29% of eighth-grade students scored at the proficient level in mathematics (National Center for Educational Statistics, 2003). Those students reaching proficiency demonstrated competency in challenging mathematics content including mathematics knowledge, application to real-world situations, and mathematics analytical skills. Thirty-two percent of the eighth-graders taking the 2003 NAEP scored below basic level demonstrating only partial mastery of prerequisite knowledge and skills that are fundamental for proficient work. Specifically, only 10% of eighth-graders could demonstrate three ways to divide an L-shaped figure in order to determine its area.

These reports of poor performance for general education students suggest that the problems facing students with MLD are even more challenging. To address these challenges, both general and special educators have begun to study more thoroughly critical components of mathematics instruction likely to improve student outcomes. Among those components most frequently associated with student achievement are the use of evidence-based instructional methods, the assessment of student progress, the depth of teacher knowledge, and the quality of commercial programs (National Council of Teachers of Mathematics, 2000; Simpson, La Cava, & Graner, 2004; Stein & Carnine, 1999). The purpose of this chapter is to focus attention on the last of these components.

CRITICAL COMPONENTS
OF EFFECTIVE MATHEMATICS INSTRUCTION

While this chapter focuses primarily on the quality of commercial programs, most educators agree that the integration of several critical components is necessary to improve mathematics achievement for all students. Prior to the introduction of our discussion of high-quality programs, we present a brief summary of research for each of these other components: evidence-based instructional methods, assessment of student progress, and depth of teacher knowledge.

Evidence-Based Instructional Methods

Historically, few experimental studies on the effectiveness of specific instructional methods have been conducted in the area of mathematics. In 1998, Miller, Butler, and Lee reviewed the research on mathematics instruction for students with MLD. More recently, Gersten, Chard, Baker, and Lee (in press) conducted a meta-analysis of mathematics intervention studies, also for students with MLD. Finally, Baker, Gersten, and Lee (2002) conducted a synthesis of research on teaching mathematics to low-achieving students. All of these researchers indicated that although the number of studies available for their reviews was quite small, the research was of high quality.

These research reviews had several findings in common. All of the reviewers found studies in which student performance improved through the use of peer tutoring, explicit teacher-directed instruction, and systematic feedback to teachers and students. Peer tutoring was particularly effective for students with learning disabilities when the tutors were older and had received extensive training.

Regarding explicit, teacher-directed instruction, Miller et al. found that instructional procedures that included teacher demonstrations and student modeling and practice were common to the most effective interventions. Baker et al. also found that explicit instruction in teaching mathematics concepts and procedures produced greater student achievement. Gersten et al. found that the teacher's use of visual representations and verbalization improved performance on problem solving. Notably, four of the five studies Gersten et al. reviewed used highly explicit instructional approaches to teach problem-solving strategies.

Assessment of Student Progress

All reviews mentioned above also found studies that supported the practice of using data from ongoing assessments to inform instructional practice. The assessment approach used in many of these studies was curriculum-based measurement (CBM). Reporting the results of CBM measures to students with disabilities and their general or special education teachers generally produced higher student achievement (Fuchs, Fuchs, Hamlett, Phillips, & Bentz, 1994; Fuchs, Roberts, Fuchs, & Bowers, 1996). Foegen (Chapter 6, this volume) provides detailed information about CBM and its implementation for middle school mathematics progress monitoring.

Gersten, Jordan, and Flojo (2005) have recently conducted research to determine potential early assessment measures that would predict subsequent student performance in mathematics. Their research suggests that a lack of fluency in arithmetic combinations correlates with subsequent math difficulties. Their findings have implications for the design of early intervention programs designed to prevent mathematics failure.

Depth of Teacher Knowledge

A discussion of "highly qualified teachers" has appeared recently in the legislation of No Child Left Behind (NCLB) (Simpson et al., 2004) and the Individuals with Disabilities Education Act (Council for Exceptional Children, 2004). According to NCLB, middle and high school mathematics teachers will need to pass a rigorous exam in mathematics or have a degree in mathematics (or the equivalent) to be considered "highly qualified." In 1998, of the 26 states reporting on the certification of their mathematics teachers in grades 7 and 8, only 6 states reported that 90% or more of their teachers were certified in mathematics and only 10 states reported more than 80% of their teachers were certified in mathematics (Blank & Langeson, 1999). Interestingly, as part of the TIMSS, researchers collected data on the preparation of mathematics teachers in the participating countries. Although U.S. teachers appeared to hold on average more university degrees, the number of eighth-grade students taught by U.S. teachers whose major area of study was mathematics was significantly lower than the international average.

The move to legislate requirements for "highly qualified" teachers, while considered controversial by some, represents an effort by the United States Department of Education to ensure that teachers have expertise in the subject areas they are teaching. Clearly, the requirements were developed as a response to the documented variability of hiring practices among states.

Ma (1999), in an extensive study of Chinese and American teachers' knowledge of mathematics, confirmed that the knowledge of most American elementary mathematics teachers was not nearly as robust as that of the Chinese teachers she interviewed. In her study, Ma found that while teachers from the United States displayed procedural competence with some algorithmic competence, Chinese teachers routinely displayed algorithmic competence with conceptual understanding. The Chinese teachers reported that their own elementary training, their teacher preparation, and their work as math specialists helped contribute to their understanding of mathematics.

In a discussion of Ma's book, Askey (1999) noted that it is not surprising that most elementary teachers have limited knowledge of mathematics. He suggested that teachers did not learn adequate mathematics from their own K–12 schooling. Nor did they learn mathematics from the teaching methods classes, which he described as being "light on math content." He indicated that middle school teachers often "fall between the cracks" in that they are rarely prepared to teach in either elementary or secondary classes. In fact, he pointed out that there are few courses specifically designed for middle school teachers. The recommendations articulated by both Askey and Ma include improving professional development (both pre-service and in-service teacher preparation) and using high-quality instructional programs, two of the components of effective mathematics instruction related to student achievement that are mentioned above.

In the previous discussion, we examined the research on three components of effective mathematics instruction that are all related in some way to the use of commercial programs. Ball and Cohen (1996) have suggested that commercial programs may serve as an important catalyst for improving mathematics instruction and subsequently improving student achievement. In the next section on quality of commercial programs, we present information that suggests that commercial programs can serve not only as a catalyst but also as the primary channel for the integration of the previously discussed critical components.

QUALITY OF COMMERCIAL PROGRAMS

The following discussion of commercial programs is divided into several sections. The first section on curriculum adoption begins by discussing how recent curricular discord in the fields of math and reading is similar. Given the challenges of curriculum adoption, we feel that insight into these conflicts may preclude educators from engaging in activities that inadvertently impede the curriculum adoption process. This section also contains recommendations for how to efficiently conduct more systematic curriculum adoption.

In the next section, current analyses of programs and textbooks are briefly discussed in light of their influence on student achievement. The final sections offer readers more specific recommendations for evaluating commercial mathematics programs. These sections include a process for initial screening of commercial programs, a more comprehensive framework that includes criteria for evaluating the quality of mathematics programs, and recommendations for program modifications based on the curriculum evaluation framework.

Curriculum Adoption

Math Programs

The current call for mathematics reform based on the dismal mathematics performance of students on both national and international assessments is not unlike the call for reform that occurred in the area of reading. In fact, the parallels between math and reading are quite striking and may be helpful to those trying to address poor mathematics performance. Table 7.1 outlines some of the more salient features of the conflicts in reading and math. Underlying both reading and math disputes is the question of whether educators are influenced more by philosophy or scientific research. The whole-language approach to reading instruction highlighted in the 1988 California Reading Framework contradicts the current scientific research in the area of reading (National Reading Panel, 2000). Similarly, the constructivist mathematics approach first represented in the 1989 NCTM Standards lacks a sufficient research base (Klein, 2003). Participants in the current mathematics reform movement and those who were most vocal in the reading reform movement tend to belong to an active research community. Linguists, psychologists, and other empirical reading researchers appeared at the forefront of the scientifically based reading movement. Similarly, mathematicians and scientists are among the most vocal critics of constructivist approaches to math instruction.

The content issues of both reform movements are also remarkably similar. The debate over decoding versus comprehension is similar to that of computation versus problem solving. Not surprisingly, the research communities in both areas have characterized these debates as false dichotomies. For many years, reading researchers have acknowledged that decoding is a necessary but not sufficient condition of being a good reader (Adams, 1990; Anderson, Hiebert, Scott, & Wilkinson, 1985; Chall, 1967). Likewise, mathematicians and scientists have been arguing for years that computational skills and conceptual understanding are completely intertwined (Klein, 2003; Wu, 1999).

TABLE 7.1. Parallels between Reading and Math

Reading	Math
Scientifically based instruction versus philosophically based instruction	Scientifically based instruction versus philosophically based instruction
Explicit instruction approach versus whole-language approach	Explicit instruction approach constructivist approach
Linguists and psychologists	Mathematicians and scientists
Decoding versus comprehension	Computation versus problem solving

The impact of these reform movements on classroom instruction is considerable. The design and implementation of state standards, state assessments, and curriculum adoption frameworks and, subsequently, the development of commercial programs emanate from these movements. Publishers of commercial programs are required by the adoption committees of highly populated states to illustrate how their programs meet state standards regardless of the scientific validity of the standards (Klein, 2005). In order to sell their programs, publishers must adhere to specified standards for each state.

We feel strongly that to meet the needs of those students most at risk for academic failure, utilizing scientifically based criteria for the selection of commercial programs is as important in mathematics as it has been in reading. Resolution of major conflicts in reading was accomplished by examining the experimental research in the area of reading (National Reading Panel, 2000). Currently all major basal reading programs use an explicit phonics approach to teach beginning reading based in part on the findings of the National Reading Panel. Although there is a dearth of experimental research in the area of mathematics, we recommend that curriculum adoption committees carefully consider the available research in mathematics instruction and design or select evaluation criteria accordingly.

The Curriculum Adoption Process

Since the process of curriculum adoption for both general and special education is critical to the selection of high-quality commercial programs, educators should not only employ a systematic framework for evaluating those programs but also conduct the adoption process in an equally systematic manner. Stein, Stuen, Carnine, and Long (2001) described a systematic adoption process for the selection of reading programs that can be applied to the selection of mathematics programs. Although a thorough discussion of the adoption process is beyond the scope of this chapter, we have outlined those features from Stein et al. that we believe are essential to conducting an efficient mathematics curriculum adoption. These features include time allocation, committee responsibilities, and the screening process.

Many curriculum adoption committees meet only after school for brief periods of time. Because thorough examination of commercial programs requires large blocks of uninterrupted time, adoption committee members must be given adequate release time to review the materials. Stein et al. (2001) suggested allocating approximately 15 release days for teachers on the adoption committee, some of which should occur consecutively to maintain continuity in screening and evaluation. During those days, teachers review research, generate screening and evaluation criteria, screen all submitted programs, thoroughly evaluate three to four of those programs, deliberate, and then select a program.

Teachers in most schools or districts are typically given the opportunity to vote on the selection of a mathematics program from a short list generated by the adoption committee. However, if the adoption committee members have, as mentioned above, spent considerable time reviewing research, and generating evaluation criteria, as well as examining programs, we feel that the committee members are in the best position to make an informed decision. For teachers in the school or district to feel comfortable with a committee decision, adoption committee members must communicate regularly and effectively with the groups they represent.

Members of mathematics curriculum adoption committees are often selected based on seniority and knowledge of mathematics. However, additional selection factors also should be considered when forming adoption committees. Committees should include individuals representing a range of grade levels as well as both special and general education students and members with excellent communication skills.

Introduction to Curriculum Evaluation

One of the most logical explanations of the difference in performance on international tests such as TIMSS and PISA is variation in the mathematics curricula (Schmidt, Houang, & Cogan, 2002; Schmidt, McKnight, & Raizen, 1996). In fact, according to Schmidt et al. (2002), "the curriculum itself—what is taught—makes a huge difference" (p. 12). Among the TIMSS countries, only the United States and Australia lacked national mathematics curricula. In the United States, where the choice of mathematics programs is determined by state and district adoptions, mathematics programs are considered the de facto national curriculum (Cai, Watanabe, & Lo, 2002).

Given the critical role that U.S. mathematics programs play in the classroom and the significant cost of those programs, most educators naively assume that the programs are well researched. In fact, in the majority of cases, the opposite is true. Most publishers do not evaluate the effectiveness of their programs either during development or once they are in the classroom (Reys, Reys, & Chavez, 2004). Such field testing and research would add to the existing high cost of producing mathematics programs, and since "consumers rarely demand proof" (Reys et al., 2004, p. 61) publishers choose not to engage in extensive research on their programs.

As part of the TIMSS, Schmidt et al. (2002) explored issues of curriculum along with those of student performance. They found U.S. textbooks to be highly repetitive and incoherent. At the middle school level, they found that the content in U.S. mathematics textbooks was not as demanding as the content in textbooks used in the A+ countries. Moreover, they found that the same topics were presented relatively briefly, grade after grade. The purpose of their curriculum analysis was to provide some insight into the reasons for such poor U.S. student performance on the TIMSS. Unfortunately, the criteria used in their analysis were not designed to help educators in their selection of commercial mathematics programs.

Clearly, mathematics programs need to reflect a high degree of instructional integrity. That is, the programs should present well-designed content, develop ideas in depth, and clarify the relationships among topics. To our knowledge, an objective, reliable, and valid tool for evaluating the instructional integrity of mathematics programs does not yet exist. Such a tool could be used to assist educators in evaluating the extent to which commercial programs contain instructional methods grounded in the research literature. The tool also could systematically guide the evaluation of program content.

As a precursor to the development of a curriculum evaluation tool, we have constructed a curriculum evaluation *framework* to assist educators in their analysis of the content and design of commercial mathematics programs. The criteria in this framework are derived from both current instructional research in mathematics and a theory of instructional design. Interested readers are directed to Engelmann and Carnine (1991); Przychodzian, Marchand-Martella, Martella, and Azim (2004); and Snider and Crawford (2004) for a more thorough discussion of the instructional design theory represented in the framework.

Screening Process

Because a thorough evaluation of commercial programs requires a great deal of time and training, we recommend that evaluators conduct a preliminary screening of the programs being considered in order to select a reasonable number (three or four) to evaluate more thoroughly. Table 7.2 outlines criteria that we suggest will facilitate the screening process. The criteria include questions that address three important areas: general theoretical approach, evidence of effectiveness, and critical content design. The questions in Table 7.2 under general theoretical approach direct evaluators to establish the underlying theoretical approach for each program being considered, that is, whether the program represents an explicit or direct approach, a constructivist approach, or another approach to the teaching of mathematics. The questions in the second section, on evidence of effectiveness, direct evaluators to determine if the program has been systematically evaluated in controlled research studies that have been published in peer-reviewed journals. In addition to published research, evidence of whether the program has been field tested is considered in this section, as well.

TABLE 7.2. Mathematics Curriculum Evaluation Framework: Screening Criteria

A. General theoretical approach
  1. Does the program contain explicit, teacher-directed instruction—that is, are steps in the strategies clearly identified?

      or

  2. Does the program represent a constructivist approach—that is, are student discovery and exploration emphasized?

B. Evidence of effectiveness
  1. Is there published evidence of the effectiveness of the program?
  2. Is there evidence that the program has been field-tested with large groups of students?

C. Critical content design
  1. Are the steps in the selected strategies *explicitly* identified in the program?
  2. Does the instruction follow a logical sequence?
  3. Are there sufficient practice opportunities distributed across the level?

The answers to the questions in the final section, on critical content design, can be used to compare how different programs teach important skills or concepts. We recommend that for screening purposes, evaluators compare two skills from each program at two levels. By comparing how programs teach these skills, evaluators can get a sense of the overall program design. To evaluate a selected number of programs more thoroughly, we recommend that evaluators use the curriculum evaluation framework described in the next section.

Mathematics Curriculum Evaluation Framework

Figure 7.1 illustrates the framework we have developed to assist educators in evaluating commercial mathematics programs. The framework contains three sections: general program design, instructional design, and assessment. The form in Figure 7.1 has three columns, for evaluation criteria, comments, and examples. The examples column provides space for specific references to pages that contain program examples illustrating an evaluator's comments. Evaluators can easily refer to these pages in their discussions about program quality with other committee members.

General Program Design

The purpose of this section is to guide evaluators in their analysis of program objectives and program coherence. To address the questions in this section, we recommend that evaluators examine the scope and sequence of each program level, as well as sample lessons from a given level. Program coherence in this framework refers to the extent to which the content of the program is balanced and integrated within and across levels.

Program objectives state what students should be able to do as a result of the instruction provided. Not only should objectives be aligned with the instruction, they should also be aligned also with the assessment procedures in order to help teachers determine whether students have mastered the objective. The objectives should contain a statement of a measurable behavior. Evaluators will find that many programs contain objectives that describe *teacher* behavior rather than *student* behavior. For example, we found objectives similar to this one in several mathematics programs: "Review telling time." Note that the objective identifies what the teacher does but not what the students are expected to learn. "Students will express time as minutes after the hour" is an example of an objective that contains a measurable student behavior.

According to instructional design theory (Engelmann & Carnine, 1991; Harniss, Carnine, Silbert, & Dixon, 2002), well-designed mathematics programs should be organized around major principles called "big ideas." Evaluators need to determine the extent to which these big ideas are well articulated and prominent in the program by examining its scope and sequence. The principle of place value is a good example of a big idea that is addressed differently in commercial programs. In some programs, the information regarding place value is found in one unit near

Evaluators _____

Program/Publisher/Year _____

Grade Level _____

Date _____

Evaluation criteria	Comments	Examples
General Program Design **1. Program Objectives** a. Are objectives stated as **observable** behaviors? b. Are the **"big ideas"** in the program obvious? **2. Program Coherence** a. Does the program use a **strand** or spiral design? b. Is there a **balance** between computation instruction and problem-solving instruction? ***Instructional Design*** **1. Strategies** a. Are the steps in the strategy **explicitly identified** in the program? b. Is the strategy of immediate **generalizability**— not too narrow or too broad? c. Are the necessary **component skills** (preskills) taught prior to introducing the strategy? d. Does the program **strategically integrate** the new strategy with previously introduced strategies and related skills?		

FIGURE 7.1. Mathematics curriculum evaluation framework.

Evaluation criteria	Comments	Examples
2. Examples		
a. Is there a sufficient number of practice examples for **initial mastery?**		
b. Are there opportunities for **discrimination practice?**		
c. Does the program provide opportunities for **cumulative review** of previously introduced skills?		
3. Scaffolded Instruction		
a. Is teacher **modeling** specified?		
b. Is teacher assistance **gradually faded?**		
c. Does the program recommend specific **correction procedures?**		
Assessment		
1. Assessment and Instruction Link		
a. Does the program contain *placement tests?*		
b. Do the program assessments contain recommendations **for acceleration and remediation?**		
c. Are the program assessments carefully **aligned with instruction?**		

FIGURE 7.1. (*cont.*)

the beginning of the program. After place value is initially introduced, these programs only briefly mention place value concepts when skills such as regrouping are taught. In contrast, well-designed programs would not only introduce place value but also repeatedly and explicitly demonstrate the application of place value concepts to a range of skills including numeral reading, operations, and estimation.

The second general program design feature is program coherence. Evaluators can also use the program scope and sequence to determine program coherence. As mentioned above an important aspect of program coherence is the extent to which the content of the program is systematically integrated within and across levels. One way of determining program coherence is by identifying whether the program employs a spiral or strand design. In programs using a spiral design, many topics are introduced at each level and repeated across many levels. Typically, programs using a spiral design lack adequate initial instruction and subsequent review. Lessons in these programs typically cover one different topic each day. Schmidt et al. (2002) referred to these programs as "a mile wide and inch deep" (p. 12).

For one mathematics program we examined, the scope and sequence indicated that 12 problem-solving strategies were taught in grades 1–8. In examining the program more closely, we found that 11 of these strategies were taught in grade 8. In that level, not one of the 11 strategies was presented in more than three lessons. More importantly, the strategies were taught independent of one another with no instruction regarding which strategy was appropriate for which type of problem. The fact that the same strategies are introduced in each subsequent grade level indicates that this program employs a spiral design. The lack of practice and lack of integration also reflect a spiral design.

In contrast to a spiral design, more instructional programs are beginning to employ a strand design (Snider, 2004). Programs using a strand design present fewer topics over a longer period of time, resulting in increased student mastery. A unique feature of strand design is that lessons are organized around multiple topics. For example, a lesson in a program organized around strands might include 8 minutes on column addition with regrouping, followed by 7 minutes on measurement concepts, 5 minutes on review of math facts, and 15 minutes on problem solving.

In addition to determining the kind of design used by a program, program coherence also addresses the extent to which a program contains a balance of computation and problem-solving instruction. As mentioned previously, one of the most contentious issues in math involves the teaching of computation. Whether to explicitly teach algorithms for computation and how much time should be devoted to computation are questions at the heart of this issue. Recently, mathematicians and mathematics educators agreed that students must master algorithms in order to successfully solve problems (Strauss, 2004). Therefore, we recommend that evaluators carefully examine the scope and sequence of each program to determine the extent to which the program reflects an instructional balance between computation and problem solving and the systematic integration of each with the other.

Instructional Design

The criteria for instructional design were developed to help evaluators determine how critical content is taught in the programs under consideration. We recommend that evaluators select three to four different skills or concepts for each level, preferably ones that have been identified as big ideas, and use the criteria specified in Figure 7.1 to examine how systematically those skills or concepts are taught.

A well-designed strategy is one that results in the greatest number of students correctly solving the greatest number of problems. The strategy should reliably lead to the solution of the problems for *all* students. Research cited above supports the use of explicit strategy instruction for low-achieving students and for those with MLD. Therefore, evaluators need to determine the degree to which the strategies in a program are taught explicitly. To do this, we recommend that evaluators locate where in the program a strategy is first introduced and determine whether the steps in that strategy are clearly articulated.

A practical approach for evaluating the quality of instructional strategies is for evaluators to assume the characteristics of naive learners. Evaluators should pretend that they do not already know how to solve the problem and follow the steps in the strategy as specified in the teacher manual. Assuming the role of a naive learner helps evaluators quickly determine whether the steps in the strategy are explicit and useful.

According to instructional design theory, the instructional strategies predominant in a commercial program should be of intermediate generalizability. The following is an example of a strategy for solving word problems taken from a recently published commercial program: Understand, Plan, Solve, and Look Back (Harcourt Brace, 2000). The steps in this word problem strategy are so broad that only students who already know how to solve the problem will most likely answer the questions correctly.

In contrast, a strategy for solving classification word problems is outlined in Figure 7.2 (Stein, Kinder, Silbert, & Carnine, 2006). Before students are introduced to this strategy, they are taught several component skills including the language skill of identifying class names for groups of objects (e.g., saws, hammers, and screwdrivers are all tools) and how to use a fact number family strategy to solve addition and subtraction problems (e.g., 2, 4, 6 make up a fact family). Also, prior to being introduced to this strategy, students would be familiar with the graphic conventions used during instruction (i.e., big and little boxes). This classification strategy is one of intermediate generalizability in that students can use it to solve many different problems of that type.

An example of a strategy of limited generalizability is one in which students are taught to find $\frac{1}{3}$ of 9 by dividing 9 by 3. This strategy works only for fractions with a one in the numerator. After being taught this strategy, low-performing students are likely to overgeneralize the application of the strategy to problems such as $\frac{2}{3}$ of 9. Programs should not allocate valuable instructional time to narrow strategies that are of limited use. According to instructional design theory, evaluators

There are 8 children. Three are boys. How many are girls?

    →
        Total
        (children)

1. Read the problem. The problem talks about children, boys and girls. Which is the big class?
2. If children is the big class then children is the total number. Write children on the line under the total box.
3. Does the problem tell how many children? So the total number is given. What is the total number? Write 8 in the box for total number.
4. Now we write the values for boys and girls in the boxes over the arrow. How many boys? Write 3 in the first box. We don't know how many girls so we don't write anything in the other box.
5. Is the total number given? So what do you have to do to work the problem? (Start with 8 children and subtract 3 boys.) Write the equation and figure out the answer.
6. If there are 8 children and 3 are boys, how many are girls?

FIGURE 7.2. Solving classification word problems.

need to attend to issues of generalizability when examining instructional strategies.

Often mathematics programs introduce the prerequisite (or component) skills necessary for understanding a new strategy and the new strategy simultaneously. For example, some programs introduce estimation at the same time as long division, a skill requiring the use of estimation. Most students need time to master the component skills *prior* to being introduced to a strategy that requires the application of those skills. Determining when the component skills for an instructional strategy are introduced addresses the quality of the strategy instruction for a given program.

Although there are advantages to introducing new strategies in isolation, students must learn relationships among strategies to fully develop mathematical understandings. Therefore, one of the features of a well-designed program is the strategic integration of mathematics strategies throughout the program. One way to determine the extent of integration is to look for evidence that the newly taught strategy has been integrated with related previously taught content. Strategic integration is particularly important for integrating computation with problem solving. For example, well-designed programs carefully integrate long division into word problems after students have demonstrated mastery of solving long division problems in isolation. Because integration is a salient feature of strand design, programs that employ a strand design are more likely to strategically integrate important skills and concepts.

Once evaluators have examined carefully the quality of the instructional strategies, we recommend that they consider related features such as examples and scaffolding. Addressing questions about the adequacy of student practice examples technically can only be answered using information about student performance (i.e., did students master this skill with the number of practice examples available?). For practical purposes, evaluators should compare programs with respect to the number of examples provided. When selecting programs for students with MLD, we recommend educators err in selecting programs with more rather than fewer examples. Reducing the number of practice examples presented is far easier than creating additional examples for students who need more practice.

In addition to the amount of practice, evaluators need to examine the *type* of practice provided. Discrimination practice refers to a set of examples that requires students to determine when to apply a strategy. For example, after the introduction of subtraction with regrouping, the program should provide practice in subtraction problems for which only some problems require regrouping. Without that practice, low-performing students will try to apply the regrouping strategy to all multidigit subtraction problems they encounter.

Cumulative practice and review refers to the notion that all strategies taught should be systematically introduced and reviewed throughout the program. Cumulative review is related to the notion of strategic integration in that the review of newly introduced strategies should be integrated and reviewed with previously introduced strategies. Well-designed programs alert both the teacher and the students to the fact that this review is cumulative and that it requires careful attention to when as well as how a strategy should be applied.

Traditionally, mathematics programs suggest teachers demonstrate a strategy with a couple of problems, then direct teachers to have students complete a number of problems independently (Harniss et al., 2002). In contrast, one of the most critical teaching procedures derived from instructional design principles is the use of scaffolded instruction. Scaffolded instruction begins with the teacher modeling a strategy followed by the gradual fading of support until students can implement the strategy independently.

Evaluators should examine the initial instruction provided for a skill or concept to determine whether the program includes procedures that clearly require the teacher to model the steps in the instructional strategy. It should be noted that some programs may suggest teacher modeling but may not explicitly provide the steps for the strategy in the teacher manual, making modeling more difficult for teachers.

Scaffolded instruction provides temporary support to students as they begin to apply their new strategies. Scaffolding may take several forms. Programs might provide a series of questions for the teacher to use in guiding students through the steps necessary to complete problems. As students become more proficient, the teacher asks fewer guiding questions. Alternately, the program may supply graphic support for students in applying their new strategy. For example, a graphic organizer may prompt students to find the common denominators prior to adding or subtracting fractions. Scaffolded instruction provides teachers with the support necessary to ensure that students solve mathematics problems with fewer errors as they become more independent.

Although modeling and carefully scaffolded instruction reduce the number of errors students make, the program should provide correction procedures. A correction procedure may suggest that teachers return to using the support provided in earlier instruction, such as guiding questions or graphics. Other correction procedures may involve simply modeling the correct answer and repeating the question. The most important consideration for evaluators is whether the program specifies correction procedures.

Assessment

The quality of the placement and assessment procedures and the link between assessment and instruction are important. Evaluators will need to examine the teacher manuals as well as any supplementary assessment materials to answer the following questions. First, evaluators need to determine whether programs contain a placement test with alternative placement options allowing students to be placed at appropriate levels of the program. Options for placement are particularly important for students who are receiving remedial instruction in order to maximize their instructional time. Next, evaluators should determine if recommendations for acceleration and remediation are provided based on the program assessment results. Finally, evaluators need to establish the extent to which program assessments are aligned with instruction. This alignment is necessary in order for teachers to use the program assessments to make informed instructional decisions regarding student progress and mastery of the content.

Curriculum Modification

The curriculum evaluation framework outlined above consists of three parts: general program design, instructional design, and assessment. In our opinion, the section on evaluating strategies, found under instructional design, should be given the greatest consideration when using the framework to select appropriate commercial mathematics programs for several reasons. First, of the topics addressed in the three sections, clearly instructional strategies are the most difficult for teachers to modify. To modify these strategies, teachers would need the requisite knowledge of mathematics that the literature suggests so few have (Ma, 1999; Schmidt et al., 2002). Second, even if teachers have been extensively trained in the area of mathematics, few teachers have had course work specifically in instructional design. Finally, teachers who have the adequate mathematical knowledge and instructional design expertise rarely have time to design new instructional strategies, let alone field test those strategies to determine if they are effective. Therefore, a mathematics program that contains well-designed instructional strategies should be given greater consideration in the selection process.

Program modification for elements of general program design is relatively straightforward. If an instructional program does not include measurable student objectives, teachers will need to review the program content and construct these objectives. Those teachers working with students on IEPs are more practiced in this type of modification. In designing measurable student objectives, teachers should examine the program assessments so they can align their student objectives with available progress-monitoring options.

Changing the general program design of a commercial mathematics program from a spiral design to a strand design in order to increase program coherence is, on the other hand, quite onerous. However, modifying aspects of the instructional design of individual instructional strategies is less complicated. As mentioned above, we recommend that educators select programs that contain well-designed strategies. However, even if the strategies are sound, the program may lack sufficient practice and review examples. Educators often need to supplement these programs by adding more practice examples during initial instruction to ensure student mastery. Once students have demonstrated mastery, teachers may need to systematically build into their lessons review of previously introduced content.

Another aspect of instructional design that is relatively easily modified is scaffolding. When working with low-performing students, educators frequently need to provide additional modeling and support to students before requiring that they perform independently. Ensuring mastery by providing increased opportunities for practice and review are modifications of commercial programs commonly required for low-performing students.

The third part, assessment, is possibly the easiest to modify in that if progress-monitoring measures are not readily available from the program, teachers can construct a series of mastery tests with minimal effort to help them assess student progress. The purpose of progress monitoring is to help teachers make more informed instructional decisions and assist them in differentiating instruction. Therefore, progress monitoring must be aligned with program content. The assessment items should address both newly taught skills and concepts as well as previously introduced content. Teachers can use mastery tests to make instructional decisions regarding acceleration and remediation as well as placement decisions.

SUMMARY

The disappointing mathematics achievement of middle school students in the United States on national and international assessments has been well documented (e.g., TIMSS, PISA). The impact of poor mathematics performance on future academic and vocational options available to these students has also been widely recognized. Mathematical competency at the middle school level is a prerequisite for success in mathematics at the high school; completion of more advanced high school mathematics courses is in turn associated with attending college and becoming fully employed (Snider & Crawford, 2004). Not surprisingly, middle school students with MLD are at an even greater risk for the negative impact of low achievement in mathematics.

In this chapter we addressed the challenge of improving the mathematics achievement of students with MLD and other students who are risk for mathematics failure by outlining several components of mathematics instruction associated with student achievement: evidence-based instructional methods, assessment of student progress, depth of teacher knowledge, and quality of commercial programs. Among these components, we assert that the quality of commercial programs plays a central role. Comparative research on different mathematics textbooks suggests that this may be the case (Schmidt et al., 2002). Quality mathematics programs have the potential for becoming the vehicle by which educators can integrate all of the previously mentioned components. Quality mathematics programs should incorporate evidence-based instructional methods; the programs should include useful assessment procedures; and finally, quality mathematics programs should provide assistance to those teachers whose mathematics preparation was insufficient. A well-designed program assists students and their teachers in developing the mathematical understanding necessary for performing complex mathematics.

Because of the influential role that commercial mathematics programs play in U.S. classrooms, assistance in the selection of these programs is a central focus of this chapter. No single commercial program is the solution for the problem of poor student performance in mathematics. All programs have strengths and weaknesses. However, some programs require more modification than others in order to meet the needs of low-performing students.

A reasonable goal for curriculum selection should be the identification of those programs that require the least amount of modification. Clearly, modifying a commercial program that contains well-designed, explicit instructional strategies and may need only additional practice opportunities is less burdensome than modifying one that requires teachers to develop these strategies.

Research on valid and reliable instruments for evaluating commercial programs is long overdue. Until such instruments are available, we suggest that the framework for the evaluation of commercial programs provided in this chapter offers both general and special educators a practical method to more thoroughly examine program quality. While the criteria included in the framework are by no means exhaustive, they should help educators not only to select quality programs but also to identify areas in programs that require modification.

REFERENCES

Adams, M. J. (1990). *Beginning to read: Thinking and learning about print.* Cambridge, MA: MIT Press.

Anderson, R., Hiebert, E., Scott, J., & Wilkinson, I. (1985). *Becoming a nation of readers: The report of the commission on reading.* Washington, DC: National Institute of Education, U.S. Department of Education.

Askey, R. (1999). Knowing and teaching elementary mathematics. *American Educator, 23*(3), 20–28.

Baker, S., Gersten, R., & Lee, D. S. (2002). A synthesis of empirical research on teaching mathematics to low-achieving students. *Elementary School Journal, 103*(1), 51–73.

Ball, D. L., & Cohen, D. K. (1996). Reform by the book: What is—or might be—the role of curriculum materials in teacher learning and instructional reform? *Educational Researcher, 25*(9), 6–8.

Blank, R. K., & Langeson, D. (1999). *State indictors of science and mathematics education 1999: State-by-state trends and new indicators from the 1997–98 school year.* Washington, DC: Council of Chief State School Officers. Available at http://ccsso.org

Cai, J., Watanabe, T., & Lo, J. J. (2002). Intended treatments of arithmetic averages in U.S. and Asian school mathematics textbooks. *School Science and Mathematics, 102,* 391–404.

Chall, J. S. (1967). *Learning to read: The great debate.* New York: McGraw-Hill.

Council for Exceptional Children. (2004). *The new IDEA: CEC's summary of significant issues.* Washington DC: Council for Exceptional Children. Available at http://cec.sped.org

Engelmann, S., & Carnine, D. (1991). *Theory of instruction: Principles and applications.* Eugene, OR: ADI Press.

Fuchs, D., Roberts, P. H., Fuchs, L. S., & Bowers, J. (1996). Reintegrating students with learning disabilities into the mainstream: A two-year study. *Learning Disabilities Research and Practice, 11,* 214–229.

Fuchs, L. S., Fuchs, D., Hamlett, C. L., Phillips, N. B., & Bentz, J. (1994). Classwide curriculum-based measurement: Helping general educators meet the challenge of student diversity. *Exceptional Children, 60,* 518–537.

Geary, D. C., & Hoard, M. K. (2003). Learning disabilities in basic mathematics: Deficits in memory and cognition. In J. M. Royer (Ed.), *Mathematical cognition* (pp. 93–116). Greenwich, CT: Information Age Publishing.

Gersten, R., Chard, D, Baker, S., & Lee, D. L. (in press). Experimental and quasi-experimental research on instructional approaches for teaching mathematics to students with learning disabilities: A research synthesis. *Review of Educational Research.*

Gersten, R., Jordan, N. C., & Flojo, J. R. (2005). Early identification and interventions for students with mathematics difficulties. *Journal of Learning Disabilities, 38,* 293–304.

Harcourt Brace School Publishers. (2000). *Math advantage.* Orlando, FL: Author.

Harniss, M. K., Carnine, D.W., Silbert, J., & Dixon, R. C. (2002). Effective strategies for teaching mathematics. In E. J. Kame'enui, D. W. Carnine, R. C. Dixon, D. C. Simmons, & M. D. Coyne (Eds.), *Effective teaching strategies that accommodate diverse learners* (2nd ed., pp. 121–148). Columbus, OH: Merrill/Prentice Hall.

Klein, D. (2003). A brief history of American K–12 mathematics education in the 20th century. In J. M. Royer (Ed.), *Mathematical cognition* (pp. 175–225). Greenwich, CT: Information Age Publishing.

Klein, D. (2005). *The state of state math standards: 2005.* Washington, DC: Fordham Foundation.

Ma, L. (1999). *Knowing and teaching elementary mathematics.* Mahwah, NJ: Erlbaum.

Miller, S. P., Butler, F. M., & Lee, K. (1998). Validated practices for teaching mathematics to students with learning disabilities: A review of the literature. *Focus on Exceptional Children, 31*(1), 1–24.

Mullis, I. V. S., Martin, M. O., Gonzalez, E. J., & Chrostowski, S. J. (2004). *TIMSS 2003 international mathematics report: Findings from IEA's Trends in International Mathematics and*

Science Study at Fourth and Eighth Grade. Boston: International Association for the Evaluation of Educational Achievement. Retrieved from timss.bc.edu

National Center for Educational Statistics. (2003). *The nation's report card.* Washington, DC: Department of Education, National Center for Educational Statistics. Retrieved from nces.ed.gov/nationsreportcard/mathematics/

National Council of Teachers of Mathematics. (2000). *Principles and Standards for school mathematics: Executive summary.* Retrieved from standards.nctm.org

National Reading Panel. (2000). *Teaching children to read: An evidence-based assessment of the scientific research literature on reading and its implications for reading instruction.* Washington, DC: National Institute of Child Health and Human Development.

Organisation for Economic Co-operation and Development. (2004). *Learning for tomorrow's world: First results from PISA 2003.* Retrieved from pisa.oecd.org

Przychodzian, A. M., Marchand-Martella, N. E., Martella, R. C., & Azim, D. (2004). Direct instruction mathematics programs: An overview and research summary. *Journal of Direct Instruction, 4,* 53–84.

Reys, B. J., Reys, R. E., & Chavez, O. (2004). Why mathematics textbooks matter. *Educational Leadership, 61*(5) 61–66.

Schmidt, W., Houang, R., & Cogan, L. (2002). A coherent curriculum: The case of mathematics. *American Educator, 26*(2), 10–26.

Schmidt, W. H., McKnight, C. C., & Raizen, S. A. (1996). *A splintered vision: An investigation of U.S. science and mathematics education.* Boston: Kluwer Academic.

Simpson, R. L., La Cava, P. G., & Graner, P. S. (2004). The No Child Left Behind Act: Challenges and implications for educators. *Intervention, 40,* 67–75.

Snider, V. E. (2004). A comparison of spiral versus strand curriculum. *Journal of Direct Instruction, 4,* 29–40.

Snider, V. E., & Crawford, D. (2004). Mathematics. In N.E. Marchand-Martella, T. A. Slocum, & R. C. Martella (Eds.), *Introduction to direct instruction* (pp. 206–245). Boston: Pearson/ Allyn & Bacon.

Stein, M., & Carnine, D. (1999). Designing and delivering effective mathematics instruction. In R. J. Stevens (Ed.), *Teaching in American schools* (pp. 245–269). Columbus, OH: Merrill/Prentice Hall.

Stein, M., Kinder, D., Silbert, J., & Carnine, D. (2006). *Designing effective mathematics instruction: A direct instruction approach* (4th ed.). Columbus, OH: Merrill/Prentice Hall.

Stein, M. L., Stuen, C., Carnine, D., & Long, R. M. (2001). Textbook evaluation and adoption practices. *Reading and Writing Quarterly, 17*(1), 5–23.

Strauss, V. (2004, December 21). Math educators find common denominators. *The Washington Post.* Retrieved from www.washingtonpost.com

Wu, H. (1999). Basic skills versus conceptual understanding. *American Educator, 23*(3), 14–19, 50–52.

CHAPTER 8

Facilitating Teacher Collaboration in Middle School Mathematics Classrooms with Special-Needs Students

RENE S. PARMAR and JANET R. DESIMONE

Mr. McManus, the special education teacher, rushes into the sixth-grade classroom, 5 minutes late. "Sorry," he mumbles under his breath to the mathematics teacher, Mrs. Cordoba. She gives a slight frown as her train of thought is interrupted but then carries on with her lesson. Mr. McManus is late because he had to stop by the school office to meet briefly with the principal regarding a disciplinary infraction by one of his students who has emotional and behavioral problems. The lesson is on finding the surface area of pyramids, and he is comfortable with the formulas and procedures. "Whew! Saved!" he thinks to himself, glad the topic wasn't something beyond his experience and knowledge.

Mrs. Cordoba is handing out a variety of small plastic models of regular pyramids (triangle, square, pentagon, hexagon) to groups of students. All the included students form one group at the far left of the room. Mr. McManus approaches Mrs. Cordoba. "Excuse me," he says softly, "but my kids need to be mixed in with the other groups." She gives him an annoyed look. "OK. Class, don't start just yet. I'm reassigning the groups." The students give a collective groan. She calls on each included student and assigns her or him to an existing group.

As the students measure the pyramid bases and faces, Mr. McManus walks around, seeing if any of the included students need help. He observes that they are mostly spectators, while each group has one or two general education students who are controlling the activity. "Everyone take a turn measuring," he says to one group. "Nina, look at how Jen has organized her information and make a chart like that," he says to a student in another group. "Peter,

154

watch your addition. Remember to count the number of sides." Mrs. Cordoba walks up. "Peter really should be using multiplication," she says. "He's going to use repeated addition for this one," replies Mr. McManus. Some children in the group snicker. Both teachers ignore them. Peter chews his pencil with a red face.

"We have a math teachers' meeting after school today," Mrs. Cordoba informs Mr. McManus. "Sorry, can't make it," he replies. "There's a CSE [Committee on Special Education] that I've got to go to. Do you have notes for next week's topics?" Mrs. Cordoba sighs deeply. "We were going to make them at the meeting—but I'll get you a copy later. I was really hoping to talk to you about some of the kids' levels of participation, but another time, I guess," she says and walks away. She avoids him for the rest of the class period.

It seems obvious that two teachers working together in a classroom to meet the needs of all students are better than one. However, while numerous books and papers have been written on the benefits of teacher collaboration, recent research seems to suggest that it is only sporadically implemented, with mixed results. In programs where inclusion is being effectively implemented, general education teachers felt that their colleagues were their most important resource (DeSimone, 2004). Many other sources suggested (e.g., McLeskey & Waldron, 1996) that inclusion is often not well implemented. In these cases, administrative and regulatory structures combine with the personal and professional characteristics of teachers involved to form barriers to inclusion. In order to create an environment where inclusion works successfully in middle school, changes are necessary at (1) the preservice level where teachers prepare for the challenges of teaching in the current environment, and (2) the in-service level where teachers adapt to new teaching arrangements and standards. Preservice teachers need support from teacher educators, and in-service teachers need support from school administrators. Successful inclusion programs have demonstrated that professionals working together can make inclusion work for the benefit of all students. In this chapter, we offer suggestions that can be used by teachers to build a collaborative working relationship. We emphasize that there is no model program that can be readily adopted. Each school and each district must use approaches and programs that are appropriate to its setting and situation.

Among the questions raised about the effectiveness of collaborative teaching is that of impact on students. Gable, Mostert, and Tonelson (2004) reviewed the literature on collaboration and found that there is a dearth of data on actual academic and behavioral outcomes for students. They further pointed out that the majority of research studies report only short-term outcomes, and few have examined the long-term effects of collaborative teaching programs. Finally, many research studies do not provide reliability data on the consistency and quality of implementation of collaborative teaching (Murawski & Swanson, 2001). Regardless of student educational outcomes, however, the current policies and legislation for education of students with mild disabilities encourage maximum inclusion and mandate participation of students with disabilities in high-stakes standardized testing.

In the present educational context, the debate is no longer whether or not collaborative teaching arrangements work. They are already present in many schools, and in many cases mandated by district or state policies. The important question is how to implement effective collaborative or coteaching models so that all students in a classroom can benefit from high-quality instruction.

DEVELOPING TEACHER COLLABORATION

General Education and Special Education Teachers

In a review of research on teacher collaboration, Weiss and Brigham (2000) identified several barriers to the implementation of collaborative programs. One of their conclusions was that special education teachers and general education teachers often do not share the same definition of collaboration. A survey on coteaching practices by Austin (2001) revealed that the majority of respondents felt that the general education teacher conducted most of the actual teaching, while the special education teacher typically made modifications for included students. However, teachers felt there was a disconnect between beliefs about sharing and the actual reality where necessary administrative supports did not exist. In fact, in some schools, special education teachers teach in separate buildings and, at best, send the general education teachers written plans or suggestions (Snyder, 1999).

In order to facilitate the development of common understandings of collaboration, some issues need clarification, including the roles and responsibilities of the teachers involved, knowledge of curriculum and instructional methods, and organizational structures necessary to implement a collaborative program (Cook, Tarkersley, Cook, & Landrum, 2000).

Roles of Special Education Teachers in General Education Mathematics Classrooms

Boudah, Schumaker, and Deshler (1997) defined four roles that special education teachers might take in a general education program. Figure 8.1 provides illustrations of teachers in the various types of collaborative roles. In general, if the special education teacher is comfortable with the content, then coteaching is possible; otherwise lower levels of participation are observed. Briefly, the roles are described as:

- *Role 1:* The special education teacher provides support to the general education teacher. In this case, the special education teacher may function as no more than an assistant, passing out materials, monitoring student behavior, writing out information dictated by the general education teacher (Figure 8.1, Role 1), and ensuring that activities are completed.
- *Role 2:* The special education teacher takes responsibility for teaching the content, thus having a more active teaching role, but operates parallel to the general education teacher. This may be through teaching the material in the resource

Role 1: Special Education Teacher Supports General Education Teacher

GE: Let's review the vocabulary for today's topic. [As GE speaks, SE prints the definitions on the board.]

> *factor*: a number that goes into another number *evenly*
> *prime*: a number that has *exactly* two factors: one and itself

GE: What are some examples of prime numbers? [SE writes down the students' examples.]

Ex.   3 = 1,3   5= 1,5   11 = 1,11

No one is working with the included students as SE is busy printing information on the board, as directed by GE. The included students are copying the notes from the board, but no one is checking on them to see if they understand what is being taught.

GE: OK, next is a composite number, which is . . . . [SE writes more definitions on the board.]

> *composite*: a number that has *more than* two factors
> Ex.   6 = 2,3,1,6   20 = 1,2,4,5,10

A girl walks in late. SE says loudly, "I was worried about you." The girl smiles sheepishly and sits down. In the second row from the window, second desk, one of the included boys keeps yawning and staring into space.

Role 2: Special Education Teacher Reteaches Content in the Resource Room

SE: Let's review the concepts you covered in class today. OK, it's about numbers that are prime numbers and those that have factors. Let me give you some tricks to help you remember the terms.

First, there's *unique*. Now this is a number that has exactly one factor. Like "1." There's a hint here, see? [She points to the word *unique* and the *i* in the word that looks like the number 1.] This is how you remember that it is a 1.

Role 3: Special Education and General Education Teachers Cover Different Topics

GE: Today Ms. E will introduce our next unit on reasoning about quantity. I have some activities related to the topic that we'll do over the next few days.

SE: OK, let's start with looking at a problem that uses what you learned about percents and proportions.

Ninety-six percent of people are exposed to the flu virus, but only 20% of them fall ill. In a town of 45,000, how many people will fall ill?

Of the people that fall ill, 72% are either over the age of 65 or under the age of 4. Since there's a flu vaccine shortage, these people should definitely get it. What's the minimum number of flu vaccines that the town health officials should order?

GE: [a few days later, after students have worked through several percentage problems with SE] Now we're going to take what you learned about percents and apply it to probability.

Role 4: Special Education and General Education Teachers Coteach All Topics

GE: [Already has the following displayed on an overhead projector] How many triangles do you count in each figure? Start with the figure that is composed of one small triangle. Then go to 2 and 4. Stop there, and we'll talk about the more difficult ones before doing them.

(cont.)

FIGURE 8.1. Possible roles for a special education teacher. GE, general education teacher; SE, special education teacher. Some illustrations are adaptations from observational data reported in DeSimone (2004).

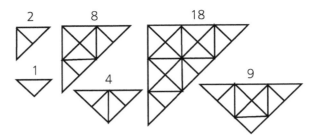

SE: To organize your work, take a blank page and make three columns. One will be the number of small triangles, type 1; then the number of type 2 triangles; then type 4.

[Both teachers walk up and down the rows, checking the children's work; everyone is busy working on the problem. GE and SE assist both included and general education students. When an included student mutters a curse word, GE, who happens to be close by, softly taps his desk, which is a sign that he has to make a check on his behavior card, which is on his desk.]

GE: OK! Great! Do you notice any pattern in the number of triangles? [Students provide responses.] Do you think you can make any predictions about triangle type 8?

SE: [Standing at overhead projector.] Let's work this out together and see if your predictions came true.

FIGURE 8.1. *(cont.)*

room or to a segregated group within the regular classroom. The special education teacher attempts to reteach the material, sometimes providing the students with strategies or helpful hints (Figure 8.1, Role 2).

• *Role 3:* The special education teacher teaches some parts of the content to the whole class, alternating with the general education teacher (Figure 8.1, Role 3). The teachers divide the curriculum, and one teacher either assists or is free, while the other teaches.

• *Role 4:* The special education teacher truly coteaches each topic with the general education teacher (Figure 8.1, Role 4), based on joint planning and a common understanding of curriculum priorities and required instructional modifications.

Similar role assignments were observed in middle school science classrooms with inclusion (Piccillo, 1994), where special education teachers often took on assisting or behavior management roles but occasionally took on alternate teaching or coteaching roles, depending on their relationship with the general education teacher and comfort level with the topic.

When making decisions about relative responsibilities and roles, one of the topics to be considered by teachers is the balance between behavior management and instructional activity. The special education teacher tends to have more strategies and experiences with the former, and the mathematics teacher with the latter. Both professionals can work together to share responsibility for both behavior management and instruction. Teachers need to agree upon management strategies that are feasible in the classroom and fit into the instructional plan. The strategies should be unobtrusive, easy to implement, and age appropriate. For example, complicated token economies are not as feasible in middle school inclusion classes as in self-contained elementary classes. Instead, teachers should design systems where students are encouraged to self-monitor their behaviors so that teacher attention can stay focused on instruction. Both rewards and discipline strategies should be easy to administer and age appropriate.

In general, positive behavior management approaches are preferable to negative ones. Such approaches have been described in numerous texts and articles (e.g., Abramowitz & O'Leary, 1991). One suggestion is to plan instruction so that there is a high rate of student engagement, with novel information introduced in small chunks rather than as a large unit. Other approaches include organizing the classroom so that students with disabilities are in closer proximity to teachers and have opportunity for individualized work when necessary. Cognitive-behavioral approaches are also effective with this age group, including those where students self-monitor and decide on their reinforcements (e.g., free time, choice of activities, homework reduction) and those where students learn positive self-management strategies and problem solving. When students experience academic success, their behavior problems decrease and their self-efficacy increases.

Further, both general and special education teachers need to consistently apply the agreed-upon behavioral plan. Students are best served in environments where the teachers hold a common understanding of goals and procedures and are consistent in their implementation. If students understand that both teachers hold the same expectations, they will be more likely to observe the class rules and participate in class activities.

Negotiating Shared Responsibilities

While a great deal of attention is directed toward the attitudes of general education teachers, some researchers have considered the views of special education teachers as well (e.g., McLeskey & Waldron, 1996). Both sets of teachers have to surrender some traditional aspects of their responsibilities and assume new roles and responsibilities. To facilitate conversation between teachers, a chart such as Figure 8.2 may form the basis for discussion. We have provided some suggestions of issues, but at each site teachers would articulate issues emanating from their own unique situations.

Once teachers have shared their perspectives, it is more likely that strategies can be developed to address areas of need. General education teachers could be provided with more information on the unique learning needs of various inclusion students. Special education teachers can agree upon their role and status in the classroom. Teachers can negotiate and honestly discuss where they might be able to assist each other for the most effective use of their time. They can decide on modifications that could benefit all students. For example, if included students are allowed to bring a sheet with formulas on it for an exam, other students may benefit from this as well. Or, if a study period is offered during or after school, it could be made available to all students experiencing difficulties. This would also avoid

Special Education Teacher		General Education Teacher	
Advantages	**Disadvantages**	**Advantages**	**Disadvantages**
• Colleagues to discuss programming • Access to more curriculum materials • Opportunity to learn more about content-area instruction • Observe academic success for students	• Give up autonomy of own classroom • Give up ability to make own curriculum decisions and set own standards • Develop and maintain coteaching relationships with (several) general education teachers • Face change in role to no longer being main teacher • Have to adhere to general education curriculum and standards	• Colleagues to discuss programming • Increase in repertoire of instructional and behavior management strategies • Having an extra adult in the room during instruction • Opportunity to learn more about special needs	• Increase the range of academic needs in the classroom • Modify curriculum and instruction • Develop and maintain coteaching relationships with special education teachers • Increase the amount of planning time and paperwork • Create multiple versions of lessons and tests

FIGURE 8.2. Discussion chart for collaborating teachers.

stigmatizing the student with special needs and benefit the general education students directly.

In a middle school where inclusion is practiced widely, special education teachers may be providing consultation to a number of general education teachers in the content areas (science, social studies, mathematics, health education, English language arts, technology education, etc.). It is not reasonable to expect the special education teacher to be a content area specialist in all of these diverse subjects, across the grade levels of middle school. However, it is essential that he or she have ready access to curriculum guidelines and standards and to instructional resources for the various topics. To the extent possible, special education teachers should be present at content-area meetings among mathematics teachers in order to gain information on upcoming topics. Over time, they will become more comfortable with the various topics to be covered and be able to take increasingly active roles.

Classroom Structural and Organizational Models That Facilitate Mathematics Inclusion

In many middle schools, content-area classes are still set up on traditional lines, with a large proportion of time devoted to whole-group instruction, followed by individual assignments. Working together, the general and special education teachers could identify times when small group activities are appropriate, taking care to devise small groups where various student strengths and weaknesses are balanced. They could also divide the class into heterogeneous groups and each teach a smaller section if feasible. Another approach that has had some success is to set up a "buddy" system as additional support for the included student.

Seating arrangements for included students also need to be carefully considered. A structure where all included students are together in one part of the room may work from the perspective of management but does not meet the goals of inclusion. Other aspects of the classroom structure that impact seating also need to be jointly negotiated by the teachers, such as use of computers, access to learning materials, access to the chalkboard, avoidance of distractions, and so forth.

Additionally, the classroom structure should be organized in a way that conveys to students that the general education teacher and special education teacher are equal partners when delivering instruction. Both teachers should have desks or workspaces and be jointly responsible for information that is posted on the bulletin boards or around the classroom. This would also help in creating an atmosphere of shared ownership among teachers.

Discussing Philosophical Differences

A possible source of friction between collaborating teachers may be differences in instructional philosophy that impact their actions and their educational plans for specific students. Some examples are provided below. There is no "correct" position on these issues, as elements of each philosophical stance can benefit students. However, it is important for teachers to understand and discuss different perspectives. Such a discussion could lead to a better understanding of various points of view and the development of a learning plan that works for the specific students being served.

Inquiry-Based versus Directed Learning

In recent decades, the field of mathematics education has been stressing inquiry-based approaches to learning (e.g., NCTM, 2000). Students are presented with challenging problem situations and use their prior knowledge, appropriate manipulative materials, and cooperative learning strategies to uncover solutions. On the other hand, many of the strategies used with special education students emphasize directly providing the student with the needed information and then supporting her or his learning through practice activities and application problems. As an example, when teaching about combinations and permutations, one teacher may prefer to begin with teaching the formula and providing some examples. The other teacher may prefer to present students with a group of materials, such as different-colored blocks, and ask them to determine how many combinations can be made, leading them through developing a chart of the information to the eventual development of the formula. Collaborating teachers need to blend the approaches so that students benefit from the strengths of each.

Intrinsic versus Extrinsic Motivation

Throughout their own schooling, many educators have felt intrinsically motivated to learn their subject area and do not always understand students who do not feel like learning. From the perspective of a special education teacher, it may be necessary to set up age-appropriate motivators (e.g., points that can be traded in for later rewards or free time) that will encourage students to persist at learning. The teacher may believe that since students have not experienced a great deal of success in academic areas, they need additional motivation, or that point systems help students self-monitor their attention and behavior, leading to the development of important social skills. The mathematics teacher may not be accustomed to providing external motivators and may resist such programs or fail to implement them consistently in the absence of the special education teacher. For example, many teachers have "Do Now" activities on the board that students begin as soon as they enter the classroom. These serve as a time for students to settle in and develop a cognitive set for learning mathematics. At this time, the mathematics teacher may be engaged in grading tests, reviewing homework, or planning activities. For the teacher to monitor behavior for a point or token system could be an additional burden that he or she does not want to undertake. Teachers should communicate about the importance of motivational systems to the students involved, the importance of consistency of implementation, and the use of systems that are easy to implement in the mathematics classroom.

Staying on Schedule

A special education teacher may find it beneficial if the curriculum is covered according to a particular sequence and pace so that she or he can better prepare and organize supplemental materials. The mathematics teacher, who usually delivers the majority of the instruction, may want to take advantage of "teaching moments," where a student's question or comment can lead to a digression to explore an interesting concept. For example, students may bring in a problem they saw in a magazine or an issue from a real-life experience related to planning their own finances or designing and measuring something they will construct. The collaborating teachers can discuss the extent to which they wish to provide enrichment and the extent to which they want to stay with the prescribed curriculum.

Cooperative Groups

Many teachers are in agreement that students can learn effectively in cooperative groups within the classroom and even complete homework assignments cooperatively. However, some research (e.g., McLeskey & Waldron, 1996) indicates that there are differences in the amount of cooperative learning and the structure of cooperative groups within classrooms that affect the learning of included students. At the middle school level, many mathematics teachers emphasize individual learning as a way to ensure that each student understands the needed concepts. She or he may feel that included students will copy the work of their peers or simply observe rather than be truly engaged if placed in groups. General education teachers may also believe that it places an undue burden on able students if they are frequently paired with included students who are struggling with the content. Special education teachers may feel that included students would benefit from the modeling provided by their peers in cooperative groups. Teachers who collaborate need to devise a plan for the balance of cooperative versus individual learning, the composition of groups, and the assignment of roles to students within groups to ensure that all are active participants and gain the conceptual knowledge necessary.

Grading Systems

Another major area is how to implement a grading system that maintains standards while reflecting the capabilities of the included students. Prior research has indicated that general education teachers are concerned about maintaining standards when modifying grades for included students (Schumm & Vaughn, 1991). Several authors have forwarded suggestions for modifying grading while ensuring that the included students still maintain the curricular standards of the classroom. Some considerations that could form the basis for discussion among teachers have been suggested by Munk and Bursuck (2001) and include (1) varying the percentage of the grade based on tests and quizzes versus homework assignments; (2) including classroom participation in grading systems; and (3) modifying grading to cover fewer items, with more problem-solving components. Other suggestions are to have more open-book tests for the entire class, have a balance between solving numeric problems and writing out explanations, have all students highlight important information on tests, and have a reader read the problems to all students. Figure 8.3 provides an example of a class activity for which teachers can discuss alternate grading.

Many teachers express concern about alternative grading, feeling that it falsely conveys to students that they are achieving at acceptable levels when they are actually below standards. Following the implementation of inclusion, special education teachers sometimes find that their expectations for their students are very far below grade level and that they do not have a realistic idea of what their students should achieve (McLeskey & Waldron, 2002). Given the current move toward having all included students participate in high-stakes assessments and master the general education curriculum, conversations among teachers on the tension between standards and modifications are crucial.

Parking at the Mall

Parking Lot Recommendations

	Dimensions	Percent of Spaces
Regular parking spaces	9 feet × 12 feet	
Handicapped spaces	15 feet × 20 feet	3

1. The new shopping mall advertised that parking space is available for 5,000 cars. How many spaces at the new shopping mall would actually be needed for handicapped parking?

   Actual space _____

   How do you know? Explain.

2. How many other parking spaces would be available? _____

   How do you know? Explain.

3. A large sale was scheduled at the mall, and the parking lot was full. Estimate the number of shoppers in the mall. _____

   Tell how you determined your estimate.

For Teacher Discussion: For the student with special needs, how would you modify the way in which this class problem is graded?

Adaptations: Student can use a calculator; aide can record verbal explanations.

Possible Suggestions:
1. Decide the percentage of grade based on the calculation versus the written explanation parts.
2. Give partial credit for correct process with incorrect answer due to careless errors.
3. Give a problem with smaller numbers to be done without calculator and average that grade.

FIGURE 8.3. Collaborating on changing the grading system. Problem adapted from Fennell (1998), illuminations.nctm.org.

Teachers and Paraprofessionals

Frequently, inclusion programs involve the assignment of paraprofessionals to classrooms with included students. This is particularly the case when students have physical and medical needs but also occurs when students with cognitive or behavioral impairments are included. An effective collaborative relationship with a paraprofessional requires planning and preparation. It is important that the paraprofessional be encouraged to work with all the students in the classroom rather than just focusing on the included students. This will help prevent the special needs students from becoming segregated or stigmatized within the classroom.

First, both general and special education teachers need to determine the paraprofessional's level of comfort with the content to be taught and the specific instructional modifications for included students. Paraprofessionals may need time to learn the content themselves and may need copies of the textbooks and teaching guides so they can understand the concepts and the instructional process that is being used. They can also be provided with instructional plans and outlines that detail how they might help students who are experiencing difficulties. Teachers can consider the continuum of assistance levels (Figure 8.4) and discuss with the paraprofessional where they expect that individual to be and what actions constitute the appropriate level of assistance.

Second, paraprofessionals need to be part of the discussion of specific behavior management plans so they can implement them along with the teachers. Like the teachers, they should focus on the instructional program, rather than being designated as disciplinarians for students. They may need to be taught specific strategies to encourage self-monitoring by students and redirect student attention in a positive way.

Third, it is important to include paraprofessionals in lesson planning meetings, even if they just listen and observe as the general and special education teachers discuss instruction and curriculum. When paraprofessionals are simply asked to carry out lessons without seeing how they were created, they may not fully understand the importance of the lessons, the connection between the lessons, or the ways in which the activities promote student progress (Rueda & Monzo, 2002).

It is well worth the effort, at the beginning of the school year, for teachers to take the time to discuss their plans with their paraprofessionals and to establish their classroom expectations and guidelines. This will ensure that inappropriate roles are not assumed and that the paraprofessional's time is used effectively. It will also make certain that students recognize that all adults working with them are in agreement on standards for learning and behavior, and that all are working together toward a common goal. It will also help teachers think of ways in which the paraprofessional can most effectively meet the needs of the included students. For example, the paraprofessional could have the responsibility for ensuring that large-type handouts are available for students who need them because of visual impairments or that tests are read to students whose IEPs indicate this modification.

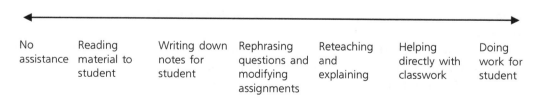

FIGURE 8.4. Levels of assistance by paraprofessionals.

Guaranteeing that the teacher is matched with the same paraprofessional for at least a few years can also be beneficial, since developing collaborative relationships happens over time. However, with constant shifts in grade-level assignments each year and the often high turnover in paraprofessional positions, this is not always possible. Teachers who have effective relationships with certain paraprofessionals may ask their building administrators to ensure continual placement of these paraprofessionals.

CHANGING THE ENVIRONMENT TO FOSTER COLLABORATION

School Structures

Teachers in collaborative teaching situations need to be aware of aspects of the typical middle school that need change in order for successful inclusion programs to operate. Teachers can use this knowledge to develop a common understanding with building administrators to work toward any needed change, modification, or adaptation. Some of the structures of middle schools that interfere with collaborative teaching arrangements were identified by Schumaker and Deshler (1988) and still serve as barriers. Among them are the large amount of content that needs to be covered, limited opportunities for teacher–student contact outside the specific class, outside pressures that often focus on raising test scores, and the autonomy of teachers (Weiss & Lloyd, 2002).

Teachers need to engage in joint curriculum planning, where topics are prioritized and integrated. All students who can complete the general education curriculum should be presented with the opportunity to do so. Students for whom the grade-level curriculum is too vast for one year's coverage should receive more instructional time and learning activities in prioritized topics. Topics that are not a priority could be integrated into the more important areas to build familiarity but given less emphasis.

New systems of communication need to be developed so that all mathematics teachers at a middle school can easily access information on student learning needs and strategies that work for specific students. At present, there is often little communication across grade levels, as well as across general and special education programs. With today's technology, it is easily possible to construct an electronic portfolio for each student with special needs, which can indicate to his or her math teachers the student's present level of performance, learning strengths and weaknesses, and specific instructional strategies that bring about the best response.

The issue of high-stakes testing must also be taken into consideration. Since all students, with very few exceptions, are required under the current legislation (No Child Left Behind) to participate in high-stakes exams for performance monitoring, teachers must include this requirement in their planning. Very often, the supports put in place to help included students succeed (e.g., after-school programs, study guides, problem-solving strategies) can benefit all students in the program.

Relationships among Teachers

Some studies indicate that when teachers have a good working relationship, inclusion is more likely to be successfully implemented (e.g., Marable, 1996). Teachers need to be more proactive in demanding from their building administrators time to meet together outside the classroom and develop a working relationship. For example, teachers may want to go together to local or regional conferences, go for joint professional development sessions, or arrange meeting times in school. If meeting times are scheduled during school, they should be at times when the special education teacher does not have other commitments, such as special education conferences with parents and professionals, writing IEPs, or attending to other professional responsibilities.

During the school year, teachers need to advocate for sufficient time for collaborative lesson preparation and frequent communication regarding the learning needs of students. In all respects, collaboration needs to become an integral component of the school climate. During departmental or schoolwide meetings and in-service training sessions teachers could take turns sharing their reflections on collaborative processes and models. Such a presentation would open the lines of communication among all of the teachers, and the presentation's collaborative format would act as a model for everyone. Arranging time to visit other classrooms and observe a variety of team-teaching models within their own schools or districts is also valuable. It is vital that teachers take the lead in presenting administrators with strategies for promoting collaboration and simultaneously enhancing the curricular offerings.

Managing the Schedule

During a 40-minute period, it becomes a challenge for teachers to cover the required material, implement modifications, and ensure that learning outcomes are being met. Block scheduling creates greater flexibility in teachers' planning, materials, assignments, curriculum, and instructional choices. Teachers are given more time to deliver explicit and cohesive lessons, integrate collaborative strategies, foster student involvement, emphasize higher-level problem-solving activities, and implement instructional and curricular modifications. Often general education teachers become frustrated because they do not have adequate planning time to meet with their special education coteacher and the rest of their team (paraprofessional, aides, etc.). Through block scheduling, general and special education teachers will benefit from common planning periods where they can share ideas, create lesson plans together, and make joint instructional decisions. In addition, block scheduling allows students to receive a more continuous flow of material that is not fragmented due to the constraints of shorter class periods. There is some controversy regarding the effectiveness of block scheduling, and its drawbacks for a given school or situation should be weighed and considered. However, there are many instances where it may provide an effective system of service delivery.

MAKING MODIFICATIONS AND ACCOMMODATIONS

Engaging in Practice Activities

Many middle school mathematics teachers have not had a great deal of experience making instructional and curricular adaptations for students with special needs. At the preservice level, future mathematics educators do not receive much exposure to inclusion or the learning needs of special education students. In their teacher education programs, they may have been exposed to only a single course on students with disabilities. Frequently, this is a survey course on various areas of special needs and special education law, without any content-specific information on ways to appropriately modify instruction. Special education teachers typically receive only a limited overview of mathematics instruction. Very often the strategies they learn are related to increasing computational proficiency and incorporating manipulatives into teaching.

The following is an activity that could be useful in developing an understanding of modifying curriculum and instruction. Teachers take a sample lesson plan (either one of their own or one downloaded from the Internet or another source). They then take the learning profiles of three or four included students and plan for their full participation. The students would be varied in their needs, for example (1) a student with a severe visual impairment who needs materials presented up close, print in large type, and extra time for completion; (2) a student with reading and writing disabilities who frequently needs to have material read aloud, needs assistance with note taking, and needs to have tests and assignments provided on audiotape; or (3) a student with emotional problems who frequently cries in frustration and stops working, gets angry at peers and uses inappropriate language, and ignores the teacher's instructions.

The lesson guidelines could include the following components from Jitendra, Edwards, Choutka, and Treadway (2002): (1) organize overall unit content; (2) adapt curriculum but keep the "big ideas"; (3) incorporate levels of understanding (e.g., Bloom's Taxonomy); (4) identify instructional activities for small-group and whole-class learning; (5) identify accommodations and modifications for included students; and (6) identify appropriate assessment procedures and standards, including appropriate procedures to use with students who have learning disabilities (difficulties with memory, organization, etc.), attention problems (distractibility, hyperactivity, resistance), and developmental disabilities (lack of comprehension, etc.). Figure 8.5 provides a sample unit outline and some activities. Mathematics teachers could work with colleagues in mathematics and special education to identify areas of potential difficulty for included students and generate strategies to assist such students.

One important aspect when adapting instruction is to distinguish between surface-level modifications (e.g., highlighters, outline sheets, overhead projectors), which can benefit all students, and curricular and instructional modifications specifically aimed at students with unique learning needs. Table 8.1 provides some instructional modifications, mainly for students with learning disabilities, which teachers can use in their mathematics inclusion classes.

Unit Theme: Measurement, Estimation, Statistics

Big Ideas: Understanding speed; displaying information graphically; making comparisons

Unit Map:

Activity	Modification	Assessment
Day 1: Marking hallway into feet, with 5-feet markers up to about 30 feet. |___|___|___|___|___| 0 1 2 3 4 5 Students create their recording sheets. Students estimate how far they can walk in 8 seconds. Students get into groups of 3; each group has one stopwatch. Students time each member of their group walking, designate the fastest walker in their group, and compare their actual speed with their estimate.	• Student with ADD uses tape measure and takes other active roles. • Student with DD needs each foot unit numbered; also needs a demonstration by a student. • Student with LD needs buddy to help develop recording sheet. • Student with LD needs check on time noted from stopwatch. • Student in wheelchair measures wheelchair speed (can build this into whole-class discussion). • Student with ED/BD needs to have self-monitoring card with him or her.	• Can students compute the difference between their estimates and the actual distance? • Can students accurately record their group's timings?
Day 2: Students determine their own rate of walking (speed = distance/time). Students discuss why rates differ (e.g., length of legs, length of stride, weight, motivation). Students get into groups again and measure how far they can walk in 8 seconds; they compare rate with previous day's rate. Students measure distance for 16 seconds, 32 seconds, and 64 seconds.	• Students with LD and DD need formula in front of them. • Student with LD needs buddy to assist with recording. • Student with DD and student in wheelchair need aide's assistance. • Make sure all students have turns during group discussion.	• Can each student correctly fill in the numbers and solve the formula? • Can each student measure (make sure they take turns)? • Can each student accurately record information on chart?
Day 3: Students create a line graph of their speed over the time periods. Students make observations about their graphs (e.g., they are not perfectly linear) and discuss reasons why (e.g., fatigue over time). Students calculate average speed, and compare it to speed calculated previously for 8-second time.	• Student with LD needs graph with intervals on X and Y axes marked. • Make sure all students have turns during group discussion. • Student with DD may need explanation of key terms (e.g., linear, curvilinear). • Students with LD and DD need formula for average and may need assistance putting in correct values.	• Can all students correct graph values? • Do students understand the concept of nonlinear trends? • Can all students calculate averages? • Can all students understand reasons for differences in rate over longer times?

FIGURE 8.5. Instructional plan for inclusion. DD, developmental disability; LD, learning disability; ED/BD, emotional or behavioral disability.

TABLE 8.1. Examples of Instructional Modifications for Students with Special Needs

Instructional strategy/ modification	Targeted areas of special needs	Targeted mathematical areas	Benefits
Graphic organizers	• Difficulty with processing and organizing • Difficulty with following a sequence of steps to solution	• Computation • Word problems • Problem solving • Real-world applications	• Helps clarify mathematical functions
Review of prior math concepts (includes spiraling lessons and homework)	• Difficulty recalling mathematical facts	• Computation • Fractions • Decimals	• Strengthens understanding of prior concepts and reinforces skills necessary for future lessons
Self-regulation	• Difficulty attending to tasks • Difficulty with following a sequence of steps to solution	• Computation • Word problems • Problem solving	• Clear guidelines so students can monitor and assess their thinking and performance • Fosters independence
Strategy instruction (includes teacher modeling; think-aloud models and cues; simplifying and reducing strategies)	• Difficulty with processing and organizing • Difficulty attending to tasks • Difficulty with following a sequence of steps to solution	• Computation • Word problems • Problem solving • Algebra • Fractions	• Specific step-by-step processes for problem solving and computation • Strengthening estimation skills
Hands-on devices and visual aids (includes manipulatives; graphing calculators; graph paper; flash cards; drawings; number lines)	• Difficulty interpreting pictures and diagrams • Difficulty with oral communication • Difficulty correctly identifying symbols or numerals • Difficulty maintaining attention	• Computation • Word problems • Problem solving • Algebra • Fractions • Geometry	• Clarifies abstract concepts and processes • Increases accuracy • Enhances understanding of higher-level mathematical concepts
Cooperative learning (includes small-group instruction; teaming; peer-assisted tutoring)	• Difficulty attending to tasks • Difficulty maintaining attention	• Computation • Problem solving	• Fosters oral communication and interpersonal relationships • May be less threatening for students than speaking in front of the whole class
Goal structure	• Difficulty attending to tasks • Difficulty with following a sequence of steps to solution	• Computation • Problem solving	• Enhances motivation • Teaches students to set appropriate and specific goals

(cont.)

TABLE 8.1. *(cont.)*

Instructional strategy/ modification	Targeted areas of special needs	Targeted mathematical areas	Benefits
Scaffolding (includes guided teacher practice and questioning)	• Difficulty with processing and organizing • Difficulty with following a sequence of steps to solution • Difficulty with oral and written communication	• Computation • Word problems • Problem solving	• Fosters independence and self-direction • Enhances understanding of higher-level mathematical concepts
Simulations (includes role-playing or acting out mathematical concepts)	• Difficulty interpreting pictures and diagrams • Difficulty correctly identifying symbols or numerals • Difficulty using a number line • Difficulty with following a sequence of steps to solution • Difficulty maintaining attention	• Computation • Fractions • Decimals	• Forms a kinesthetic awareness of an idea or process • Creates concrete illustrations for abstract ideas
Computer-assisted instruction	• Difficulty attending to tasks • Difficulty maintaining attention • Difficulty with oral communication	• Computation • Problem solving	• Enhances motivation • Increases attention • Increases coordination

Note. Derived from Steele (2002); Jarrett (1999); Miller, Butler, and Lee (1998); and Carnine (1997).

Advocating for Better In-Service Programs

In many districts, in-service training consists of periodic workshops for teachers, organized by building or district administrators. There is often no systematic organization of topics based on current needs; rather they are planned based on topics in the news and/or available speakers. Teachers need to become more proactive in requesting specific workshops that address their needs and identifying resources through their professional organizations or other available resources.

In a recent study, middle school mathematics teachers indicated that a frequently addressed special education topic was working with children with attention-deficit disorder (ADD) and attention-deficit/hyperactivity disorder (ADHD) (DeSimone, 2004). While these disabilities are often found in included classrooms, there are many other areas that need coverage as well, particularly difficulties with memory and organization, and social or emotional disabilities. The relatively low-incidence disability of autism has also been extensively addressed, although many middle school teachers may never have a child with that particular condition in their class. Cook (2001) found that general education teachers are often more accepting of students with severe disabilities than those with mild disabilities, although the latter are more frequently included at the middle school level.

Another finding was that in-service workshops frequently presented some broad and general strategies. However, teachers would benefit more if they could see some more specific exemplars, along with follow-up in the actual classroom, with feedback and suggestions. Other studies on successful in-service programs have also suggested that in-class demonstrations with follow-up visits and feedback make up the most effective approach.

Among the topics that could form the foundation of in-service training for collaborative teaching is that of curriculum modifications. Teachers can work together to identify big ideas in mathematics. Comprehending big ideas will make learning the secondary, less complex mathematics strategies easier and more significant for students (Carnine, 1997). Teachers can then prioritize objectives so that they devote adequate time to central concepts that form the foundation of mathematical concepts. They can then decide how much time to allocate to skill development. Curriculum modifications include prioritizing topics to stress important concepts early in the school year and integrating topics so that all topics can be covered in the allotted time, taking into consideration the learning needs of the included students. Decisions about using a spiral or intensified curriculum model based on student needs could be part of the discussion. Students with attention difficulties often find intensified models easier to deal with, as they can stay focused on a topic for a period of time. Students with memory or comprehension difficulties may benefit from some spiraling, as they can have frequent repetitions of concepts built in.

CONCLUSION

In many school districts across the United States, inclusion is the mandated service delivery model for a large percentage of students with disabilities. Following dissatisfaction with pull-out programs, many sites have turned to coteaching approaches. However, many aspects of the existing system hinder the effective implementation of teacher collaboration. These include insufficient teacher preparation for collaboration, varying goals of general and special education teachers, inflexible administrative structures, lack of continuing support, and individual and personality characteristics of teachers and paraprofessionals. All of these issues can be addressed at the local level if there is open communication among teachers, administrators, and teacher educators. Each school needs to find its unique model, building upon research and guidelines available from successful programs.

REFERENCES

Abramowitz, A. J., & O'Leary, S. G. (1991). Behavioral interventions for the classroom: Implications for students with ADHD. *School Psychology Review, 20,* 220–235.

Austin, V. L. (2001). Teachers' beliefs about co-teaching. *Remedial and Special Education, 22,* 245–253.

Boudah, D., Schumaker, J., & Deshler, D. (1997). Collaborative instruction: Is it an effective option for inclusion in secondary classrooms? *Learning Disability Quarterly, 20*(4), 293–316.

Carnine, D. (1997). Instructional design in mathematics for students with learning disabilities. *Journal of Learning Disabilities, 30,* 130–141.

Cook, B. G. (2001). A comparison of teachers' attitudes toward their included students with mild and severe disabilities. *Journal of Special Education, 34,* 203–213.

Cook, B. G., Tarkersley, M., Cook, L., & Landrum, T. J. (2000). Teachers' attitudes toward their included students with disabilities. *Exceptional Children, 67,* 115–135.

DeSimone, J. R. (2004). *Middle school mathematics teachers' beliefs and knowledge about inclusion of students with learning disabilities.* Unpublished doctoral dissertation, St. John's University, Queens, NY.

Fennell, F. (1998). Mathematics at the mall. *Teaching Children Mathematics, 4,* 268—274.

Gable, R. A., Mostert, M. P., & Tonelson, S. W. (2004). Assessing professional collaboration in schools: Knowing what works. *Preventing School Failure, 48,* 4–8.

Jarrett, D. (1999). *The inclusive classroom: Mathematics and science instruction for students with learning disabilities: It's just good teaching.* Portland, OR: Northwest Regional Educational Laboratory.

Jitendra, A. K., Edwards, L. L., Choutka, C. M., & Treadway, P. S. (2002). A collaborative approach to planning in the content areas for students with learning disabilities: Accessing the general curriculum. *Learning Disabilities Research and Practice, 17,* 252–267.

Marable, M. (1996). Identifying best practices for including students with serious emotional disturbances. *University Microfilms International,* AAT 9634468. *Dissertation Abstracts International, A57/06,* 2435.

McLeskey, J., & Waldron, N. L. (1996). Responses to questions teachers and administrators frequently ask about inclusive programs. *Phi Delta Kappan, 78*(2), 150–157.

McLeskey, J., & Waldron, N. L. (2002). Inclusion and school change: Teacher perceptions regarding curricular and instructional adaptations. *Teacher Education and Special Education, 25,* 41–54.

Miller, S. P., Butler, F. M., & Lee, K. (1998). Validated practices for teaching mathematics to students with learning disabilities: A review of the literature. *Focus on Exceptional Children, 31,* 1–24.

Munk, D. D., & Bursuck, W. D. (2001). Preliminary findings on personalized grading plans for middle school students with learning disabilities. *Exceptional Children, 67,* 211–234.

Murawski, W. W., & Swanson, H. L. (2001). A meta-analysis of co-teaching research: Where are the data? *Remedial and Special Education, 22*(5), 258–267.

National Council of Teachers of Mathematics. (2000). *Principles and standards for school mathematics.* Reston, VA: Author.

Piccillo, B. (1994). The inclusion of students with disabilities in general education science classrooms: A qualitative analysis. *University Microfilms International,* AAT 9509142. *Dissertation Abstracts International, A55/11,* 3475.

Rueda, R., & Monzo, L. D. (2002). Apprenticeship for teaching: Professional development issues surrounding the collaborative relationship between teachers and paraeducators. *Teaching and Teacher Education, 18,* 503–521.

Schumaker, J., & Deshler, D. (1988). Implementing the regular education initiative in secondary schools: A different ball game. *Journal of Learning Disabilities, 21,* 36–42.

Schumm, J. S., & Vaughn, S. (1991). Making adaptations for mainstreamed students: General classroom teachers' perspectives. *Remedial and Special Education, 12,* 18–27.

Snyder, R. F. (1999). Inclusion: A qualitative study of in-service general education teachers' attitudes and concerns. *Education, 120*(1), 173–181.

Steele, M. M. (2002). Strategies for helping students who have learning disabilities in mathematics. *Mathematics Teaching in the Middle School, 8,* 140–143.

Weiss, M. P., & Brigham, F. J. (2000). Co-teaching and the model of shared responsibility: What does the research support? In T. E. Scruggs and M.A. Mastropieri (Eds.), *Advances in learning and behavioral disabilities* (Vol. 14, pp. 217–245). Stamford, CT: JAI Press.

Weiss, M. P., & Lloyd, J. W. (2002). Congruence between roles and actions of secondary special educators in co-taught and special education settings. *Journal of Special Education, 36,* 58–68.

Index

9 781593 853068